5th Edition

Divorce After 50

A Guide to the Unique Legal & Financial Challenges of Your Divorce

Attorney Janice Green

FIFTH EDITION	FEBRUARY 2022
Editor	JANET PORTMAN
Book and Cover Design	SUSAN PUTNEY
Proofreading	IRENE BARNARD
Index	VICTORIA BAKER
Printing	SHERIDAN

Names: Green, Janice, 1948- author.
Title: Divorce after 50 : a guide to the unique legal & financial
   challenges of your divorce / Attorney Janice Green.
Other titles: Divorce after fifty
Description: 5th edition. | Berkeley : Nolo, 2022. | Includes index.
Identifiers: LCCN 2021033801 (print) | LCCN 2021033802 (ebook) | ISBN
   9781413329551 (paperback) | ISBN 9781413329568 (ebook)
Subjects: LCSH: Divorce--Law and legislation--United States--Popular works.
   | Middle-aged persons--United States--Handbooks, manuals, etc. | Older
   people--United States--Handbooks, manuals, etc.
Classification: LCC KF535.Z9 G738 2022 (print) | LCC KF535.Z9 (ebook) |
   DDC 306.89--dc23
LC record available at https://lccn.loc.gov/2021033801
LC ebook record available at https://lccn.loc.gov/2021033802

This book covers only United States law, unless it specifically states otherwise.

Please note

This book's accurate, plain-English legal information can help you solve many
of your own legal problems. But this text is not a substitute for personalized
advice from a knowledgeable lawyer. If you want the help of a trained
professional —and we'll always point out situations in which we think that's
a good idea—consult an attorney licensed to practice in your state.

Acknowledgments

There are those who contribute to a book and don't have the foggiest idea they are doing so, like—

My longtime law partner, whose inventive legal acumen and insight, high ethical standards, and wit contributed to the foundation from which these pages sprouted—thank you, my dear friend, Jim Farris.

My family law mentor, who drove me nuts when he insisted on carrying my trial briefcase and who modeled excellence in advocacy—thanks to you, Jon Coffee.

My family law clients, whose difficult voyages through divorce taught me about the humanity and the humility of family law. My professional brethren who supported me in untold ways: Joe Milner, Kris Algert, and my fellow collaborative family lawyers.

There are those who contribute knowingly, like—

My treasured buddies, whose encouragement helped me keep my toe in the writing waters—Gayle Gordon, Dorothy Baum, Paul Scott, Kate Culligan, Carole Taxis, Mary Matus, David Wahlberg, Anne Wynne, and Nancy Scherer (who also kept me out of the ditch on estate planning). Thank you and thank heavens none of you charged per hour for our porch chats!

Those lovely people who wrote so from-the-heart about their late-life divorce experiences, you know who you are, even though no one else does. Thanks to each of you for your time and compassionate participation.

Then, there are those whose "bizness" is books and who graciously and gracefully guided this project to completion from the East Coast to the West Coast, like—

My agent, Katharine Sands of the Sarah Jane Freymann Literary Agency in NYC. A sharp, talented rep whose devoted energy and astute judgment guided and buoyed this project, even when life threw me a curveball.

My first editor, Emily Doskow, who wields her editing machete with skill, patience, and a steady hand, and who turned me from a passive into an active—Emily, who really made it all shine and who never grumped at me! You've been a jewel to work with. My editor through three editions, Lina Guillen, whose discerning eye fine-tunes the updates and revisions, has been a delightful and patient cohort. And a big thanks to Janet Portman, who edited this edition, for her patience and knowledge of grammar.

And my publisher, Nolo, whose professional staff made this experience joyful and glitch free: Marcia Stewart, Helena Brantley, Sheri Lent, Lexi Elmore, the production folks, and so many others including Andrea Burnett, publicist, who was vital in jump-starting public awareness of the book. To all of you, a huge hug of gratitude.

And finally, there's Will Secrest, who saw this book coming long before I did, whose love for me and the written word encouraged my finger-thinking, and whose words, "Keep the twinkle in your Zen, Janice," echo eternally from his spirit. I miss you, my dear Mountain Man. Thank you, thank you.

Dedicated
to
Will

About the Author

Janice L. Green, www.JaniceLGreen.com, is a family law attorney who has practiced in Austin, Texas, for more than 46 years—32 of which as a partner in the AV-rated boutique family law firm, Farris & Green. During her career, she was board certified in family law by the Texas Board of Legal Specialization, named a Fellow in the American Academy of Matrimonial Lawyers, listed in *Best Lawyers in America*, noted as a *Texas Monthly* Super Lawyer, and frequent lecturer and published author of more than 65 articles on family law. Green is an Honors graduate of the University of Texas School of Law and Phi Beta Kappa cum laude graduate of the University of Texas at Austin.

While continuing to reside in Austin, she makes time to escape to her cabin-home outside Pagosa Springs, Colorado, to write, garden, and relish mountain sunsets.

Table of Contents

Your Late-Life Divorce Companion

D ivorce at any age is a time of upheaval. But after age 50, divorce has a different feel, a different context, and a collection of issues not encountered by younger spouses. You can sense the difference—that's why this book is in your hands. You know that having more years behind you than ahead of you is a truth that shifts priorities and refocuses the lens through which you experience life, and now, through which you are considering divorce.

That recognition is what sets this book apart from others. *Divorce After 50*, now in its fifth edition, is your guide through the legal and financial issues relevant to your late-life marriage crisis. It includes the tools you'll need to navigate the circuitous route through separation and divorce, with or without a lawyer, no matter the size or complexity of your finances. What's at stake now and for your future will be shaped within the framework of the nuts and bolts of divorce rules.

I practiced family law for over 40 years. More than a decade ago, I began noticing more "mature" clients in my family law practice. In fact, the divorce rate among adults over 50 has doubled since 1990 and tripled for those over 65; after the 2020 U.S. Census data is analyzed, we will know more about the continuation of these trends. Unlike couples divorcing in their 20s, 30s, and 40s, these clients were thinking about divorce in relation to their health, their retirement security, and their adult children's response to the news. Many couples evidenced the heightened anxiety that can accompany the awareness of fewer years ahead to recover emotionally and financially from divorce. And now, the COVID-19 pandemic adds fuel to this anxiety; though its end seems within reach, we are constantly reminded of the possibility that virus variations and low vaccination rates might result in more disruption and loss.

The first and last chapters of this book serve as bookends for the more technical chapters—bookends created by the voices of people like you, who faced a divorce later in life. In Chapter 1, their words are distilled into the themes running through many late-life divorces. At the other end is Chapter 13, consisting of a collection of survival stories written by people who moved through a late-life marital collapse. They wrote not only about life on the other side of their crucible, but also how they handled some of the same challenges you face. By the way, it's perfectly all right to jump into the last chapter, sooner rather than later, to tap into their words of experience.

Between the bookends are chapters that cover, in more or less chronological order, the issues that most couples face (you can hopscotch through the chapters, depending on what you need to know at the moment and what's relevant to your situation). First, you'll select the people who will steer you through a divorce—both professionally and personally—and glance at the roles adult children play in their parents' divorces. You'll also see what can happen when questions about mental capacity surface and the need arises for a surrogate decision maker, such as a guardian.

Next, you'll look at the ways people divorce—through litigation, arbitration, mediation, or collaboration—to find the process that best fits the personalities, personal facts, and pocketbooks involved in your divorce. Some late-life couples stop short of divorce and opt for long-term separations or postmarital agreements, and that's covered, too.

The nitty-gritty legal information is arranged around four important verbs—identify, characterize, value, and divide—that make it easier for you to figure out which assets will benefit you most at this stage of life. *Divorce After 50* also leads you through critical health care changes and the Medicare puzzle; potential income streams; the interaction between estate planning and divorce; and financial strategies that will inform your settlement negotiations or trial preparation.

Divorce later in life has the potential to be a creative turning point and a positive beginning for you. You've made the important first move to pick up this book and learn about the legal aspects of this life-changing event—an empowering step. Make sure you don't overlook what you bring to this experience: a mature perspective and wisdom accumulated over the years. These will be of great benefit to you as you move through your late-life divorce.

Get Updates to This Book and More on Nolo.com

When there are important changes to the information in this book, we'll post updates online, on a page dedicated to this book:

www.nolo.com/back-of-book/DIVL.html

You'll find other useful information there, too, including author blogs, podcasts, and videos.

How Did I Get Here? The Rhyme and Reason of Late-Life Divorce

Starting in middle age and even more strongly in our later years, most of us plan to pull our foot off the accelerator and begin to coast on the fruits of our lifelong efforts—in the best-case scenario, settling in to a pleasant retirement or semiretirement. It can be shocking and confusing to have this expectation turned upside down by a divorce—even if you're the one initiating the split. You might be wondering why this is happening when you feel you are in the prime of your life and have finally reached the moment you have been waiting and working for. What you're learning is that age does not provide immunity from divorce, nor does a long-term marriage protect you. According to Pew Research Center, about 34% of those divorcing after 50 have been married at least 30 years and 12% for over 40 years.

You might be reading this book because you've recently had the shock of hearing from your spouse that a divorce is in the wind. You might be the one who wants the divorce. It's also possible that you are considering divorce but need to gather more information before making a final decision. No matter your situation, you are probably feeling anxious and isolated, and desire to understand what is happening—and why.

Why Is This Happening?

Late-life divorces and long-term separations can happen for the same reasons that result in relationship breaches of younger adults: infidelity, family violence, substance abuse, financial pressures, regrets about earlier decisions, or the desire for independence. However, many of these reasons are reframed and have new meaning when they surface in the context of a graying divorce—and some late-life divorces are the result of realities unique to older adults.

Reflecting on the "why" might be your first step in this difficult process. It can help you make decisions in the near term and can shape your negotiation strategies later. More important, understanding why and knowing that others have come before you with the same concerns, issues, and feelings can help you feel less isolated and confused. This chapter covers some of the most common answers to the question I asked new clients: "What brings you to my office?" The answers provide insight into some of the most common circumstances underlying the graying divorce.

Grappling With the Realities of Time

"I turn 60 in a few months. It's hit me that I am not immortal. I want an authentic life. To get there I need to end this marriage."

"My parents lived into their nineties. I'm 75 and I feel like I have many more years ahead of me. My wife has given up at 70. I haven't. We see things too differently to stay together."

"We've been separated for 20 years. I think it's time to make it final."

The average American life expectancy now is 79—up from 47 in 1900. Over 13% of the U.S. population is 65 or older; at the time of the last census in 2010, the over-65 crowd numbered 40.3 million. The projection for this age group in 2040 is 21% of the U.S. population. (According to one mind-boggling statistic, 65% of the people who have passed age 50 in the entire history of mankind are still walking the earth today.)

Aging can play a significant role in a decision to divorce later in life. Along with the reality that we are all living longer, our "can-do" culture offers incentives to tackle challenges at any age. An emphasis on individual fulfillment sometimes seems to encourage the idea that we can achieve happiness at any age if only we follow our hearts, even if that means switching partners after many years. A person staring at a 60th birthday might choose to end an unhappy marriage and make a fresh start, stepping out of marital turmoil to seek happiness and live a life that feels more authentic.

With modern medical advances, it's easy to believe there will soon be a cure for many of the conditions that accompany aging. Thanks to advertisements for the latest and greatest pharmaceuticals and medical procedures, we begin to think that high blood pressure, diabetes, heart conditions, cancer, and other debilitating diseases will gradually cease to exist. We are inundated by reminders that we will live longer if only we stop this bad habit, start taking that vitamin supplement, or embark on a new exercise regime. We also hear that if we laugh more often, keep positive thoughts in the forefront of our minds, and reduce stress, marital happiness and good health will follow. If it looks like divorce will help generate these elements in one's life, then it's not a big leap to the idea that divorce will lead to a longer and happier life.

There's even some scientific support for this idea. An American Medical Association study involving 42 married couples found that hostile marriage partners take longer to heal from physical wounds, such as surgical incisions, than nonhostile couples. (The hostile behaviors that were measured included belligerence, glowering, threatening speech, hostile tone of voice, criticism, and dramatic eye-rolling.) This study involved a relatively small number of subjects, but its conclusions mirror findings in earlier research that show troubled marriages contributing to depression, heart disease, and even death. All of these realities can act as motivation to seek what appears to be a healthier lifestyle on the other side of a divorce.

Reacting to Illness

"My cancer is in remission. But my life isn't. I want to make the most of the time I have left. I'm ready to file for divorce. I've put it off long enough."

"My wife has Alzheimer's. What happens if I divorce her? I love her dearly, but our life as a couple is over. I don't want to die a gradual death with her, and I don't want my estate going into bankruptcy because of her medical expenses. We talked about this before she became so ill. I think she would understand why I'm here."

When a married spouse becomes ill, society expects that the healthy partner will adhere to the traditional wedding vow to stick around "in sickness and in health." But serious illness can change things in a marriage. For example, when a spouse becomes seriously ill, and especially when an ailing spouse is cognitively impaired or doesn't recognize the healthy spouse (for example, with Alzheimer's disease or a severe brain injury), things can shift drastically. The healthy spouse in an unhappy marriage can experience the illness as the last straw. Spousal abandonment after a diagnosis of cancer or multiple sclerosis was the subject of a joint research study by the University of Utah and University of Washington Schools of Medicine. They found that a woman is six times more likely to be separated or divorced soon after she receives such a diagnosis than if a man is the patient. Even spouses who aren't alienated from their partners consider divorce when cognitive issues prevent them from having a satisfying marital relationship. These situations are loaded with abandonment issues, but many spouses come to believe that the ailing spouse would have supported the idea of divorce under the circumstances.

Preserving Marital Assets Through Divorce

Some spouses divorce in name only while continuing to live together, in an effort to preserve marital assets. This isn't about greed, but about protecting Medicaid or other crucial benefits. The fear of depleting a marital estate when serious illness strikes is real—over 66% of U.S. bankruptcy filings list medical bills as the reason for seeking relief, and 80% of those are people who had some form of medical insurance.

When your health is in jeopardy, as opposed to the failing health of your spouse, it can similarly lead you to take hold of your own fate. Facing your mortality naturally raises the question "What can I do to make my remaining time the best of my life?" This might be followed by another question: "Why should I spend my limited time with someone I no longer love?"

Lacking Common Purpose

"My husband just announced that he wants to end our 35-year marriage. He won't tell me why. Says he can't explain it. He retired a couple years ago. I've been a housewife our entire marriage and have never had to work outside of our home."

"I wanted him to find something to do with his time. So he got a computer. That was fine with me until he left me for the Internet. He avoided me until recently when he told me he wants a divorce."

"We didn't divorce while the kids were young. We wanted to keep the home together as long as we could. Our youngest is graduating soon. There will be nothing to hold us together. The kids are now old enough to understand."

"I am afraid of being alone. Yet, as I think about it, I'm alone in this marriage."

Social science research is clear that spouses must make emotional adjustments when a partner retires or children leave home for college or to begin their own adult lives. Much has been written about the "empty nest" syndrome and the sound of silence that accompanies it when parents have nothing to say to each other because substantive communication has always been tied to their children. The children are gone, interests once fed by the workplace vanish, friends move away, and spouses find themselves without common purpose. Some parents who always lacked common purpose but resisted divorce because of their children give themselves permission to divorce when the children reach adulthood.

Retirement can also have enormous impact: A retired husband might demand the same mothering as a long-departed child, and his wife might be reluctant to take on a new full-time caretaker role. Older men, too, might flee a marriage after retirement when they feel inadequate to handle the close proximity of a needy or dependent wife.

This bleak picture isn't the only possible outcome—many spouses return to interests shared earlier in life, like travel; and many develop new common interests and projects. But problems can arise, and even lead all the way to divorce, when one spouse blames the other for late-life tedium and decides to end the marriage instead of searching for new ways to relate.

Divorce filings driven by a lack of common purpose frequently come as a surprise to the abandoned spouse, who soon learns how many complaints have been stored in the other's memory bank. When the loss of purpose drives a divorce, it is often coupled with another reason, such as recognizing one's own mortality or discovering (or rediscovering) a romantic connection outside the marriage.

Rediscovering Sexuality

"He's got a Sweet Young Thing he wants to marry! He's 72. At his age? How can this be happening?"

"I just discovered that my wife is having an Internet affair on a senior citizen dating site. I had no idea that's why she was spending so much time on our computer! I had no idea that kind of thing even existed."

"He went to his 40th high school class reunion and met up with an old girlfriend who is widowed. Now he wants to pick up where they left off, and our marriage is going to end as a result of this foolishness."

"Our father wants to marry his secretary, who is many years younger. Our mother is devastated. And I'm so angry that I want you to nail it to him. I'll pay your fees. Just take care of our mother."

Infidelity can be a cause of divorce in itself, or it can be symptomatic of another problem in the marriage. A late-life divorce is no exception. Research tells us that sexual drive does not stop at some predetermined age. A 2001 survey of 1,300 Americans over the age of 60 found that nearly half reported having sexual relations at least once a month, and 40% of those wanted to have relations more often. The first comprehensive national survey of sexual attitudes, published in 2007, concluded that most active people ages 57 to 85 experience only a slight decline in the frequency of sexual activity from the 50s to early 70s, and that many men and women remain sexually active well into their 70s and 80s. These attitudes were again reflected in the 2018 National Poll on Healthy Aging by the University of Michigan: 40% of adults aged 65–80 are sexually active, and 54% say sex is important to quality of life.

It turns out that older Americans cheat more than younger Americans. According to University of Utah sociologist Nicholas Wolfinger, who noticed these age differences when reviewing the General Social Surveys, "[p]eople born between 1940 and 1959 report the highest rates of extramarital sex. These are the first generations to come of age during the sexual revolution."

When intimacy with a spouse has been dormant, it is not unusual for desire to start clamoring for expression outside the marriage. Class reunions, Internet chat rooms, and social media are prime arenas for that expression. There's no data on the frequency of infidelity in the lives of older adults, but we do know that older spouses frequently report lack of sexual relations as the reason for wanting to leave the marriage (or the justification for an affair).

In my view, the power of sexuality—and the corresponding fear of losing it—can cause people to act in ways that seem surprising from an outsider's view. Time and again, I have seen older clients who are ready to walk away from a long-term marriage because of an affair or new relationship (or the corresponding client who is shocked to discover a spouse's affair). As these cases progress, extramarital acting out is often explained by revelations of weak or nonexistent common interests, problems with communication, or health conditions interfering with sexual relations.

The Possibility of Reconciliation

When an older divorce client in a long-term marriage is experiencing a marital crisis sparked by a single act of infidelity (rather than a pattern in the marriage), there might be merit to waiting or stretching out the divorce process to give the spouses time to work through the impact of the event. I have seen many such situations that ended in reconciliation, with the infidelity serving as a wake-up call rather than a death knell.

Social and Cultural Forces

"For almost 40 years I've taken the abuse. My friends tell me it is time for me to end this charade. But I am afraid to try to get out. He'll be enraged if I even mention divorce."

"My divorced daughter has been urging me for years to leave her father because of how he treats me. I've always thought of divorce as a young person's option, not something for someone my age to seriously consider. But what if I were to take the plunge after all these years? ... I can't believe I'm thinking about this."

"I have lived with an alcoholic for over 40 years. Don't ask me why, but I just woke up and realized that I am not going to spend the rest of my life tiptoeing around him. I thought he would mellow with age. But it's getting worse."

Just as every divorcing spouse is responding to conditions within that person's own marriage, nearly everyone is also driven by social forces. Significant cultural transformations can be particularly powerful for a spouse divorcing later in life, suggesting new options and ways of living.

Gender Equality. Greater gender equality in recent decades, both in the workplace and in the home, has precipitated many graying divorces. The increase in opportunities outside the home has led women to seek fulfillment and independence later in life and to reject the traditional woman's role of caretaker, especially once children are grown and gone from home. As more women establish successful careers, they also create their own sources of retirement income, removing a barrier to divorce. Women who remain more financially dependent on husbands might be slower to initiate a divorce.

Economic Climate. Economic conditions affect the timing of divorce, too. During short-term economic downturns, spouses sometimes put divorce on the back burner. During longer downturns,

divorce can be perceived as a remedy to ease financial stressors—
or can be rendered impossible by the reality that there's simply not
enough money to get divorced. This is especially present when the
economic outlook includes a poor real estate market, rendering a
couple's most valuable asset less flexible.

No-Fault Divorce. A no-fault divorce can be filed and finalized
when only one spouse believes that the marriage is broken and
irreconcilable. No-fault laws do not require proof of cruelty, infidelity,
or abandonment, the traditional grounds for divorce. The growth
of no-fault laws in the 1970s—a reflection of society's changing
attitudes toward divorce—gradually made divorce less stigmatizing,
as the increasing divorce rate has done as well. This social change can
have an effect on older spouses, who see acceptance of divorce around
them. And if an older adult's grown child gets divorced, the parent
might look differently at marital disharmony and see divorce as a
real possibility. No-fault divorce is now available in every state in the
United States.

Spousal Abuse and Substance Abuse. A study by the American
Association of Retired Persons (AARP) cites verbal, emotional,
and physical abuse as a primary reason for divorce in couples
between 40 and 79 years of age. More than 20% of the 1,147 men
and women surveyed cited drug or alcohol abuse as a major cause of
the divorce. Substance abuse often goes hand in hand with physical
and emotional abuse.

Despite increased public awareness of the prevalence of spousal
abuse and the development of better intervention and prevention
services, it is not easy to shake off entrenched aggressor-victim roles
that have been played out for decades in a long-term marriage. It takes
tremendous courage to break this abusive cycle later in life. These are
some of the most difficult cases to see to completion, because frequently
an abused partner abandons the process and returns to the familiar.
Nevertheless, my experience is that more and more long-term victims are
deciding to stop the abuse.

The Revolving Door of Serial Divorce

"Hello, again. I should have listened to you the last time you represented me. Marrying my girlfriend back then was not a smart move. You told me to wait a couple years before I married her. I should've listened."

"This is my third marriage, and I learned not to waste any time when it is clear that things are not working. I can recognize a mistake when I see one. Let's get the ball rolling and file."

Divorced persons tend to remarry—and, statistically, to divorce again. About two-thirds of divorced women and 75% of divorced men give marriage another try. And those who have a history of divorce appear to be less willing to stay in a subsequent unhappy marriage—the divorce rate for second and subsequent remarriages is higher than for first-time divorce—60% or more. Of people over age 50 who divorce, 53% have divorced at least once before. For those aged 50 to 64, having been previously married doubles the risk of divorce; for those 65 and older, the risk quadruples.

According to the anecdotal observations of family law attorneys, older divorce clients who are repeat customers are typically one of two types. The first is the older adult who has the financial means to marry and divorce repeatedly. The second is the client who remarried within the first few years after a previous divorce. Psychologists describe the two years following a divorce as a crisis period during which the divorced person experiences intense emotional upheaval, continuing conflict among family members, and difficulty adjusting to a new lifestyle. When in the throes of such turmoil, it is natural to seek solace in a new relationship. Unfortunately, the solace is often short-lived.

Again anecdotally, this pattern seems to affect men more than women. With the clock ticking loudly, men seem eager to extricate themselves from struggles on the home front so that they can move quickly into new relationships that they expect to be more peaceful. Women, on the other hand, seem more adept at creating postdivorce support systems instead of remarrying quickly: circles of friends, formal counseling groups, and involvement with family members, particularly grandchildren.

Motivating Loss

"This is my second marriage. I'm 82; she's 34. I was widowed the first time around. It was a mistake to marry her so quickly after my wife died, but I was lonely."

"When we married he was a Silver Fox. Handsome, wiser. He is 15 years older than me. I honestly do not know what happened to his looks. Despite the financial security he offers, I can't shake the image of his aging body and aging attitudes. I feel guilty about this, but I don't want to be married to a father figure."

"My first wife died about five years ago. She was the love of my life. But soon after losing her, I knew I didn't want to go it alone. We had such a wonderful marriage that I was sure I could find someone else like her. Then I met my second wife and she seemed like she was going to be another perfect partner. Was I ever wrong about that! Maybe because we dated for only four months and I didn't really know her and her kids. They never approved of me, and I didn't particularly like them. She always sides with them, and we always seem to be at war. I can't handle this tension any longer. Anyway, this was all a big mistake. I married her too fast."

"Both of my parents are now deceased. While they were alive, I never would have considered divorce. It would have destroyed them. Now I feel free to do so."

We all know people who have remarried too soon after losing a spouse, when the grief and loneliness felt too great to face alone. Remarriage is a way to end isolation and loneliness—but it can be unwise if it's too soon after the loss. The grief process from the first marriage—whether it ended in death or divorce—must run its course.

The death of a parent can also be a motivating loss precipitating divorce. What had served as a buffer between self and death is removed when a parent dies—thus it is yet another opportunity to confront one's mortality and open the door to contemplating divorce. The death of a parent can also be a trigger if the parent's approval was important:

When that parent was alive, the adult child—even as an older adult—might have rejected the idea of divorce because it would draw the parent's disapproval and judgment. When the parent dies, the option of divorce becomes more real.

Finally, there is the loss of youth and health. Try as we might to surgically lift our sagging parts and tuck our folds away, age catches up with us. Youthful appearances start to recede, and unhappy spouses begin to look anywhere and everywhere to recapture them, blaming the loss of youth on an unsatisfactory marriage and assuming that good times will roll again if the marriage ends.

COVID-19's Effect on Divorce

As this book goes to press in late 2021, it's too early to know what the long-term impact of the pandemic will be on divorce rates and rationales. During the height of the COVID scenario, many couples who would otherwise have filed for divorce instead hunkered down. The number of divorce filings dropped. But as the pandemic moves into our rearview mirrors, change is afoot.

"For couples over 50 in particular, counselors say, the pandemic has amplified the soul-searching that often hits people at this age," according to a May 5, 2021 *Wall Street Journal* article, "Bill and Melinda Gates Divorce Highlights Rise of Older-Age Splits." This article cites findings from The National Center for Family and Marriage Research at Bowling Green State University, which suggest that the pandemic suppressed divorce rates in 2020 in five known states (Arizona, Florida, Missouri, New Hampshire, Oregon). Nationwide divorce statistics are not yet available, but divorce attorneys report that divorce consultations and filings are now on the upswing.

It makes sense that the close proximity of spouses and lack of social interaction during the pandemic would exacerbate many of the underlying rhymes and reasons for divorce highlighted in this chapter, especially for those couples lacking common purpose.

Other by-products of the pandemic are a heightened sense of vulnerability, watching a society in flux, and a daily reminder of mortality —all of which play into the themes behind gray divorce.

Bitterness Is Not Your Friend

Have you found elements of your own story here? There is often overlap, sometimes a great deal, among these themes in the late-life divorce; rarely does a marriage fall apart due to a single cause. Any divorce has the potential to create feelings of bitterness, self-righteousness, and victimization. This is normal, and especially likely in a late-life divorce, where the very length of the marriage can give rise to an intense sense of betrayal. You will need time to work through these feelings, but work through them you must. If you don't, they will make your inner life more difficult and painful for a longer time. They'll also stand in the way of your divorce process. Bitterness interferes with sound judgment and makes it harder for others to listen to what you have to say during negotiations. And many judges discount the testimony of a bitter and angry witness.

This is not to say that finding your way out of bitterness is easy; you may well need help. Consider reading some of the excellent books available, either on divorce specifically, on grief or loss, or simply about handling life in general. Join a divorce support group, or start or resume counseling. Make sure you keep up your friendships with the people who really support you, and take good care of your physical health. In other words, try any and every constructive avenue that will help you be calm and focused as you ride the emotional and legal rollercoaster of divorce.

Getting Guidance—The Professional Side

Whether you are just starting to consider divorce, are committed to going forward, or have been surprised by your spouse announcing plans to end your marriage, you are embarking on a journey to unknown places. You are sure to have company on your journey, in the form of friends and family members with a great deal to say about their view on the law, the court system, and how you should proceed.

You may get some valuable information from these personal advisers, and Chapter 3 addresses ways you can get assistance on the personal level. But personal advisers are no substitute for professional guidance. It's never too early to sit down with a legal adviser called a divorce lawyer, domestic relations lawyer, or family law attorney. Even if you intend to represent yourself in your divorce, a consultation with an attorney at the outset will put you on the right track with accurate information about your state's laws and local court rules, intelligence about the propensities of local judges, and specific guidance for your situation. If you're unrepresented, having a lawyer review your settlement agreement at the end of the process can also give you peace of mind about the legality and finality of your settlement arrangements.

The Role of Lawyers in Divorce

Assuming you have an initial consultation with an attorney at the beginning of your case, you will have a few choices about how to move forward.

You can retain the attorney to represent you during your entire divorce from start to finish. That's mostly what "Working With a Divorce Lawyer," below, is about.

If you're in mediation with your spouse, you can ask the attorney to serve as a coach or adviser in the background—known as a consulting attorney—while you attend mediation sessions alone, armed with the lawyer's advice and a plan for negotiating with your spouse. A consulting attorney may also be involved in drafting or reviewing documents that cement any agreement you have reached in mediation. This saves money because you are not paying the attorney to be present in mediation.

It is an option if the issues in your case are straightforward and if you are comfortable negotiating solo. This option is covered more in the discussion of mediation in Chapter 4, "Your Divorce Options."

You can ask a lawyer to take on specific tasks in your divorce or advise you in particular situations, while you represent yourself. (See "Unbundled Legal Services: The a la Carte Approach," below.)

Regardless of how you're going to work with your attorney, but especially if you are going to have an attorney represent you throughout your divorce, choose that person carefully. Possibly more than any other area of law, the arena of divorce law is emotionally laden, personally intrusive, and demands a good match between the lawyer's and client's personalities. Because it's so important, the majority of this chapter is devoted to walking you through the process of finding and hiring an attorney.

The quality of your attorney, and of the connection you have with your lawyer, is crucial to how you experience a divorce. For example, you do not want to be kept in the dark and then required to make a major life-changing decision at the last minute and on the spot. You do not want to have sleepless nights because your deposition is approaching and you have not been appropriately prepared for it. Instead, you want an attorney who will minimize the stress of the divorce by keeping you informed and ensuring you are prepared to participate. Your attorney should also have a good "deskside" manner, a focus on good communication and client service, and the intelligence, experience, ethics, and skill to represent your interests well.

Working With a Divorce Lawyer

To help you make the important choice about who will represent you, this section explains the process of choosing an attorney and focuses on what you could do to prepare for the initial consultation with an attorney. I've also included some notes about the process from my perspective—that of an experienced family law attorney. A glimpse from my side of the desk will help you evaluate the other half of your potential attorney–client partnership.

Many people consult an attorney before taking any other action or even talking with their spouse about a divorce, so that's where we'll begin.

Consulting Before a Crisis

You might have been served with legal papers or otherwise learned that your spouse has filed or is seriously considering filing for a divorce; or perhaps you are the one who is ready to file or you want to explore the possibility of divorce. In either event, getting early advice and assistance from a lawyer might be invaluable. It does not pay to put your head in the sand. Instead, lessen the fear of the unknown and educate yourself about the realities of your situation sooner rather than later. Remember, just talking with an attorney does not mean divorce is inevitable. I've had many clients consult with me over a period of years without ever deciding to go forward with their divorce.

An attorney might provide advice on an as-needed basis before a divorce case is ever filed—and that early advice might prevent a crisis. You might consult a lawyer just once or have a series of office meetings covering a variety of topics. Talking to a lawyer might help you in a number of ways by:

- alleviating your fears
- averting problems before they arise
- educating you about your rights and the divorce laws in your state
- offering suggestions about what you should and should not do (predivorce planning), and
- highlighting potential bumps in the road.

Again, consulting with an attorney does not make it inevitable that you will divorce, nor is it set in stone that you will hire that lawyer. You might decide to retain the attorney to represent you in a divorce, you might decide not to hire that particular attorney, or you might conclude you do not need to retain an attorney at all. Whatever the outcome is, you have to start by getting some information.

Finding an Attorney

How do you find the right attorney for you—not just any attorney, but one who is a good match for your circumstances and your personality? In late-life divorces, your financial future depends on the decisions you make. This is not the time to blindly walk through the first page of a Google search—nor is there any need to do that, as there's a wealth of more informative resources available.

 TIP

Conflict of interest rules prevent one attorney from representing both you and your spouse. It's a cardinal rule of professional ethics that one attorney must not represent both spouses in a divorce case, because of potential conflicts of interest. No matter how simple your case might be, rest assured that you and your spouse will have different viewpoints on some issues. An attorney's allegiance is to one client. Even if one spouse elects to be self-represented and the other spouse retains an attorney, that attorney advises only the one client.

Certified Specialists

Like physicians who specialize in certain areas of health care, most attorneys specialize in an area of the law. State regulatory agencies that license attorneys (or other designated commissions or agencies) offer expert certification to attorneys in certain specialities, often including family law. Certified specialists have practiced for a required number of years, have met certain criteria relating to their experience, and have passed a written test. All of these requirements assure you that the attorney is experienced and knowledgeable in the complex and ever-changing field of divorce law. Certified specialists often charge a higher rate than other attorneys, and you might not need or want a specialist for your case—but it's a good thing to ask about when you're interviewing attorneys. If your state bar does not certify legal specialists, then consult with someone who has a track record of handling divorce cases.

No matter how or where you search for an attorney, look for indicators of competence, such as membership in professional organizations, honors received, published articles, and a good reputation among peers. There's more detail below about the questions you'll need to ask.

Six Avenues of Referral

You can look for an attorney in a number of ways, and I suggest you try them all. If an attorney's name pops up in more than one place, that's a good sign.

Here are six ways to search for an attorney:

- **Referrals from legal professionals.** If you know an attorney or a judge, ask for at least three referrals to experienced family law attorneys. A member of the legal community is one of the best resources because news of an attorney's reputation, both positive and negative, spreads quickly.

- **Other professionals and advisers.** Ask other professionals for recommendations. Therapists and counselors hear daily about good and bad experiences their patients have with attorneys in family law matters. Bankers and businesspeople also have experience with attorneys—and even if those lawyers aren't family law attorneys, they might have good referrals to lawyers in that area. Pastors, rabbis, and priests can be good referral sources as well.

- **American Academy of Matrimonial Lawyers (AAML).** Check the membership directory on the website of the AAML at www.aaml. org. Membership is by invitation and is subject to peer review, testing, and screening; to be accepted, an attorney must have demonstrated expertise in family law over time. You might not need—or be able to afford—an attorney with such a high skill level. If that's the case, you could ask one of the attorneys listed in the directory, or the attorney's office staff, to recommend another skilled and reputable lawyer in your community, probably one who's been practicing for a shorter time than the AAML attorney.

- **Lawyer directories.** With the growth of the Internet, lawyer directories have proliferated. Some ways of searching for a lawyer electronically are really no better than using the old-time yellow pages, but others will gather you some useful information. Nolo has a lawyer directory at www.nolo.com/lawyers. The attorneys who advertise there prepare a comprehensive profile that includes their education, experience, philosophy of practice, and fee schedule—a great deal more information than most other online legal directories. Another reputable resource is the Martindale-Hubbell Legal Directory at www.martindale.com or www.lawyers.com. Attorneys are rated by their fellow professionals, including judges, on their competence and professional ethics. Finally, www.justia.com also has a directory of attorneys.

- **Referral services.** Many local city and county bar associations operate attorney referral services. A referral service is not a legal directory—a directory allows you to choose among attorneys who pay for a listing or advertisement in the directory, while referral services will match you with a particular attorney—sometimes based on the facts of your case, but often simply by matching you with the next attorney on the referral list. Sometimes, these attorneys are very new to the practice of law and are using the referral service as a way to attract clients. This isn't necessarily a deal-breaker—many new attorneys are smart and talented, and often they have mentors who will advise them on matters that are new to them. But you should always find out as much information as you can about the lawyer's background, experience, and resources, and make sure you feel comfortable with that lawyer. Employers' legal services plans, akin to health insurance, can also be referral resources—and the same caveat applies.

- **Family, friends, and networks**. Family, friends, and social and professional networks are always a resource for finding attorneys. It is rare not to know of someone who has experience with a family law attorney. But keep in mind that the facts in someone else's case will be different from your situation, and the attorneys involved might be very different from what you need. Always cross-check the attorneys through the other networks, peer review listings, and referral resources suggested in this section.

Do Some Online Research

Before scheduling an appointment with an attorney, do some online research. Start with the attorney's website to review the biographical and professional information, including that of other family law attorneys in the firm. Is the website user-friendly? What is your impression and reaction to the site?

Google the attorney's name for other professional links and reviews. Keep in mind that online reviews, be they of restaurants or professionals, are easily gamed by websites that offer their services as "real" reviewers. And remember that attorneys have a tendency to make people mad—even the good attorneys. Especially in the field of family law, I'd be suspicious of an attorney with nothing but 5-star ratings.

To sharpen your skills in evaluating an attorney's reviews, consider the following:

Fake reviews tend to include these elements:
- extreme black or white opinions
- terrible grammar and poor spelling; frequent use of exclamation points
- anonymous (you should be able to check out the reviewer's profile)
- sarcastic or satirical or inflammatory user names or rhetoric, and
- frequent use of "I" and "me" and a lot of verbs.

Genuine reviews tend to have these characteristics:
- middle-of-the-roaders who have positive and negative feedback
- specific examples leading to the reviewer's conclusion
- timing is recent,and
- reviewer's profile shows thoughtful reviews for other services, and repetitive phrases do not show up in other businesses or professions reviewed.

TIP

Check for disciplinary action. Most state attorney licensing agencies keep records of attorneys licensed to practice in the state, often including disciplinary actions taken by the state bar. Enter your state's name and "state bar association" or "attorney licensing" into a search engine to find the licensing agency, and follow the links to check your potential attorney's record.

Scheduling Your First Appointment

When you call a law office for an appointment, it's unlikely you'll talk to the lawyer right away. Instead, a legal secretary, legal assistant, or paralegal will ask you some initial questions to screen for conflicts of interest. A conflict of interest exists if the attorney has already consulted with or represented your spouse about this or another matter. The attorney might even be representing your spouse now, unbeknownst to you. If the attorney has a conflict, the attorney should not talk with you at all, even for a brief time. If the lawyer or staff do not ask you for the name of your spouse immediately, provide it and ask them to check for a potential conflict of interest before you give any details on the telephone.

> EXAMPLE: Spouse A calls the attorney's office and schedules an appointment, or maybe that spouse has already met with the attorney. Spouse B calls the same attorney's office and gives extensive information to a staff person, including B's expectation of an impending pay increase. Spouse B has given information to Spouse A's attorney that the attorney could use to that spouse's advantage, which could influence the case strategy.

Asking for a conflicts check might be beneficial in another way: By learning that a conflict exists, Spouse B in our example discovered that Spouse A has already consulted with an attorney—valuable information.

Once you're past the conflict screening, the office staffer will probably ask you a number of other questions to find out whether your case is the type the attorney handles. This is also your opportunity to ask questions about things like the fee for an initial consultation, the retainer, and basic background information about the lawyer's education and experience. Remember that you are the consumer and in the driver's seat. You are just as entitled to receive information as you are required to give it.

If either you or the attorney's employee comes to the conclusion that this lawyer isn't the right one for you, ask for referrals to other attorneys.

If you have the option of having an online Zoom appointment or an in-person appointment, go with the in-person format unless health issues make in-person meetings unworkable. Too many subtle clues about compatibility could be lost on both sides of an online screen.

Pay for the Privilege

Family law attorneys usually charge for all consultations, even the initial one. That is a good thing for you because paying for the initial office visit underscores your intent to create an attorney–client relationship. Why is evidence of this intent important? This relationship is the cloak of confidentiality that protects all information shared with an attorney in the context of a lawyer–client relationship. This protection means that the lawyer should not tell anyone else anything that you told the lawyer—or any advice the lawyer gave you—without your permission. The privilege is very broad—the only exceptions are when you told your lawyer something that was "in furtherance of a crime or fraud" or that demonstrated your intent to cause serious physical harm to someone else.

The purpose of the attorney–client privilege is to encourage candid discourse between the client and the attorney. It allows you to speak freely knowing that the information is secure, and it assures the attorney that all relevant facts are in the open between the two of you.

Paying an attorney for legal services does not mean that you have to hire the attorney to represent you in the long haul; it means that for this single consultation, you have established an attorney–client relationship. In addition, once an attorney–client relationship exists, the attorney has a potential conflict of interest with your spouse and should not reveal to your spouse what you say to the lawyer, or represent or advise your spouse.

Taking Someone With You to the Meeting

You might feel that you want a friend or a family member, such as your adult child, to accompany you to the first meeting with an attorney, to serve as moral support or to take notes for you and help you ask the right questions. Particularly when we are under stress, we might have difficulty processing and remembering information, forget questions to ask, or be too submissive, and the presence of a third person can indeed be helpful. But before you take another person with you to the attorney's office, consider some potential problems.

First of all, the attorney–client privilege might not apply if a third person is present in the room. If the third person is not a client, the lawyer has no obligation to keep what that person says in confidence, or to keep confident what you say in the presence of that person. And if that third person is called to testify about what happened in the meeting, there's no privilege—everything that went on in the meeting is fair game. The only exception is if the third party is an agent or representative of either the lawyer or you. Your friend or adult child is not your agent unless he or she is your legal guardian or conservator.

If you really feel you need to have someone there with you to help you interview the attorney or ask questions about the process, consider limiting the discussion to things your spouse already knows and that you don't care about keeping private. When you dive into the nitty-gritty of the facts and you need to tell your attorney things your spouse might not know, ask the third person to leave the room. If you don't, you might not be able to be completely candid—and an attorney's advice is only as good as the facts presented.

Preparing for the Meeting With the Lawyer

You can increase your chances of having a successful and cost-effective encounter with the attorney, so that you get quality advice and counsel from the outset. Here are some tips to help you be a smart consumer of legal services:

> **Tip #1: Bring important documents.** If you have received correspondence or legal papers from your spouse or your spouse's attorney, or if you and your spouse signed a prenuptial agreement before your marriage, take these documents with you to your appointment or send or deliver them to the lawyer's office in time for the lawyer to review them in advance.

> **Tip #2: Bring a financial overview.** If you have a financial statement that lists your assets and liabilities, take it with you. This type of summary helps to focus the meeting and ensures that you will not forget key information. Even if it's not current, historical information can highlight activities that you'll need to ask your spouse to explain, such as expenditures or asset transfers. If you do not have a financial statement, create a list of your assets and liabilities as best you can. If you do not know your financial circumstances, do not panic. What you do not know could be as important to the attorney as what you do know.

> **Tip #3: Bring tax returns.** Provide a copy of your tax returns, including schedules and worksheets, for the last three years.

FROM THE LAWYER'S PERSPECTIVE

Preparing for the first client meeting. The more information an attorney reviews before meeting with a potential client, the better. It saves the client time and money, as the client does not have to wait while the attorney reads through a stack of papers provided at the initial office visit. Advance preparation lets attorneys hit the ground running in the first meeting and gives time for details to sift through their mind and percolate fresh ideas and questions.

Tip #4: Make a timeline. Take time to write a chronology of major events during your marriage. Include the following information:

- how and when you and your spouse met and how long you knew each other before you married
- whether either of you was married before and if so, whether the prior marriage ended in an amicable settlement or a contested case
- whether you and your spouse signed a prenuptial agreement before your wedding or a postmarital agreement after you married
- the names, birth dates, and Social Security numbers of your spouse and children, noting if any of your minor children are from a previous marriage
- career and educational milestones for you and your spouse
- residence locations throughout your marriage
- financial milestones and significant financial transactions
- dates when changes in health occurred
- points when you began noticing changes in your spouse's behavior
- if and when affairs, or suspected affairs, occurred
- acts of violence or abuse, and
- comments your spouse has made concerning the divorce.

If you think something might be important, include it. Err on the side of too much detail rather than too little. Giving this information to your attorney at this early stage is the most efficient way to explain your history. It also helps you begin to see the bigger picture and notice patterns and trends that you might otherwise overlook.

Be sure to write at the top of the first page of the chronology the words "Attorney–Client Communication." That notation invokes the attorney–client privilege and should protect the chronology from being disclosed later in your case.

FROM THE LAWYER'S PERSPECTIVE

The value of chronologies and the three lists. The marriage chronologies prepared by my clients were extremely helpful. I referred again and again to a chronology throughout a case. Both what a client chooses to write, and what the client omits, reveal useful information. Another exercise I frequently asked clients to do was to make three lists: 100 Things I Want To Have, 100 Things I Want To Do, and 100 Things I Want To Be. Clients told me how hard it was to complete these lists, but also said that when they did, they learned a great deal about themselves and what was really important to them. For example, by the time most of them completed 40 items on the list of 100 things they want to have, it changed from a list of things into a list of characteristics, such as having a sense of humor or a sense of accomplishment. Divorce clients need help in shifting their focus away from the unhappiness of their situation and toward what is really important. There were also times when the lists shaped decisions that my clients and I made together about how to structure a settlement.

Tip #5: Make a list of questions for the attorney. If you want to know all about the divorce process, then ask. If you want to know about alternatives to divorce, such as legal separation or postmarital agreements, ask. Also inquire about the attorney's professional education, experience, philosophy of practice, and all available methods the lawyer uses to resolve and address marital dissolution. Ask how the attorney views his or her professional role: as the Decider or the Adviser? What happens when the client and attorney disagree about strategy? What decisions, if any, will the attorney make unilaterally without first consulting with the client? The answers to these questions will shed light on the attorney's style of communication.

FROM THE LAWYER'S PERSPECTIVE

My function, your facts. The cornerstone of legal advice is to give the client information, alternatives, and guidance. The function of an attorney is not to make decisions for you, but to provide what you need to know so that you can make well-informed decisions yourself. Time and again I explained to clients that a decision is theirs to make—theirs alone, not mine. If they wanted to hear my recommendations, I would tell them. If a client chooses to ignore my advice, so be it. In the end, all decisions are made by the client.

Why Do This for A Living?

The enjoyment of a family law practice has to come from within, because it is not a popular profession. No one who came into my office wanted to be there. Clients usually arrived full of dread, misconceptions, and a lot of anger. They had little idea of what to expect, and what they did expect, they didn't think they would like. This discomfort was even more prevalent in older clients. They intuitively knew the stakes were higher for them. But I loved my job because I saw every day that divorce is not just an ending. In fact, divorce could be a creative turning point in people's lives, bringing positive change. My role was to lead clients through the legal quagmire and help them come out on the other side in one piece, ready to reap the positive aspects of the transition. The resilience of the human spirit is something I witnessed many, many times, and witnessing this resilience made this line of work fulfilling.

During the Consultation

After you explain why you scheduled the office appointment, the attorney will ask you questions to elicit facts and will start to broadly evaluate the major issues in your case. The lawyer should give you an overview of the stages of the divorce process and an explanation of fees and billing policies. If you do not understand something the attorney says, ask to have it repeated and explained until you understand. Lawyers are so familiar with the details of what they do that they easily digress into lawyer-babble. If the attorney seems annoyed with your questions, you might want to factor that into your consideration of whether this is the lawyer for you. An attorney who isn't supportive of clients' full understanding of what's going on in their divorces is likely to be a difficult lawyer to work with.

Expose the Skeletons

Telling your lawyer the full story of your marriage might be painful and difficult. But remember that you are not being judged; your case is simply being assessed. Do not sugarcoat the truth. Your attorney must know your shortcomings. Try to imagine what your spouse will say about you, too. You could certainly explain or defend yourself, but you must tell the attorney what you anticipate hearing. For example, do you have health problems or a history of emotional problems? Does your spouse complain about the amount of alcohol you drink? What medications do you take? Did you lose interest in sex with your spouse? Have you ever been physically violent or been on the receiving end of family violence? Have you been arrested or charged with a crime? Are you estranged from your children? Have you been fired from a job?

Assume that any and all skeletons in your closet will come out. It is always best if the attorney learns about your shadow side from you, rather than from your spouse's attorney. Above all, be truthful in your version of the facts and when answering the attorney's questions. No attorney wants a client who lies, and the attorney might withdraw from the case if you aren't completely truthful. Ethical attorneys will not put their law licenses or professional reputations on the line by knowingly lying to a judge or opposing counsel.

FROM THE LAWYER'S PERSPECTIVE

Musical chairs. A marriage in freefall has at least two sides. In our first meeting, I always asked the question, "What would I be hearing if your spouse were sitting in that chair instead of you?" Asking a client to project the beliefs of a spouse creates a distance from the information relayed. The information might not be "true" in the client's mind, but the question is not about what is true, but rather what will be said. I asked clients to visualize an auto accident at an intersection with four witnesses, each standing in a different quadrant of the intersection. All four people see the event from a different angle. No two views are the same, just as no marriage is experienced the same by the two people involved. A client is best served by understanding the other spouse's point of view. If I could coax a client into that frame of mind, then the client wouldn't be thrown for a loop every time a ridiculous allegation came up during the divorce process.

It is difficult to talk about things like this, especially to a stranger. That's why it is so important to feel comfortable confiding in the lawyer you choose. This is no time to be modest, timid, or embarrassed. Rest assured, much of what you say has been said before in the very office you're sitting in. If the attorney acts shocked or appears judgmental, you might want to look for someone else to work with.

Take Notes

Don't hesitate to take notes before, during, and after the meeting with the lawyer. You might be stressed and later find it difficult to remember all you hear. Jot down your impressions, noting what you liked, what wasn't comfortable about your experience with the attorney and staff, and information about the divorce process that the attorney explains to you.

You might wonder whether it's okay to record conversations with your attorney. I discouraged recordings because they seemed to find their way into the hands of the wrong people more often than written notes did. If you really want to record the interview, first ask the attorney if it's okay—it's illegal in most places to record conversations without the other person's consent. If the lawyer balks, you'll have to settle for taking good notes. If the attorney agrees, then for heaven's sake, stash the recording in a secure place outside your home and not on a device that's accessible to your spouse.

Inquire About Using a Team of Specialists

Attorneys can specialize in family law, estate planning and probate (wills and conservatorships, for example), and elder law (Social Security, Medicare, and Medicaid benefits). Divorce financial analysts specialize in working with divorcing couples to determine the best way to divide assets and debts. You might need any or all of these professionals to help with your case. The idea of having a team of lawyers and other professionals working on your case might seem overwhelming, especially if you're thinking about costs. But the assistance of specialists can be invaluable. When you are interviewing attorneys, find out whether they are willing to work with other professionals if the need arises, or whether they do so as a matter of course.

Look for a Good Fit

Remember that you are interviewing the attorney not only to obtain legal advice, but also to find out whether you and the attorney are a good fit. It's very likely that you will spend a significant amount of time with your attorney if your divorce is complex. Look around the attorney's office for impressions about whether the attorney seems like someone you wouldn't mind spending time with. If you see awards or honors displayed on every inch of wall space, ask questions to find out whether the lawyer's ego is likely to come before your interests. Try to discern what personality traits might be in conflict or be compatible with yours. Your goal is to hire an attorney who will put your concerns first and with whom you'll be comfortable discussing every square inch of your private life. And pay attention to your gut feeling—ideally, you should actually like your lawyer.

FROM THE LAWYER'S PERSPECTIVE

Transference. Transference is a redirection of unconscious feelings toward a counselor. You usually hear about it in the mental health professions, but it is alive and well in the family lawyer's office. For example, if a client's spouse has not given them the time of day for many years, the client might interpret my professional interest and attention as a different kind of interest and consider seeking a personal relationship. Because divorce attorneys are in counseling roles where intimate experiences are discussed, transference might occur—it's entirely understandable. And it's also temporary—it usually passes quickly after the client is presented with the first bill for my services.

Do Not Get Involved With Your Lawyer

You've probably read about or heard of divorce clients who become intimately involved with their lawyers, on a sexual or financial level, or both. When I hear stories like these, I shudder on behalf of the lawyer and the client. Nothing is more damaging to the reputation of lawyers than the violation of professional boundaries. Divorce clients are vulnerable and there is no excuse for taking advantage of them. If you are concerned that your lawyer is behaving inappropriately, make a report to the state bar or other professional authority. And if you find yourself tempted, don't act on an impulse. Step away from the moment and consider the messy consequences. This, too, shall pass.

Keep It Private

It's possible that you and your spouse have already agreed that you each will consult a lawyer before you move forward with your divorce. But if you haven't discussed attorneys—or if you haven't even brought up the subject of divorce yet—deciding not to tell your spouse that you're going to consult with an attorney is not necessarily a sneaky move. It might be smart. You might need more time to decide whether you even want to pursue a divorce or to decide which process—litigation, mediation, or collaboration—is best for your situation. You might need more time to gather information. And you might want to consult with more than one attorney in order to decide which one you want to hire. It's perfectly legitimate to keep this process to yourself if you don't feel that you want to tell your spouse yet.

At some point, though, you'll need to tell your spouse that you have a lawyer and who the lawyer is. Once hired, your lawyer will help you plan for how, when, and what to tell your spouse.

Risky Business: Wiretapping, Digital Sleuthing, and Electronic Surveillance

Ours is a tech-infused culture; every day we hear about new apps, software, social media platforms, and digital devices that challenge our ideas about privacy. Nowhere is that more apparent than in the divorce arena, where breach-of-privacy claims between spouses and between former spouses are becoming quite common. These claims can be brought as separate causes of action within a divorce suit or filed as the basis of a separate civil lawsuit known as a tort (an intentional or negligent causing of harm). At a minimum, the threat of such claims might create leverage in divorce negotiations.

Here are examples of activities that can lead to allegations of privacy breaches: attaching a tracking device on a spouse's vehicle without the spouse's knowledge or consent; the invasion of online email or social media accounts without the account holder's consent; accessing or duplicating files on a spouse's digital devices without that spouse's consent.

Because overzealous cyber-sleuthing can result in serious consequences—criminal and civil offenses, confinement in prison, and hefty fines—I'll address these topics now, rather than later in the book. Similarly, if you're considering becoming an amateur spy in your divorce, it's a good idea to discuss these issues with your attorney first, to make sure you don't violate any state or federal laws.

Many people try their hand at digital snooping before they have any idea of the serious blowback they could face. I want to alert you to the reality of the risks and encourage you to discuss specific topics with a lawyer, especially if you think your spouse has compromised the privacy of your email and texts or placed a tracking device on your car or other personal property, or if you have engaged in this type of activity. Even an attempt to commit an offense could itself be an offense.

Laws Protecting Privacy

Since the 1960s, the U.S. Congress has enacted a matrix of legislation, including the Wiretap Act, Stored Communications Act, and the Computer Fraud and Abuse Act, which aim to protect our expectations of personal privacy. These laws together are called the Electronic Communications Privacy Act (ECPA), and Congress updates them to reflect new technology. When you add the multitude of state laws on these subjects and the fact that judges' decisions interpreting these rules have been all over the map, you end up with a confusing framework of guidelines about what you can actually do.

In the 1970s, a federal appeals court concluded that the Wiretap Act was not intended to reach inside a home, to disputes between spouses; but a couple years later, another court concluded the opposite. Many of these cases have turned on the following inquiries:

- Was spyware installed before or after the divorce was filed?
- What was the motivation for the wiretapping?
- What type of data was retrieved? For example, was the invasion limited to emails between lovers, or all emails, including a spouse's confidential communications to an attorney?
- Was the computer separate property (belonging to just one spouse) or community property (jointly owned)?
- Was consent provided, and what was the scope of that consent?
- Was the spying technology even in existence at the time the law was passed?

If you obtain evidence illegally, in violation of a privacy law, you might find that it won't do you much good—and it might expose you to prosecution by the state for violating a criminal law. Divorce judges in some states will admit the evidence, reasoning that your illegal act does not detract from the credibility or relevance of the evidence itself; but others will find a way to exclude it. And even if the court allows the evidence to come in, the manner in which you obtained it (such as by theft) could be brought to light during your cross-examination at trial, if you give a different explanation as to how you came upon this evidence. Being exposed as a sneaky individual who pilfered private information could be more harmful than any benefit the evidence might bestow.

Now, suppose you are the *victim* of your spouse's illegal intrusion into your emails, texts, or other private communications. You might be tempted to threaten to report your spouse's illegal act to the local prosecutor unless your spouse agrees not to use the evidence gathered during the invasion. Don't do it, and don't expect your attorney to do it (in some states, such a threat would be a violation of the attorney's ethics rules).

A Lawyer's Vulnerability

You're not the only one at risk. You could expose your attorney to civil or even criminal liability by using or disclosing information that was obtained illegally. For example, if your lawyer uses your evidence in court documents, such as pleadings or affidavits, threatens to use the tainted information, or uses the information to get a better settlement, then your attorney might also be named as a defendant in your spouse's breach of privacy lawsuit. In one reported case, Spouse A "guessed" the correct answers to security questions on Spouse B's computer and gained entry into Spouse B's Yahoo email account; Spouse A copied emails between Spouse B and their lover, then gave a copy of those emails to Spouse A's attorney, without explaining how Spouse A got them. Spouse A and Spouse A's attorney were both held liable and fined with civil penalties for violating wiretap laws. No doubt, this attorney should have asked how the client got such sensitive information.

On another front, attorneys are being held to higher standards due to technology advances. Many states' attorney disciplinary rules now require lawyers to stay abreast of benefits and risks associated with relevant technology, and to understand how the use or misuse of social media might affect a client's case.

Preserve the Privacy of Your Attorney–Client Communication

Communications with your attorney are protected from discovery, unless you disclose them to a third party, such as your spouse. Here are some steps you can take to prevent disclosure and preserve the confidentiality of your communications:

- Ask what your attorney's policies are regarding emails and texting.
- Let your attorney know if you don't want to communicate via email or text.
- Set up an email account just for attorney–client communication, or be sure you have a new and good password on an older secure account.
- Don't send emails to your attorney from an address you do not want to use for replies.
- Communicate via secure email websites and preferably not on public Wi-Fi.
- Don't rely on email communication if your matter is urgent.
- Encrypt financial data sent over unsecured avenues, such as public Wi-Fi.
- Don't send or open sensitive documents on smartphones, because they're usually less secure than computers.
- Don't text your attorney about sensitive matters.

Protect Your Own Privacy

- Use secure passwords that your spouse doesn't have; update them frequently.
- Don't leave your computer on when unattended; do not leave your smartphone unattended.
- Check and tighten your security and privacy options on all social media and email accounts and cellphone data options.

- Do not use public Wi-Fi networks unless you want the information "reachable" by others.
- Enable "Find My Phone" features on smartphones.
- Consider disabling location features on your smartphone. Remember, it's difficult to clear all GPS tracking capabilities from a smartphone.
- Don't use computers that your soon-to-be ex uses; it's very easy to retrieve passwords entered into a shared computer.

Let Your Attorney Know ...

Let your attorney know the skeletons in your closet before your attorney finds out about them from the opposing side, specifically whether you:

- have used key loggers, GPS trackers, or imaging or copy hardware on any person's computer or other digital device (cellphone, smartphone, iPad, notebooks, laptops, or computers)
- have deleted relevant emails or other Internet communications and photos; remember, pressing the delete key does not remove the item's footprint from computers and other digital devices. You can purchase "scrubbing" software online, and a simple Google search will lead you to them. However, be aware that data retrieval experts work quickly to develop counter-technology.
- have a profile on a social network (Twitter, Facebook, or Instagram) or post on YouTube
- have your own website or blog
- use your cellphone or other devices for texting, video or audio recording, Internet browsing, or emailing
- use encryption software
- back up your files and data, and how you do it
- keep files in iCloud, DropBox, or other "cloud" type resources
- share a computer, cellphone, or other device with anyone, not just your spouse
- have given other people access to your passwords
- keep track of your passwords, and how often you change them
- have ever been hacked on any of your devices, and
- have any adult material on any device.

Don't Play Cyber Detective

You can avoid the serious, costly, and time-consuming civil and criminal consequences discussed above if you get legal advice before you:

- Change or delete documents, emails, or other data relevant to your case
- Try to mine a spouse's social media, personal, or business email accounts
- Videotape or audiotape conversations or situations to which you are a party and definitely those to which you are *not* a party
- Install malware or keystroke logging programs (or have someone else do so)
- Install GPS tracking devices on your spouse's vehicles or devices, or
- Hire a tech-savvy private investigator.

Interesting Networking Statistics

- 50% of adults over 65 use social networking sites, per the Pew Research Center Survey, Social Media Use in 2021.
- The American Academy of Matrimonial Lawyers (AAML) surveyed attorneys and found that 4 out of 5 used evidence derived from social networking sites in divorce cases, with Facebook leading the pack. Additionally, 81% of the responding lawyers have used or encountered evidence taken from a social media site.
- People who use Facebook more than once an hour are more likely to "experience Facebook-related conflict with their romantic partners," according to a study by R. Clayton, published in the *Journal of Cyberpsychology, Behavior and Social Networking*, June 6, 2013. Of the subjects, network users ranging in age from 18 to 82, 79% reported being in a romantic relationship .
- Previous studies have shown that the more people use social media sites, the more likely they were to monitor their partners.

Understanding How Attorneys Charge

This might be your first experience as a consumer of the intangible product called legal services. Even if you have worked with an attorney before, perhaps in a real estate transaction or on estate planning, you might have a very different experience in the family law context, which is often less predictable and more open-ended.

This section covers common billing practices in depth. The reason for including so much detail is that many complaints filed against attorneys involve misunderstandings (or shenanigans) about fees, and divorce almost always costs more than you think it should. You might avoid a lot of problems if you understand in detail how attorneys charge.

Factors Affecting Fees

It may seem strange that it's so difficult for lawyers to predict how much your divorce might cost. But there are a number of variables that can affect the cost of a divorce:

- the temperaments of both spouses
- the actions taken by the opposing attorney
- whether you need to trace commingling of marital and separate assets
- whether you need to hire appraisers and valuators
- the type and complexity of assets involved
- the influence of each spouse's advisers, and
- how much knowledge each party has about the relevant facts.

Hourly Rates

Most family law attorneys charge an hourly rate for their time and often charge a lower rate for work done by certain staff members, including other attorneys in the office, law clerks, and paralegals. Rates vary depending on where you live and on the attorney's experience and reputation. In addition, you'll pay for expenses related to your case, like filing fees, copies, postage, travel, delivery, and the like (see "Expenses," below).

Your lawyer should agree to keep records of time spent on every activity related to your case, from telephone calls and digital communication to office visits and time in court. Most lawyers measure time in either six-minute (one-tenth of an hour), ten-minute (one-sixth of an hour), or quarter-hour increments. The smaller the time segment, the lower the fee, so be sure you ask about this. For example, if your lawyer bills in quarter-hour segments, a six-minute phone call will cost you $50, while it would cost only $20 if the lawyer used six-minute increments. Ask how frequently you will receive periodic billings. You might even ask to see a sample bill to see how detailed the lawyer is about explaining the tasks that each staff person accomplished.

Expenses

Your case will undoubtedly involve expenses, which might include court filing fees, photocopies, postage, travel, research expenses, delivery services, and similar case-related charges. If your attorney hires an expert, such as an appraiser or a forensic accountant, you'll pay for that as well. Talk with your lawyer at the outset about how the office handles these expenses. Does the lawyer front the costs and then bill you for reimbursement, or do you pay some of the costs directly—for example, by writing a check to an expert who will testify about the value of an asset? The fee agreement that you sign should set out the specific rates for things like photocopying and printing emails. If you want to try to save money by doing some of that administrative work yourself or paying for copies somewhere else, ask your attorney to agree to that at the outset.

Fees for Consultation as Needed

You might consult an attorney on an as-needed basis only, with each appointment standing alone. If you do, you will probably be expected to pay at the end of each office meeting—and this might work better for you as well, especially if the consultation occurs before you file for divorce, because it means you won't receive a bill in the mail. If you hire the attorney later to represent you in a case or transaction, your financial relationship will probably change to a retainer arrangement, discussed below.

Flat Fees

A flat fee is a lump sum that covers all charges from the beginning to the end of your case. A flat fee is designed to give both you and the attorney some degree of security about what to expect in terms of cost. The difficulty is that in setting the fee, the lawyer must try to estimate how complex your case will become; it's not very common for a divorce attorney to charge a flat fee for an entire case because of the difficulty of predicting the number of hours your case will take. All of the variables described in "Factors Affecting Fees," above, contribute to this difficulty.

If the lawyer overestimates this, you'll pay more than your case warrants. On the other hand, if the attorney underestimates the time, then after a certain point the attorney will be working for free, which might not work well for you in terms of having the lawyer's full attention. Either way you look at it, you stand to lose with flat-fee representation unless you have a very simple set of facts.

Contingency Fees

A contingency fee means that the attorney receives a percentage of the award if the case is won, and nothing if it's not. The word contingency refers to the fact that the fee is contingent on a positive outcome. Contingency fees are most commonly used in personal injury cases.

In a divorce, using a contingency fee means you would pay the attorney a percentage of the value of the marital assets that you are awarded. Many states don't allow contingency fees in divorce cases at all, and even in places where they're allowed, they are frowned upon. It is easy to see why. If an attorney's fee is dependent upon the valuation of assets, the negotiation takes on a personal aspect for the lawyer, who might be less than objective during negotiations and might have a hard time keeping an eye on what's best for the client.

Retainers

A retainer is money that you pay to your attorney to cement your contract and guarantee the attorney's time on your case (and from the lawyer's perspective, to guarantee payment). Although you're likely to pay the retainer at or soon after the first meeting, you won't pay just for that appointment. In fact, the amount will be much more than what you owe for the initial consultation, because it's a deposit against fees that will be due later. The lawyer will put your money into a special account called a trust account, where it remains yours until the lawyer earns it, at which point the lawyer transfers the amount owed into the attorney's own bank account. Some lawyers have a standard retainer amount; with others the amount is based on the issues involved in your case or on other factors listed in "Factors Affecting Fees," above.

FROM THE LAWYER'S PERSPECTIVE

It matters who's on the other side. Your spouse's choice of attorney influences both the tone and the cost of a divorce—and might even dictate the retainer required. For example, if your attorney knows the opposing attorney has a reputation for being unethical and fee gouging—or even ethical and extremely aggressive—the retainer could be higher. In that situation, your attorney might predict that they'll have to spend lots of time responding to groundless accusations, oppressive discovery, and pointless hearings—and that will increase the cost to you. Likewise, if your attorney knows that the opposing attorney has no experience in family law, understand that it's likely that they will expend more time because they will have to educate their opposing counsel. On the other hand, if your attorney knows their opposing attorney is experienced, honest, knowledgeable, and open to compromise, the road will be much smoother, and the retainer will likely be at the lower end.

The Fiduciary Relationship

Because a refundable retainer is your money, not the attorney's, until it is earned, most states require attorneys to follow strict accounting procedures for money held in trust. Retainer funds must be deposited into a special trust account that is separate from the attorney's business operating account. The attorney has a fiduciary relationship (meaning a relationship of high trust) with you as to funds held in a trust account, must always be able to account for those monies, and must never withdraw funds from the retainer except in accordance with your fee agreement. "Borrowing" funds in trust accounts is theft and lawyers can be suspended or disbarred for doing it.

Nonrefundable retainers—which are not related to fees or costs but are intended only to ensure the lawyer's availability—are rarely used and are prohibited in some states. The much more common refundable retainer is a deposit to be applied against future fees and expenses, with any remaining funds returned to you at the end of the case. Refundable retainers can work in a few ways:

- The retainer might be held on deposit to be applied to the final bill upon conclusion of your case. As your case progresses, you will receive monthly bills and will be expected to pay those when you receive them.

- The retainer might be used each month to pay the fees and costs for that month. When your initial retainer is exhausted or gets down to a specified amount, you might be required to replenish it.

- The retainer might be called an "evergreen" retainer. This means you deposit a specified sum with the attorney, and you always maintain that balance. Your monthly billing charges are deducted from the retainer funds, and you replenish the retainer to maintain the specified minimum balance. At the end of your case, any unearned part of the retainer is refunded to you.

Written Fee Agreements

Unless you consult the attorney just once or on an as-needed basis, a written fee contract is an absolute must. The agreement should spell out all details about retainers and billing procedures, along with the specifics about fees and expenses. In some states, consumer contracts, such as divorce attorney fee agreements, must be in writing. But even if your state does not require that, you want the details of your fee and representation agreement to be in writing to avoid misunderstandings down the road.

Many clients hiring a divorce lawyer are distraught, distracted, or embarrassed to ask questions about accounting and billing procedures. They might even feel intimidated by the attorney or staff. When presented with the fee contract, they sign quickly and without thought or question.

Don't let that hesitant person be you. Instead, pause for a moment. You do not want disagreements about fees to interfere with your relationship with your attorney later. The best way to avoid them is to read the contract with care, ask questions if you do not understand something, and require that any clarifications be written into the contract. If you are presented with the fee contract at the end of your initial consultation, take time to look it over carefully—or consider taking it with you to review when you are rested and have time to absorb it. You might even want to have another attorney, or at least a trusted friend, review the contract before you sign it. If the lawyer doesn't want you to take the time to review the contract and ask questions, find another lawyer.

Who Pays the Attorney

Most attorney–client relationships are direct: It is the client's responsibility to pay the attorney. However, in some cases, a third party is involved—for example, an adult child who agrees to pay the parent's attorneys' fees. In that case, the contract should explain that person's financial obligation and make clear that even though someone else is paying the lawyer, all decisions still rest with the client. The only exception is if the client is incompetent and the third party has the authority to serve as an agent, guardian, or representative of the client.

Even if someone else assumes primary responsibility for your fees, you will probably remain liable as well. You'll likely have a hard time persuading a lawyer to sign a contract that absolves you of responsibility and makes a third party solely responsible for paying your fees.

If you need help paying your attorney and you borrow money from friends or family, talk with your lawyer beforehand so that the transaction is documented as a loan rather than a gift. A loan for attorneys' fees might be credited to you when you calculate the final division of assets and liabilities, putting some of the burden on your spouse.

Can You Make Your Spouse Pay Fees?

If your spouse is the person in control of all the money and you don't have access to any money to pay fees, a lawyer might work with you to ask a judge to order your spouse to pay your lawyer a retainer. But if you are expecting your spouse to pay your attorneys' fees in a divorce, raise that issue with the attorney in the beginning. Rarely will an attorney accept a client who can't pay, in the hope that the court will order the opposing party to pay the bill.

Last Words on Lawyer Shopping

Attorneys' fees in a divorce case can balloon beyond your or your attorney's expectations, because of the time consumed by unpredictable, emotionally driven conflicts. That is why you must trust your lawyer's ethics and judgment. Pay attention to your instincts and your gut reactions to the attorneys you interview. If in doubt, keep on shopping; it is essential that you feel safe and comfortable. Consider consulting with more than one attorney when you're looking to choose someone to work with. Yes, it is expensive to pay for more than one initial consultation, but it will be worth it. You will learn something from each attorney you meet (and you might also create a conflict of interest with an attorney your spouse might otherwise retain). Most important, by observing different styles and personalities, you will find the right lawyer for you.

Unbundled Legal Services: The a la Carte Approach

Many people planning a divorce experience sticker shock when they learn about steep hourly rates and high retainers for legal representation. Often, they consider self-representation or using an attorney only for some parts of a case. Advances in computer technology (such as "virtual law office" software) also support a trend toward self-representation or using so-called unbundled services.

In the legal world, "unbundling" refers to breaking down the attorney's role into separate, definable tasks. Other terms for this concept include limited representation, limited-scope representation, and discrete tasks legal representation. Instead of retaining an attorney to represent you in all stages of a divorce, you might contract with an attorney to provide only specifically delineated services. Think of it as an a la carte menu where you pick and choose distinct activities you want a lawyer to perform, as needed.

Not all states allow or encourage limited representation by attorneys. In those places where unbundled representation is an option, the client must give informed consent in a written legal services contract that sets out exactly what the lawyer will and won't do for the client.

Unbundled Legal Services in a Divorce

An attorney does so many different tasks when representing a client in a divorce that the menu of unbundled services is quite extensive. The client might choose from a long list of options, including the following tasks:

- **Preparing the initial pleadings.** A full-service attorney would go on record as your attorney by filing the initial petition or response with the attorney's name on the papers; the attorney would thus become answerable to the court. In the unbundled service situation, the attorney prepares the pleadings, but your name appears on them as representing yourself (you're referred to as "in pro per" or "pro se"), and the lawyer isn't accountable to the court. The lawyer could also prepare other court documents for you to file as the divorce progresses.

- **Document preparation for the discovery process.** A lawyer could help you prepare or answer requests for document production, interrogatories, written depositions, requests for admissions, and discovery motions. Once the documents are drafted, you would be responsible for signing them, filing them with the court (if required), and serving your spouse with a copy.

- **Office consultations, telephone calls, fax, email, or mail.** You might try doing everything in your divorce yourself with help from an attorney behind the scenes giving you advice and instructions. This is also called coaching. The lawyer might assess the strengths and weaknesses of your case, offer advice on the law, explain the options available for resolving your divorce, and advise you on how to prepare a property inventory, how to hire experts, what documents you might want to prepare, and other strategic issues.
- **Reviewing documents drafted by the client.** If you're doing your own divorce, you could still have a lawyer look over whatever you write, whether it's a letter or a set of discovery requests.
- **Doing legal research and analysis.** The lawyer might help you look up legal rules or do the research for you.
- **Investigating facts, contacting witnesses, and reviewing records.** Lawyers often work with investigators and might refer you to someone who could help with some of the legwork on your case.
- **Reviewing terms of a settlement agreement.** This is a crucial function and if you have a lawyer do nothing else, hire one to make sure your settlement agreement is complete and legally adequate.
- **Preparing documents necessary to transfer property between the spouses in accordance with their final agreement.** You might need help preparing transfer documents, such as deeds, or setting up liens to guarantee support or buyout payments.

If you think you might want to represent yourself with coaching from an attorney, you should discuss the possibility at the outset with attorneys that you interview. Not all lawyers are open to it, and although it does happen, it's rare to go from full-service representation to unbundled representation with the same attorney. Ask each attorney you interview some important questions:

- Does this jurisdiction allow limited legal representation?
- Do you have experience in limited-scope representation?
- Is the judge friendly to pro se litigants?

- What are the critical deadlines?
- Is discovery necessary in my case?
- When do I have to appear in court?
- When should I begin negotiating with my spouse?
- What can you tell me about my spouse's attorney?

Is Unbundling for You?

Unbundling isn't for everyone. Doing a divorce involves a lot of picky legal tasks and a lot of information gathering. You need to have the time to devote to it and you must be comfortable with paperwork, rules, and doing research. Red flags should alert you that unbundled legal services are less than ideal in your case. You should probably have a lawyer representing you if:

- Your spouse is dishonest or is an uncompromising bully, or has been diagnosed with a personality or character disorder.
- You know very little about your marital finances or assets and liabilities.
- Your spouse is not willing to share financial information.
- Speaking in front of others is a high-anxiety situation for you.
- Confrontation unnerves you.
- Your marital estate has complicated issues of valuation or characterization.

Pros of Unbundling

Contracting with an attorney to provide unbundled legal services usually costs less than full-service representation. That is its major selling point. It also gives you more control over the process. And working on your own divorce might create a history of working with your spouse to resolve issues, a history that you might build upon to help you in the future should disagreements arise.

Cons of Unbundling

From both the client's and the lawyer's perspective, unbundled legal services carry some downsides:

From a client's viewpoint. Representing yourself in court in anything other than an uncontested divorce can be risky. The judge might have a bias against pro se litigants; you might even run into a judge or court staffer who simply tells you that you should go hire an attorney (a statement you should never accept, as you have the right to represent yourself). On the other hand, some judges give litigants who are representing themselves the benefit of the doubt. Some jurisdictions even provide volunteers or staff lawyers to assist self-represented litigants.

If you and your spouse both started out self-represented but your spouse suddenly appears in court with an attorney, you will probably want to respond in kind. In contested hearings where one spouse has a lawyer and the other one does not, the unrepresented spouse usually operates at a distinct disadvantage.

Clients using unbundled legal services assume a lot of responsibility, along with the concurrent opportunity to make mistakes. If your coaching attorney is not available to advise you during an unexpected crisis, you might have no recourse. Without the knowledge and experience of an attorney, significant matters could fall through the cracks. With full-service representation, the attorney has an ethical obligation to represent you, examine your issues thoroughly, and proceed appropriately. If hired for a limited purpose, what you've signed on for is all you get.

From the lawyer's viewpoint. Some lawyers feel that preparing documents or giving advice in an information vacuum doesn't give them enough familiarity with the case facts to do a good job at their piecemeal assignment. Or, they might feel that their limited role gives them little control over what actually happens in court. In each case, they might worry that they're not able to serve clients effectively. Lawyers also worry that clients, who do not have calendaring systems reminding them to comply with rules and time limits, will miss important deadlines—and in an unbundled situation, it's not the lawyer's job to notify you of deadlines.

Attorneys are also concerned about liability exposure if something goes awry. For example, if a client doesn't give a lawyer-coach all the facts, the attorney might unwittingly offer faulty advice—and if the client relies on the advice and the case suffers, the client might come back seeking recourse against the lawyer. (This concern might be eased somewhat by a very detailed legal services contract that provides clarity about the role of the attorney. It could allow the client to give informed consent and even waive the right to sue the attorney over the advice given.)

Due to the accelerating costs of divorce and rising number of self-represented parties in family law in the last decade, unbundled services offer a valuable choice to the well-informed consumer. If you're considering self-representation, review some of the following additional resources:

- *Nolo's Essential Guide to Divorce*, by Emily Doskow (Nolo)
- *Divorce & Money: How to Make the Best Financial Decisions During Divorce*, by Violet Woodhouse and Lina Guillen (Nolo), and
- *Represent Yourself in Court: How to Prepare & Try a Winning Case*, by Paul Bergman and Sara J. Berman (Nolo).

Working With Other Advisers

You've heard the phrase, "It takes a village." This concept of collective effort also applies to a divorce. Your village most certainly will include your personal advisers and your lawyer. In addition, it might grow to encompass professional advisers who help you uncover facts, value assets, manage debts, and plan for your financial future, as well as support your emotional well-being. How large a village you'll have, and how closely these advisers will be involved, depends on your circumstances.

Your lawyer will talk to you about other professional advisers you'll need during your divorce; their advice might well influence your lawyer's strategy and, ultimately, the outcome of your case.

Legal Advisers or Experts

Your case might benefit from legal advisers in other areas of law, including estate planning; and probate attorneys and elder law attorneys as described in "Inquire About Using a Team of Specialists," above. If you need a Qualified Domestic Relations Order (QDRO) to divide a retirement account, it's likely you'll hire a lawyer with specific expertise in that area, and experts in real estate or business transactions might help your attorney prepare complex asset transfer documents.

Investigators

If you don't understand your family finances, or if you suspect your spouse of financial wrongdoing or of hiding assets, you might need to hire a private investigator, forensic accountant, or computer data collection expert at some point during your divorce. There's a longer discussion about when to use this type of expert in Chapter 7, "More About Assets—And What They're Worth to You." It's important to be careful not to engage in misconduct of your own when you go into this type of investigation, so be sure you and your lawyer are on the same page before you ask for help from investigator types.

Experts in Asset Valuation

Professional asset evaluators are frequently required by law to have licenses issued by the state or other licensing agency. For real estate, you'd turn to property appraisers and realtors. For retirement plans, you'd engage actuaries and accountants. For businesses, you'd look for valuators with specialized training. Personal property appraisers examine art, antiques, and collectibles. Chapter 6, "The Big Ticket Items: Your Home, Your Retirement, and Your Family Business," and Chapter 7, "More About Assets—And What They're Worth to You," will give you more details about the qualifications and referral resources for asset valuation professionals.

Financial Experts

Financial professionals might help you decide what you want to negotiate for, including which assets to keep and how to deal with your debts. Certified divorce financial planners, independent investment counselors, tax planners, and stockbrokers all have information that could prove useful, and if your debt situation is complicated you might want to consult with a debt counselor, bankruptcy attorney, tax attorney, or other tax specialist. There's more about these professionals in Chapter 5, "Marital Property: Steps to a Fair Division," Chapter 8, "The Bad News: Debts and Taxes," and Chapter 10, "Your Financial Survival."

Mental Health Professionals

Mental health and counseling professionals—physicians, psychologists, marriage counselors, therapists, substance abuse specialists, negotiation coaches, and career counselors—provide a wide scope of services. Many people find it very helpful to engage in some form of counseling during the divorce process, which can be enormously stressful. You might get help managing the process, as well as support, ideas, and feedback about your future plans, as you move through the divorce and on into your new life. As you digest the following chapters, you will learn more about the roles of professional advisers in divorce. It is comforting to know their expertise is out there, should you need it. ●

Getting Guidance—The Personal Side

Y ou do not go through divorce in a vacuum. In fact, in addition to the professional advisers discussed in the previous chapter, you probably have many other voices offering you advice—advice that is sometimes helpful, sometimes confusing, and sometimes contradictory. It can be difficult to discern which advice you should follow, especially if age, health problems, or other circumstances leave you feeling particularly vulnerable. This chapter focuses on making sense of the cacophony and helping you figure out how you want to deal with your spouse, how to assemble a network of friends and family to support you, and how to relate to your adult children about your divorce. We'll also address issues of competency—in other words, what to do when the need arises for a surrogate decision maker, such as a guardian or conservator.

What You Might Hear From Your Spouse, and How to Respond

Some divorcing spouses can relate to one another in a civil manner from the outset and calmly work through their issues. If you're in that situation, congratulations. You should be able to use mediation or a collaborative process to complete your divorce quickly and without spending a fortune. Chapter 4, "Your Divorce Options," explains those ways of completing your divorce.

But in some situations, one spouse has preconceived ideas about how the cards should fall and attempts to bully the other spouse into agreeing to those ideas. In other words, you might be confronted with antagonism and browbeating before you even have the opportunity to consult with an attorney. Try not to let this shake your equilibrium.

Instead, in the early going, it's important that you take things slowly, refrain from making decisions until you have all the information and advice you need, and resist any pressure you might be feeling from your spouse.

Difficult spouses tend to use particular tactics in a contentious divorce. The following sections are a preview of some of the things you might hear from your spouse at the start of your divorce. In each case, you'll see examples of what you might hear, a reality check about what you could expect to actually happen, and some advice about how to deal with what you're hearing.

"Don't Hire a Lawyer—or Else"

The first thing your spouse might do is threaten you with dire consequences if you consult an attorney instead of simply accepting what your spouse thinks the settlement should be. For example:

- "If you don't take what I offer, I'll fight you tooth and nail and leave you penniless."
- "I was going to be fair with you, but now that you've said you want a lawyer, I'm going to play hardball, and you'll end up with nothing."
- "If you hire a lawyer, I'll file bankruptcy and nothing will be left for you."

These are threats, and you should consider them a neon sign pointing you toward the lawyer's office—sooner rather than later. No matter what your spouse might say, you cannot resolve anything until you know your rights and understand how the law applies to the facts in your case. There is absolutely no reason you have to negotiate before you consult with an attorney. When faced with confrontational badgering, remove yourself from the situation. If you stay and argue, you will accomplish nothing. If you feel physically threatened, call the police. This is not the time to be conciliatory.

"We'll Save Money if We Mediate Without Attorneys"

Mediation is a process in which a third person (the mediator) helps divorcing spouses reach a settlement of the issues in their divorce. The mediator doesn't have the authority to make decisions, but instead facilitates the discussion and supports communication so that the spouses might reach their own resolution. Mediators aren't permitted to give legal advice, as they're not representing either party, but they can provide legal information, such as explaining support guidelines in your county or state.

A detailed explanation of the mediation process is provided in Chapter 4, "Your Divorce Options." Right now, though, the issue confronting you is whether you should go into mediation without an attorney by your side, or even before you've consulted an attorney at all. Your spouse might make this sound very attractive by emphasizing the cost savings, and it is true that mediation could be a very cost-effective alternative to turning your case over to attorneys and having them hash out a settlement. Mediation could also have a positive effect on your relationship with your ex-spouse, because the mediator often will help you work on your communication skills so that your ongoing contact is less stressful.

These are important reasons for considering mediation as part of the big picture. However, mediation requires a level playing field in which both spouses are fully informed about the legal rules relating to property, debt, and alimony. A common strategy is for the spouse who has greater knowledge about the family finances to try persuading the other to begin mediation right away. If you're the other spouse—the one with less information—you are in a tough spot, because it's very difficult to resolve or even discuss anything substantive before you understand your financial situation and your options. You need to gather information and get some advice about your rights.

Unless you're absolutely sure that you know and understand the family financial picture as well as your spouse does, you should, at the very least, have a consultation with an attorney before going into mediation. There's much more about working with attorneys in general in Chapter 2, "Getting Guidance—The Professional Side," and on working with attorneys in mediation—and choosing a mediator—in Chapter 4, "Your Divorce Options."

"Let's Just Use One Attorney"

It's unethical for a lawyer to represent two clients with conflicting interests, and no divorce lawyer should ever represent both spouses in a divorce. No matter how amicable the divorce might seem, there's always a possibility that your interests and your spouse's may differ on some point, and a joint attorney cannot handle such a situation. The sole circumstance under which only one attorney would be properly involved in a divorce is when one spouse retains an attorney and the other spouse is self-represented. This is not the same thing as having one lawyer represent the two of you.

"Let's Just Work It Out Ourselves"

Your spouse might put pressure on you to try to negotiate a settlement without any intervention at all from lawyers, mediators, or anyone else. If your spouse wants to talk about possible terms of a settlement and you haven't seen an attorney yet, just keep two simple rules in mind:

- Get information; don't give it.
- Listen; don't commit.

There's usually no harm in having a conversation, as long as it stays theoretical. But you definitely shouldn't commit to anything until you've had a chance to consider the big picture. And if you can avoid it, don't negotiate at all until you've had a chance to consult with an adviser.

Two good reasons support this approach:

It is unwise to negotiate piecemeal until you know your goals on all issues. Issues in a divorce case are often interrelated. For example, agreements about alimony might influence the property division and vice versa; taxable assets might not be an equal trade for nontaxable assets. As a general rule, you'll do better if you treat negotiations as a package, so if you lock yourself into an agreement on one issue, it won't be available as leverage when negotiating another issue.

Also, you may make certain assumptions at the outset that you later learn are incorrect. For example, you might agree to accept a particular retirement account in exchange for giving up something else, only to learn later that the retirement account is not a cash asset but an annuity with steep surrender charges, while the asset you gave up has immediate cash value. If you had known that, you might have made different decisions.

When you commit to a position early, but later change your mind, you risk creating the impression that you can't be trusted to take and keep a position. Simply put, backtracking sours the mood of negotiations and makes it more difficult to get other things you want.

> EXAMPLE: In the initial stages of divorce, both spouses agree that Spouse A will keep the house, to which she feels emotionally tied. Spouse B wants the brokerage accounts because he plans to use those assets to purchase a new house he has already found; Spouse A agrees to this because she knows little about investing and is insecure about managing brokerage assets. Also, she wants to appease him. As the divorce moves forward and the parties gather information, Spouse A learns that the property taxes on the house are beyond her capacity to pay. She concludes that instead of keeping the house, her best option is to sell it and divide the sale proceeds with Spouse B, and also divide the brokerage accounts between them. In the meantime, Spouse B has become increasingly attached to the idea of purchasing his new home immediately with the brokerage funds. When Spouse B finds out that Spouse A has changed her mind, he becomes agitated and mistrustful because he thinks she is not keeping her word. Tensions and testiness accelerate and strain subsequent attempts to settle.

No one likes to negotiate with a moving target. You see how easy it is to create expectations that later become barriers to negotiation— you generate these expectations unwittingly in idle, seemingly friendly, give-and-take with your spouse. Before you know it, you have telegraphed a strategic position that you might end up changing later. To avoid this, simply stay away from discussions about how you might settle your divorce until you've considered the big picture and are prepared to negotiate a full resolution.

An early resolution is not always the best resolution. It is understandable that you want to put this stressful, emotional time behind you, and you might feel that you want a quick divorce settlement so you can move on with your life. In most cases, though, speed doesn't serve your best interests. This is especially true if your spouse is the one who deals with the finances and you're in the dark as far as what you own and what you owe.

That said, in some areas an early agreement makes sense. If your spouse definitely wants her grandmother's afghan, and you are allergic to wool and don't like the color, go ahead and pass it over. Agreements about small things like this might actually support a future settlement as they begin to establish common ground and create goodwill. But don't make any big commitments. If you find yourself cornered by your spouse who wants to talk before you are fully prepared to negotiate, try to listen carefully. Hear what is important to your spouse and why. Valuable information might be gained in these conversations. Just say, "That is interesting. Thanks for telling me that. I will consider it."

Family and Friends

Divorce brings with it a restructuring of your social and family networks—especially in a late-life divorce where relationships have developed and been cemented over many years. As you begin redefining yourself and your place in the world, you are also redefining your support system. You will seek solace and comfort from your family and friends. You might unload on them. You might reveal new confidences about what has been happening in your marriage. You might hear for the first time that others thought long ago that you were headed for a divorce. You will undoubtedly hear a great deal of advice and be treated to many divorce war stories. These connections wield powerful influences, for better and worse, in the process of dissolving a marriage.

The Tribe: Dealing With Family

Often, the first people you'll talk to about your divorce are family members. You might have children or grandchildren to tell, or parents and in-laws to inform—and you need to tread cautiously. Delivering news of a divorce to the family is never easy, and you can expect reactions to fall all over the map. Adult children are an issue all their own, addressed in "Adult Children and Divorce," below. But parents and in-laws need special attention in the disclosure process, too.

Talking with in-laws poses some tricky issues. You might end up maintaining a decent relationship with your in-laws after the divorce, but it's hard to predict, and the old saying that blood is thicker than water might be brought home to you now. It is common for clients to report initially that in-laws are "in my camp." But be cautious. If you end up asking for something that they feel you are not entitled to, or if you take a position they view as threatening to their blood relative, they might circle the wagons. That is why you are wise to remain circumspect about what you discuss with them. By all means, try to maintain a friendly relationship—but keep your own counsel about anything related to the divorce. In addition to being good strategic advice, this will also prevent you from burning any bridges when it comes to your future relationships with these relatives as well as your ex.

Friends

Very likely, you and your spouse have many friends who are couples— and this presents another set of potential challenges. Friends often feel that they have to take sides. If you could spare them this, you'll probably keep more of them once the divorce is over. If you don't object to your friends staying connected with your spouse, let them know that, and do what you can to support those relationships. Some amicable partners write a joint letter to friends, announcing the divorce, the couple's desire to maintain friendships after the divorce, and their intention to have a peaceful conclusion to this chapter of their lives. Some of the letters I've read are quite moving and set a tone that puts everyone at ease.

If relations between you and your spouse are acrimonious, though, this is another place to be careful about sharing information. For example, let's say that you are close to one partner in a couple and your spouse is close to the other. Talking to your friend could mean you are unwittingly feeding information right back to your spouse through your friend's pillow talk.

The Lover

Extramarital lovers might be silent partners in the decision to divorce. Clients rarely want to hear an attorney's advice on this subject, which is to keep a new partner on the back burner during the divorce. But consider it from this perspective: If you really believe your new partner is the person you want to end up with after your divorce, then keeping them as far away from the process as possible will only be to the good.

For one thing, sharing a common enemy—your spouse—provides a tenuous bond. A relationship that is nourished by the angst and anguish experienced during a divorce is on shaky ground. After the divorce is final, that particular shared interest vanishes, and the extramarital relationship might wither as a result. Also, rarely will you receive unbiased input from someone who stands to gain from the downfall of your marriage.

If you really care about your new partner, consider giving the relationship a chance to succeed on its own. Lovers could provide comfort and affection when you most need it. Accept that, but keep it separate from your divorce.

Shadow Advisers

The likelihood is high that you have family members and friends who are divorced. You might seek their advice because you assume that they know how to get through it. And these shadow advisers might welcome the chance to relive their divorce experience through your current reality. It's healthy to connect with others when you are going through a difficult time, but remember that every divorce is driven by its own facts and no two divorces are alike. The advice you receive from friends and family could be less than helpful and could even be harmful if your situation is quite different from what they've gone through. Also, you're most likely immersed in your own narrative about what's going on, and that's what you'll be telling your shadow advisers. This makes their feedback equally unbalanced.

Remember that your friends and family are not legally bound by confidentiality like your lawyer is. Take care in deciding when to share negotiating strategies developed with your attorney, and make sure that information does not travel to the other side and undermine trial preparation or negotiations.

Does it sound like I'm telling you never to talk to anyone about your divorce? That's not my intention. Certainly, I am encouraging you to be very cautious, both in what you say and in what advice you seek and follow. But of course you should find ways to talk about your emotions, your questions, and your plans. You may have friends and family members you consider completely trustworthy and who you know will not disclose information to your spouse. You might also want to consider seeing a therapist—the safest way to vent, because it's also a confidential relationship.

Adult Children and Divorce

For a long time, little attention was paid to the grown children of divorcing parents. With custody, child support, and visitation outside the court's control, the adult child was deemed a nonissue. Most often, children of parents who divorce later in life have already moved out of the family home. But it is a myth that adult children escape the effects of parental divorce.

Research shows that older children can be as unsettled by the divorce of their parents as younger children. They experience similar trauma, and they have to deal with the changing family dynamics just as younger children do. The over-18 child, though beyond the direct reach of the court, still grapples with parent–child contact and issues of financial and emotional support.

These can be very difficult, painful situations for families. If things are really going badly, family counseling might provide some help with unraveling the dynamics of the divorce; adult children might find individual counseling helpful, too.

The Boomerang Generation

The term boomerang generation describes the many young adults who return to their childhood homes after college—or who never leave in the first place. They might struggle with being self-supporting, and studies tell us they are financially dependent longer than their parents were in the previous generation. According to the Pew Research Center's analysis of July 2020 monthly U.S. Census Bureau data, 52% of adults between 18 and 29 live with their parents—the highest percentages ever recorded. This might be due, in part, to the changes in households during the COVID-19 pandemic.

A variety of theories address why so many young adults these days don't make a real break with their parents at the point when it's generally considered natural to do so. The skyrocketing costs of higher education leave some dependent on parents for their education and related housing. Some are so saddled with student loans that they cannot afford to fly the coop, and they live at home to cut expenses, or possibly to save on rent so they can buy a first home. Perhaps they return to their parents' home because they are divorced themselves and need support or help with child care. And others never developed the skills and confidence to live independently.

Whatever the reason, if young adults are living with their parents— or are significantly dependent on them financially—then the finances of divorce become even more complicated. For the adult child, divorce might raise the specter of losing financial support that seemed certain when the marriage was intact. You might have to make some difficult decisions about what comes first, your own future needs or the immediate financial needs of your kids.

Many financial planners are advising intact couples to fund retirement first, before contributing to a child's education fund, especially if money is tight. Experts have two reasons for this recommendation: (1) College loans are available for you or your child, but you cannot borrow for retirement, and (2) the likelihood of your children having to support you later in life is greater if you fail to save for retirement. This advice also applies to divorcing parents. Remember the instructions when traveling on an airplane: Put on your own oxygen mask before putting one on your child.

Coping With the Loss of Home

Even adult children who live independently hold onto their childhood memories, including the image of an intact home. They assume that if they ever need to go home, they will have a home to return to. In this context, home is more than a structure made up of rooms. It is a metaphor for the heart of a family.

Divorce is an attack on the home these adults once knew. "Was it all a lie?" "Were my parents just pretending?" "Was all that I remember about my childhood just a façade?" These are typical questions for adults who might have been unaware of their parents' marital distress even while they all were living under the same roof. Some of us edit our own childhood memories so that only the positive scenarios stand out. But once a parent announces that a divorce is in the works, many adult children feel significant shock and anger.

Parents who have become idealized over time become real people when they divorce, with real faults. It takes time for adult children to make the shift to where they can hold simultaneously their own recollections of parents and home and their parents' reality of needing to end the marriage. You might need to be patient with your adult children as they make this shift, and acknowledge how difficult it might be for them.

Divorce could also mean the end of familiar rituals and traditions— holiday celebrations, family reunions, birthday parties, family vacations, and other important events. It is painful to lose the security provided by such traditions and expectations. If your divorce is relatively amicable, then you might be able to give your children the gift of continued family traditions even postdivorce—but that's in the future, and their loss in the present is difficult to accept.

Derailing Plans and Threatening the Future

Adult children might be in the midst of major life transitions of their own when they receive news of their parents' divorce. Commitments like educational pursuits, career development, or establishing a family could make it difficult for an adult child to be supportive. If the adult child works in a family business, the strains of allegiance to one parent or the other might compound these challenges. An adult child who assumed it would be many years before a parent would need or expect financial aid or emotional support might experience resentment if parents are particularly needy.

Adult children might also experience fear for their own future if they have grown up with an expectation of receiving an inheritance or sharing in their parents' wealth as the parents age. The expectation could be explicit, unspoken but clear, or merely imagined. In any case, it could lead the child to act or fail to act—perhaps by not saving for the future because of the anticipated windfall, perhaps by counting on the parents' assistance to provide the down payment for a first home or tuition for graduate school. The prospect of a family's wealth being divided to support two separate households might create concern, and the thought of having a parent's estate depleted by attorneys' fees is not pleasant either.

Issues for Parents to Consider

At the start of your divorce, I encourage you to pause and think through how you want your adult child to be involved in your marriage crisis. Throughout the process, remember that an adult child has no easy role in a parental divorce. Here are some things to consider at the outset and as you proceed.

Sharing information. What benefits are there to sharing the nitty-gritty details of your case with your adult child? Do you really need their advice? Can you be sure they'll keep your discussions confidential? And will it benefit or harm your child to hear about these details?

Contact between your kids and your attorney. Your lawyer might want your permission to talk with your son or daughter. The children's observations and opinions might be helpful for your attorney, so if your child doesn't object and you don't see any downside, give your consent.

Leaning on your child. Are you relying solely upon the advice and counsel of your child? Is this a responsibility that is fair to place on the child, no matter how mature? Are you getting impartial feedback and advice? Or does it make more sense for you to find more objective advice from a counselor, pastor, rabbi, or friends?

Roles of the Adult Child

The role an adult child takes in the parents' divorce is forecast by family dynamics. Here is a brief overview of various roles adult children might play.

Chief Confidante and Supporter. In a late-life divorce, usually one spouse is experiencing shell shock. That parent might turn to the adult child, especially when the parent does not have an established network of friends or other family members to lean on. The child becomes the parent's chief confidante and source of emotional support.

Most adult children do not want to listen to either parent bad-mouthing the other, for the same reasons that younger children find it so threatening. In this situation, it is not unusual for young adults to shift their anger from the parent who initiated the divorce to the one who is bashing the other parent.

In another dynamic, adult children support one parent because they have witnessed abuse by the other parent. These cases continue the pattern of alignment already established in the family unit. A divorce does not come as a surprise to this young adult and is often welcomed.

The Fixer. Adult children of divorce might feel a responsibility to fix their parents' marriage. The role might arise from the child's self-blame for the marital disruption or the child's personality as a take-charge problem-solver. An adult child in this fixer role often accompanies a parent to the attorney's office for the initial consultation.

The Mediator. Children frequently engage in shuttle diplomacy between parents. The child might even participate in negotiations and mediation. This role is similar to the fixer, but more objective.

The Guide and Interpreter. If a parent suffers from a cognitive impairment, an adult child might serve as interpreter—either informally, or as the court-appointed guardian for a parent who is struggling with competency. (See "Surrogate Decision Making: When a Divorcing Spouse Needs Extra Help," below.)

The Absent One. Some adult children stay out of the parents' divorce experience. This adult child might have endured parental turmoil throughout childhood and found safety in total withdrawal—a pattern that doesn't change when the divorce occurs.

Degrading the other parent. Think before you pick up the phone and say, "Let me tell you what that SOB father of yours has done to me!" First, if there's any chance you might reconcile, it will be difficult for children to forget what has been said during the divorce process. Second, even when your kids are adults, it's just not right to interfere with their relationship with their other parent. Let them make their own decisions about this.

Being an inspiration. The best gift an adult child could receive after a parental divorce is to see both parents thrive. Knowing a parent could bounce back from one of the most troubling episodes in life is reassuring for a child—even a grown-up one.

Unintended Consequences

One of the most significant pieces of research about the effect of divorce on the adult child–parent relationship is a 1999 study by the Johns Hopkins University School of Medicine, entitled "Parental Marital Disruption and Intergenerational Transfers: An Analysis of Lone Elderly Parents and Their Children." The researchers focused on ways adult children assist parents: housing their parents; providing financial assistance; and providing informal care to disabled elderly parents.

This study shows that the fallout of divorce is far-reaching and provides a glimpse of unintended consequences of late-life divorce for parents and children alike. Other studies confirm the study's findings:

- Divorced parents provide less financial assistance to their children than intact couples.
- Disabled or frail divorced parents might not be able to count on personal and economic support from their children.
- Divorced fathers are especially vulnerable, receiving less informal caregiving later in life due to weaker ties with their children. Fathers receive fewer hours of informal care and are much less likely to live with an adult child.
- Parent–child ties are strained further by remarriage. Remarried parents receive less informal caregiving from their children, purchase more hours of formal care, and provide less cash assistance to their children than parents who were married only once.

A more recent Pew Research Center study reports that almost 40% of adults over the age 60 give money to their adult children, while only about 12% receive financial help from their kids. This study does not focus on the divorce context, but it reflects the continuing disparity between the two directions of support.

With the aging of society, families have more years of "linked lives" between generations, exacerbating these problems.

Filial Responsibility Laws

We know that all states have child support laws . But it's less widely known that 27 states have filial responsibility laws that place a legal obligation on children to support their parents under limited circumstances. Support obligations arise where a parent is indigent. You can check whether your state has a law regarding a child's duty to support a parent by using a search engine to look up "filial responsibility laws" in your state.

Issues for the Adult Child to Consider

If you are the adult child facing your parents' late-life divorce, you also have some issues to consider and choices to make.

Continuing relationships. You might be hearing information for the first time that affects your view of one parent (or both). Take some time before taking sides, in the interest of preserving both of your valuable parent–child relationships. Try to have compassion for each of your parents and remember, there are two sides to most stories. For the same reason, prejudging the parent who filed for divorce is often unfair, as the reasons for filing are likely complex and not easily deciphered.

Balancing sympathy and support. You can be sympathetic and supportive to one parent without divorcing the other parent yourself.

Setting limits. You might feel pressure to align with one parent or the other. As soon as you identify yourself strongly with one parent, the other is likely to become wary, weakening your connection and possibly preventing you from being helpful later when your objective involvement could be useful. If you need to ask a parent to leave you out of the fighting, do it. If you want to demand that your parents be civil to each other in your presence, do it.

Overlooking weaknesses. Try to forgive your parents' weaknesses, which are magnified during a divorce. Lower your expectations of their behavior and try to understand their ups and downs. Few people are paragons of virtue when dissolving a marriage.

Designing a different future. Help your parents by beginning to design new and different family rituals to strengthen and repair bonds. Two new family units can offer positive experiences. It might be different from what you expected for your family's future, but it's still possible that at the end of the day, you'll have two loving and supportive family structures.

Surrogate Decision Making: When a Divorcing Spouse Needs Extra Help

Questions about mental competence sometimes surface in the late-life divorce. Capacity might be impaired due to Alzheimer's disease, dementia, or brain injury resulting from an accident. The impairment might have led to the breakdown of the marital relationship. In other situations, concern about competence might arise during the course of the divorce, based on something more than the typical emotional upset. In either event, when a spouse isn't capable of making decisions in a divorce case, the need arises for another person to make those decisions instead. This section addresses those situations.

Incapacity

A legal finding of incapacity (or incompetence) means that a judge has determined that diminished mental abilities require the appointment of a guardian to act on behalf of an incapacitated person. Terminology varies among the states—we'll use the term guardian in this chapter, but in your state the surrogate decision maker might be called a conservator and the incapacitated person the conservatee, ward, or subject of the guardianship. Whatever term your state uses, a guardian acts in the place of the incapacitated person by making decisions about the person's finances, medical care, general well-being, or a combination of any of these issues.

Incapacity, as used in the context of a guardianship, is not easy to define. Generally, it refers to an impaired ability to recall information, understand the consequences of one's actions, plan for the future, exercise reason, and make decisions. Activities that require mental competence include entering into contracts, consenting to medical treatment, marrying, driving a motor vehicle, making a will, and signing a power of attorney. For a judge to conclude that a guardian should be appointed, the court must decide that the person requires care and supervision to keep from becoming a danger to self or others.

Just because a person suffers from a mental illness does not automatically mean that the person is incompetent. Many people with mental illness or disability are capable of making sound decisions. A person is presumed to be competent and capable until a judge decides that evidence proves otherwise.

If the need for a guardianship has arisen for the first time in the context of a divorce, a judge will have the option of appointing a general guardian for all purposes, or a limited guardianship. The latter, also known as a guardian *ad litem* (GAL), is a good choice when a person appears incompetent to make decisions concerning a legal action, but is otherwise competent. The GAL will represent the person's interests only in relation to that lawsuit—for our purposes, the divorce.

How Guardianship Works

A guardianship proceeding could be filed by a family member, friend, or an unrelated professional who recognizes a person's need for assistance. Appointing a guardian is considered an option of last resort, because it limits the most basic civil rights of the person subjected to the orders (known as the "ward").

Each state has its own laws spelling out procedures for the appointment of guardians; petitions are processed in the probate court in most places. Most states give family members priority to be named as a guardian, though a judge might name an unrelated person if circumstances dictate. Some states allow competent individuals to nominate a guardian in advance, and also allow them to name those they do not want to serve as their guardian. Guardian preferences might be stated in the course of estate planning, along with wills and powers of attorney, well before competency is in question. (See Chapter 11, "Estate Planning and Divorce.")

The need for a guardianship must be proved by certificates of incapacity from one or more doctors, which describe the degree of impairment. Physicians use a variety of tests to measure function, including geriatric assessment, mental status testing, interviews, and physical exams—all of which should be completed close in time to the filing of the petition for guardianship. The doctor's certificate must describe the functions that are affected, the degrees of impairment, and the specific activities the proposed ward is incapable of managing. The judge might also consider testimony of the potential ward, the potential guardian, and witnesses. For a judge to grant a guardianship, the evidence must meet high standards. Usually the petitioner must prove incapacity by evidence that is "clear and convincing" or even "beyond a reasonable doubt."

To ensure that the rights of the proposed ward are protected, the court might appoint an attorney to represent the proposed ward for purposes of the guardianship action only. The attorney will represent the interests of the proposed ward by appropriately questioning the evidence introduced by the party seeking the guardianship, and possibly offering evidence on behalf of the intended ward.

Even when a judge appoints a guardian, most states require the judge to shape a guardian's power around the specific needs of the ward, by listing the rights granted to the guardian and preserving all remaining rights in the ward. A guardian could serve as guardian of the estate, guardian of the person, or a combination of both. A guardian of the estate manages the ward's money and property. Powers include paying debts, paying for personal care, paying support for the person's dependents, preventing financial abuse, managing assets, and engaging in Medicaid and tax planning. A guardian of the estate must report to the court on how the ward's money is being used, and must not use the ward's money for personal gain.

A guardian of the person makes personal decisions for the ward— most significantly, decisions regarding living circumstances, health care, preventing personal abuse, determining with whom the person may associate, and other life choices.

Acting as guardian for someone during a divorce would most likely require you to qualify as guardian of both the estate and the person. Becoming guardian of the estate would allow you to make financial decisions on behalf of the ward. However, when a guardian of the estate wants to enter into a divorce settlement on behalf of the ward, the terms and conditions of the proposed settlement must be approved by the probate court first.

A court-ordered guardianship will provide for the guardian's compensation, and the guardian is required to report periodically to the judge about decisions the guardian has made on behalf of the ward.

In Lieu of Guardianships

Not all adults with mental or physical impairments need a formal court-supervised guardianship. The amount of support depends on the person's level of function and what type of support is available. Here are some alternatives to formal guardianships.

Informal Networks

Many elderly and impaired persons function perfectly well with an informal network of caregivers that might include family, friends, neighbors, and public services. The person might allow caregivers to make decisions without any formal documents being signed. A system like this could work well for quite a while, but might come to an end when a caretaker becomes unavailable, when the person is no longer capable of making even the decision to allow others to take care of things, or when a third party (such as a medical care provider or financial institution) requires formal written authorization for the caregiver to act on the person's behalf.

Delegating Authority Using Powers of Attorney and Medical Directives

Any adult who is competent to make decisions can use legal documents to designate someone to take over decision making in the event of their incapacity. Basically, it's a way of planning in advance for incapacity in the future. These documents create an agency relationship, meaning that the designated person acts as an agent for the person who can't make decisions. The agent does not have to be an attorney, but could be a trusted family member or friend, or even an institution. You can delegate financial authority through a power of attorney, or nominate someone to serve as your health care proxy through a medical directive.

Financial powers of attorney. A financial power of attorney allows your agent to act for you with regard to your finances and property. The power of attorney might authorize only one action, like the sale of a specific piece of real estate; or the authority to write checks and make deposits into your account. You can also grant someone broad authority to deal with all of your financial matters, including the right to sell and manage real estate and other important assets. Some financial institutions accept powers of attorney only if they're written on their own forms, so if you are considering creating one, check with your bank or other financial institution to make sure you're using a form that will be recognized.

Medical directives. Special powers of attorney are frequently used for providing consent to health care, including decisions to terminate life support. These medical directives are also called health care powers of attorney, living wills, physician directives, personal health care directives, medical powers of attorney, or advance directives.

A financial power of attorney or medical directive could be effective immediately upon signing, or become effective when the person becomes incapacitated or another triggering event happens. (The latter are called "springing" powers of attorney because they spring into effect only upon certain events occurring.) An elderly or impaired adult might want to make a financial power of attorney effective immediately, for example so that a friend or relative could take care of banking chores or paying bills. Powers of attorney expire upon your death (at which time the provisions of a will take over), upon revocation (usually in writing or by specific action), or on a specific date that's stated in the document. The subsequent establishment of a guardianship might also void powers of attorney.

The advantages of a power of attorney are that you are the one who chooses your decision maker, you might avoid the costs of having the court appoint a guardian, and you alleviate the burden on others to guess your wishes. The primary disadvantage is obvious—the potential for an untrustworthy agent to abuse the powers granted—so be sure you choose your agent with care.

Revocable Management Trusts

Another way to plan for future incapacity is to use something called a revocable management trust. The person who creates the trust (the trustor) might name himself or another trusted person as trustee, then name a reliable successor trustee and transfer assets to the trust for management. The trustor might also be the beneficiary. The trust could be revoked at any time as long as the trustor has capacity. If the trustor is also the trustee and the trustor becomes incapacitated, the successor trustee easily assumes management of the assets, pays the trustor's expenses, and avoids the need for a guardianship. The advantage of this approach over a power of attorney is that the trustee has legal title to the assets, so third parties could not question the authority of the trustee to deal with trust assets—unlike third parties who might question the agent's authority under financial powers of attorney. If all of this sounds like a foreign language to you, you can learn the basics about trusts in Chapter 11, "Estate Planning and Divorce."

Authority of Guardians Regarding Divorce

Issues of impairment might arise in a divorce in a number of ways. A spouse might already have a court-appointed guardian, or one spouse (or another family member) could make allegations of the other's incompetency that affect the divorce process.

Filing for Divorce

Even when an adult has a legal guardian, not all states allow that guardian to file for divorce on behalf of the ward—even when there are laws on the books that allow guardians to file other types of civil lawsuits. If no specific law authorizes the guardian to file for divorce, then the courts must step in to decide whether it's permissible—and in the past, they have mostly said no. The reasoning behind this interpretation is that the decision to end a marriage is too personal a matter for a guardian to perform, and that if the legislature intended for guardians to have this power, it would have written a law granting it.

In the last few decades, however, more states have passed laws or issued court decisions holding that an incapacitated person could file for divorce through a guardian. Many personal decisions are now made by guardians, including decisions about medical care—even those that involve life-ending medical decisions—as well as decisions about where the ward lives and who the ward associates with. Some judges have concluded that it would be unfair to deny incapacitated persons the ability to leave a marriage, especially an abusive one.

Where No Guardian Has Been Appointed

If a spouse questions the capacity of the other spouse during a divorce and the judge agrees that there's a problem, the judge will likely appoint a guardian *ad litem* (GAL), as explained above. The GAL makes decisions for the impaired person during the course of the divorce. The GAL could be a family member, trusted friend, or someone specifically trained to serve as a GAL, possibly even be a licensed attorney. Or, a licensed attorney *ad litem* might be appointed to appear in court and represent the interests of the GAL (and, by proxy, the spouse who is represented by the GAL).

A GAL makes decisions on all issues in the divorce action, including property division and support issues. The GAL often consults with the impaired spouse to the extent possible, to discern that spouse's preferences. Otherwise, the divorce proceeds like any other divorce. Importantly, judges have the power and duty to ensure that the interests of the incapacitated spouse are being well represented by the GAL, and that the GAL's efforts do not include coercion. Judicial oversight is especially critical when the GAL and the competent spouse reach a settlement.

Powers of Attorney and Divorce

Even if you've signed a power of attorney designating an agent with the authority to file or defend a divorce, a judge is likely to still designate a GAL. That designee could be the same agent designated in your power of attorney, but the court might select someone else if the judge doesn't think the original nominee has the skills to act for you in the divorce action.

The Importance of Legal Advice

If your case involves questions about impairment of either spouse, it is imperative that you seek legal advice. This is not the time to represent yourself—the judge in your case will likely stop the divorce proceedings and require that the competency issues be addressed before any other decisions will be made. The court is also likely to require that both parties have legal counsel. Only when the impaired spouse's best interests are looked after by a surrogate decision maker will the divorce move forward.

Getting the Help You Need

No two people are the same when it comes to the need and ability to recruit emotional and practical support during a divorce. You might find it difficult to ask for help from the people close to you, or you might be relying on them too much. Just make sure that you take the time to assess your own needs and find the best way to meet them.

4

Your Divorce Options

When you say "I'm getting a divorce," it's clear that you are planning to end your marriage. But within that simple sentence reside a series of choices—about how you want your divorce to go, how you are going to make decisions yourself and with your spouse, and how much money you intend to spend on the process. You even have the option to back off and examine the possibility of making a decision short of a divorce, like a legal separation.

Your options for resolving your divorce are on a continuum. At one end is sitting down with your spouse, having a conversation about how you are going to end your marriage, and agreeing to divide the pie that is made up of your accumulated property and debts. This is sometimes known as the kitchen-table alternative. At the other end of the spectrum is full-blown litigation, culminating in a trial.

The continuum offers many other options, and you can choose among them or even end up using a combination. For many people, full court litigation is the first option that comes to mind, because it's what they most often see on television and in the movies. In reality, most cases don't go that route, and you have many other, more peaceful alternatives, which also happen to be less expensive and less emotionally fraught. The possibilities include mediation, collaborative law, and limited legal representation.

This chapter gives you information about each of your options so that you can make an informed decision—in concert with your attorney, if you have one—about how you want to move forward.

Alternatives to Divorce

Not every couple with serious marital problems goes directly to the option of a divorce. It's very common for people to live apart while deciding which step to take next, and there are a number of different ways to do that. This section explains the concepts of informal separation and formal legal separation, as well as postmarital agreements, which sometimes take the place of a court divorce.

The Continuum of Separation

Just as there's a continuum of options for divorcing, various options and levels of formality exist within the concept of separation. Where you fall on this continuum depends on your circumstances. At one end is the informal separation—one spouse moves out of the marital residence for the short run, to give each of you some breathing room and a chance to assess your options. At the other end of the separation spectrum is the legal or more formal separation, possibly involving a court order that's quite similar to a divorce judgment.

A separation can be a concrete step toward divorce or an agreement between spouses who decide to stay together but want to separate their finances or divide marital property—a "nondivorce" divorce. We are going to examine the separation spectrum by looking at four possible scenarios. Your situation might fit neatly into one of them or gradually evolve through a variety of them.

Scenario 1: Informal Trial Separation

If you are having marital problems, either you or your spouse might move out of your family home even though you have no present intention to file for divorce. The court doesn't need to be involved in your family decisions at this point—you do not need a court's permission to live apart. At this stage, it is an informal trial separation, a chance to step back from conflict and decide whether divorce is really the next step. It might be a time for individual or joint counseling. The decision could be reversed at any time.

However, when one spouse moves out, you do need to work out some issues during the separation period. Who is going to pay for what expenses? Will you change the locks, or will the spouse who moved out be able to come and go at will? Will you set up forwarding for mail and telephone calls? What will you say to friends and family about the separation? Can the spouse living elsewhere remove property from the house? While you might not be ready for a formal property division, you should make working arrangements about the use of bank accounts, credit cards, and the logistics of day-to-day life. It's a good idea to write those down, even if you do it in a very informal way on the same pad you use to make your grocery list.

Even though you might not want to think about divorce, a separation —even an informal one—might affect your rights now and into the future. It's not too early to consult with a divorce attorney and learn about models of separation that exist in your state and the consequences, if any, to the arrangement you and your spouse want to make.

Scenario 2: Living Apart With a Written Agreement

You and your spouse might know the separation is likely to be permanent, even though you're not ready to file for divorce yet. In other words, divorce is a possibility or even a strong likelihood, and you do intend to continue living apart indefinitely, but for now, neither of you wants to file legal paperwork. Again, no court is involved because you're not filing for divorce or for a legal separation. However, in this situation a written agreement can provide clarity about expectations and responsibilities.

The states treat lengthy separations in different ways, so you should find out from an attorney whether a written separation agreement, signed by both you and your spouse, is a binding contract in your state. If you continue to live apart, will your property rights or your responsibility for debts change? How will the court characterize property or debts acquired during the separation? Is an agreement for alimony binding? There are many more questions that you should deal with. For a preview, look at Scenario 4, below, where we describe issues you might cover in a postmarital agreement; many of these are the same ones you'll want to consider in your separation agreement.

If you do end up divorcing, the separation agreement will often form the basis of your settlement or judgment. Before signing an agreement, you should carefully consider all the issues, make full financial disclosure, and be sure that both spouses have the opportunity to consult with lawyers.

Scenario 3: Formal Legal Separation With Court Action

In most states, you and your spouse can ask the court for a legal separation—a formal court order that addresses many of the same issues as a divorce judgment. The order sets out the ground rules for handling finances and support while the parties live apart, with an expectation that the separation will be permanent. The legal separation is instead of a divorce, not in addition to it. The only states that do not provide for court-ordered legal separation are Delaware, Florida, Georgia, Maryland, Mississippi, New Jersey, Pennsylvania, and Texas.

However, these states might recognize formal separation agreements, especially those entered into while residing in another state, such as the postmarital agreements discussed below in "Scenario 4: Making a Postmarital Agreement."

Depending on your state's laws, a legal separation order might be a final determination of the financial issues in your marriage, so that even if you divorce later, you won't have to deal with additional property issues. The order might provide that property acquired by either party during the separation is that person's sole property, and could lift duties of mutual care and support.

In states that provide for formal court-ordered separation, the order might be converted into a judgment in a later divorce; at the very least, it will carry great weight. A judge also has the power to invalidate a separation agreement if it does not comply with state law or if a spouse was subject to undue pressure or fraud in its preparation. In short, this type of separation can be as complicated and expensive as a divorce. If you're asking a court to make an order of legal separation, you'll probably need an attorney to help you negotiate the terms of the separation.

Some people choose legal separation in order to maintain the status quo for a specific reason—for example, to keep marital status intact until a spouse becomes eligible for Medicare, to allow a military marriage to reach the ten-year or twenty-year point that entitles the nonmilitary spouse to receive certain benefits, or to meet the ten-year mark that means a former spouse is eligible for Social Security benefits (all of these issues are covered in later chapters). Others decide on legal separation for personal or religious reasons.

No matter what your legal separation does in terms of affecting your rights, you are still married, and you are not free to remarry until you have a final divorce decree.

Scenario 4: Making a Postmarital Agreement

Perhaps you and your spouse decide that you will resume living together after a separation, and in the interim, you've reached some decisions about how you want to structure your financial arrangements. Or, maybe you didn't separate, and you want to try to save your marriage, and you have decided that you want a written agreement about how you'll deal with financial issues if you do divorce. A written agreement that changes your rights and duties with regard to your spouse is called a postmarital agreement (or a postnuptial agreement or a partition and exchange agreement). The "post" in postmarital means after a marriage has taken place, not after it ends.

CAUTION

The standards for a postmarital agreement are high. A postmarital agreement is subject to very strict rules about how it must be prepared and signed. There has to be evidence that the agreement was entered into voluntarily, that both spouses had the chance to consult an attorney, and that all financial information was disclosed by both spouses.

Postmarital agreements are a relatively new phenomenon. In the past, courts refused to enforce them, on the basis that a married couple was a unit, a singular whole, and therefore could not contract with itself. Postmarital agreements are available in most states now, though many courts still are very suspicious of them. In states that do not have legal separation by way of court order, postmarital agreements might serve the same function of structuring the spouses' financial relationship.

Postmarital agreements are based on the belief that putting to rest financial disagreements, uncertainties, and insecurities might allow a couple to continue a contentious marriage more harmoniously. The scope of a postmarital agreement could be very narrow, addressing only one or two issues that are bones of contention. Changing careers, receiving an inheritance, or selling a business are the types of events that can trigger a negotiation between spouses to change or clarify property ownership, entitlement to income, or finances in general. On the other hand, postmarital agreements could also have a broad scope—for example, a couple could use a postmarital agreement to plan for dividing assets, income, and debts in the event of a divorce in the future. These written contracts could also affect how property will be distributed at the death of one spouse.

As is true of legal separations, some couples sign postmarital agreements—instead of divorcing—for religious reasons, for the sake of social appearances, and to get or keep benefits not available if they divorce.

Don't Cave In

It's not always wise to enter into a postmarital agreement. Sometimes one spouse files for divorce and then proposes to drop the divorce if the other spouse signs a postmarital agreement. If the spouse who didn't file is keen to save the marriage, signing such an agreement might lead to unwise concessions. A few months after the ink is dry, the spouse who originally filed for divorce could go ahead and do so again—this time armed with favorable terms in a postmarital agreement, which has the power to influence the divorce outcome. Of course, if the second spouse could prove actual fraud in the inducement to sign the postmarital agreement, the court might refuse to enforce the terms. But you can't rely on that, so if your spouse is threatening to end the marriage unless you sign a postmarital agreement, proceed with caution.

A Separation Checklist

If you're considering separating from your spouse, make a plan before you make a move. Whatever your feelings about the likelihood that you will reconcile, or your expectations about how you'll deal with your finances, it's better to be safe than sorry. Consider doing all of the following to ensure you don't give up any of your rights during the separation period:

- Remove your name from any bank or credit card account for which you do not want to have any further responsibility. If you want to keep both spouses' names on the accounts, then freeze joint accounts.

- Agree on how to handle mail. Remember you might need to review mail related to marital assets and debts (including credit card charges).
- Remove your name from any leases and utilities that relate to property you're not living in, if the separation is going to be lengthy.
- Make a list of debts each spouse will pay. Both of you should sign the list when it's complete.
- If there's personal property you feel strongly about keeping if you do divorce later, keep it with you. Take photos or videos of household contents that are removed or left behind.
- Check health, car, homeowners', and property insurance policies to be sure that coverage is not compromised. Some insurance companies lapse coverage in case of marital separation. Be sure to read your policies carefully or ask your insurance agent about this.
- Make copies of records that you leave behind, such as tax returns, account information, and real estate documents. Make a list of addresses and account information for all financial accounts.
- List or photograph the contents of safe deposit boxes.
- Decide who is going to pay for maintenance and repairs on the cars and house, and reach an understanding about reimbursement for those costs.
- Establish agreed boundaries about privacy, and avoid unannounced appearances at the other's residence. Discuss the possibility that one or both of you might begin dating. Avoiding surprises will help with the transition.

Separations help many people to weather difficult times in their marriage and eventually reconcile; others choose separation as an alternative to divorce. Still others find that with or without a separation, their path leads inevitably to the end of their marriage. At this point, they need to choose among their divorce options.

> ### Removing Your Name from a Residential Lease
>
> When more than one person has signed a lease, usually they are each responsible for paying the entire rent (the landlord can demand it of any tenant; how the tenants allocate the rent between them is up to them). Landlords like having multiple parties liable for the rent, should one of them not be able to pay. For this reason, when a couple signs a lease, the landlord will probably be unwilling to let one spouse out of the lease. You can't do anything about this refusal unless you want to remove your name from the lease (and move out) due to domestic violence. Many states require landlords to "bifurcate" the lease, allowing the victim to move out without further liability for rent. If domestic violence underpins your divorce and you need to move out, check your state's laws on victims' rights in this situation.

Litigation

Litigation encompasses a broad range of possibilities. If you and your spouse each hire an attorney, and the attorneys file papers for each of you, send requests for information back and forth in a formal way, and then eventually work with you and your spouse to negotiate a settlement without going to court, that's a litigation process—even though you might never see the inside of a courthouse. It's also litigation if you're in and out of court constantly, fighting over every issue.

Although both of these scenarios are litigation, they're very different in terms of the financial and emotional cost to you. Litigation that ends in a negotiated resolution is by far the most common way that divorces are resolved—up to 95% of litigated divorce cases end in settlement without trial. But some do go to court—and if you do not mind your personal information being made public, if you want someone else to make decisions for you about your future, and if you want to pay lots of money for these privileges, then courtroom litigation is for you. Although I don't recommend it in most cases, it is a necessary option and the best—or only—one in some circumstances.

Why Go to Court?

The main reason a case ends up in court is that one or both parties engage in unreasonable negotiating tactics or take unreasonable positions on the legal issues. Other reasons for litigating include:

- to deal with a spouse who hides or destroys assets
- to turn over the decisions to a third party
- to experience a public catharsis
- to have a judge interpret an ambiguous law or resolve confusing factual situations or deal with a party whose behavior is egregious, and
- to seek damages for injury caused by family violence or other wrongful acts.

Whether your litigation process is a formal negotiation or a battle on every issue, it will proceed along a fairly predictable path:

1. Initiation of the divorce suit
2. Resolution of matters needing immediate attention, like who is going to live where, who is paying what bills, and whether one spouse will pay interim attorneys' fees for the other spouse
3. Discovery of significant information and facts
4. Negotiation in an effort to settle, and
5. Trial, if no settlement is reached.

Each of these stages is governed by laws and regulations specific to your state and, sometimes, to the court that you're in.

Stage 1: Initiating the Divorce

You might think it doesn't matter who files the initial papers, and in many cases, that is true. But if you or your spouse has moved to a new county or state, or if your lawyer thinks you'll gain a strategic benefit from presenting your side of the facts first to the judge, you might want to be the first to file.

Initial Pleadings

The case begins with the filing of a pleading that is called a petition, a complaint, or a request. (The document is called a pleading because it pleads the elements of your case.) The initial petition sets out limited facts and tells the court what you are asking for—usually a resolution of property rights, a determination of support, and the like. After filing, the spouse who filed the petition must deliver the papers to the other spouse, who is expected to respond within a limited time period. The responsive pleading is called a response, answer, or counterclaim.

CAUTION

Read the pleadings! If you receive a petition for divorce or any other legal document, check to see whether it contains any orders from a judge telling you to do something or refrain from doing something. It is very common for divorce papers to contain financial restrictions on both spouses. Read the document carefully and look for any timetables and hearing dates. If a court order is involved, make sure you comply with it, at least until you've had a chance to talk with an attorney.

Default Divorce

Another reason for reading papers carefully is to avoid defaulting, which means failing to respond. If you receive divorce paperwork from your spouse and you don't respond to it within the time given, the case might proceed without you. This is called a default divorce. If you fail to participate, your spouse might convince the judge to make orders that are not in your interest. If you are on the receiving end of a divorce petition, do not sit still and think, "This, too, shall pass." The clock is ticking.

Residency Requirements and Waiting Periods

Every state has residency requirements and waiting periods. The residency requirement is the length of time you must live in the state before you are entitled to file for divorce there. Residency requirements vary from six weeks to a full year.

The waiting period is the length of time you must wait between the date you file the initial paperwork and deliver it to your spouse, and the date when you could get a final judgment of divorce. Waiting periods range from 30 days to a year or more, and even if you complete your divorce negotiations earlier, you can't get a final judgment until the waiting period has passed. Until you have a judgment of divorce you are still married, and neither of you can remarry.

Grounds for Divorce

If you are initiating a divorce, the initial petition will set out the grounds, or basis, for your divorce request. Perhaps you have heard of the term no-fault divorce. It means that you do not have to state specific reasons for wanting a divorce, and neither person has to show that the other person did anything wrong (in the past, this was required). Under no-fault rules, the grounds for divorce are things like incompatibility and irreconcilable differences. The spouse filing for divorce just needs to say there's no chance of reconciliation. There's no need to present evidence of who was at fault in breaking up the marriage.

Even if the other spouse doesn't want the divorce, there's no way to contest it—the only things up for discussion are property division and support. In some states, you can argue that fault grounds, such as adultery, cruelty, or abandonment, should influence the division of property and the question of whether alimony is justified. If you think that fault is relevant in your case, talk to your lawyer about whether you could raise the issue in your state.

RESOURCE

Learn about residency requirements and waiting periods in your state. You can find this information as well as a chart of which states use fault as a factor in dividing property or determining custody, in *Nolo's Essential Guide to Divorce*, by Emily Doskow (Nolo).

Stage 2: Resolving Immediate Issues

Often, it's necessary to resolve certain issues quickly, at least on a temporary basis. Temporary orders might cover questions like who is going to live where, who is going to pay which bills, who will care for the pets, and who should pay and receive support while the divorce case is pending. Also, if a spouse has competency issues, the judge might appoint a guardian at an early stage to serve as a surrogate decision maker (see "Surrogate Decision Making: When a Divorcing Spouse Needs Extra Help" in Chapter 3).

Often, parties make temporary agreements themselves. But if the spouse in control of the money won't pay voluntarily, or if other issues need resolution right away, the other spouse must seek a court order. Generally, temporary orders are decided in a short hearing or, if the issue is complex, a minitrial, with both parties presenting evidence. Whether issued by the judge or agreed to by the parties, a temporary order establishes the status quo while the case is pending. You might have another chance later to argue the same issues, but if the issue is really important to you, take a stand at an early stage. Judges are very fond of the status quo, and you might have a hard time getting temporary orders changed later.

Automatic Restraining Orders (Temporary Injunctions)

Many states issue automatic restraining orders (also called temporary injunctions) as soon as a divorce petition is filed, to control certain aspects of the spouses' finances and family matters while the case is pending. Typical restraining orders prevent either spouse from unilaterally:

- concealing, selling, or destroying assets or incurring debts
- opening mail addressed to the other spouse

- canceling utilities or other services
- destroying electronic or financial records
- canceling credit cards
- changing beneficiaries on life insurance, retirement accounts, or any other benefit that calls for a beneficiary designation
- canceling or changing insurance coverage
- exercising a power of attorney on behalf of the other spouse, or
- interfering with the other spouse's occupancy of the family home.

Restraining orders are designed to protect personal safety and to ensure that your marital property stays secure while you work out the terms of your divorce. If you need to do something that's prohibited by automatic restraining orders, you and your spouse might agree to make a change—for example, you might agree to cancel a credit card so you're sure neither of you will make any additional charges. You should put any such agreement in writing, and if you have an attorney, get advice first.

Stage 3: Discovery

The third stage of litigation is broadly referred to as the discovery phase, because each spouse tries to discover the facts needed to negotiate effectively. During discovery, you or your lawyer will use a number of legal tools to gather information about some important questions:

- What positions is the other side taking?
- What evidence—documents and other material—supports those positions?
- Who will be called as a witness or an expert to testify to relevant facts?
- What value does the other side assign to marital property?
- What are the marital assets and liabilities?
- What are the other spouse's expectations about support, and what evidence supports those expectations?

What Happens During Discovery

The discovery stage is the time when theories are developed, documents are provided for the other side's inspection, assets are evaluated, inventories are prepared, witnesses testify at depositions, expert witnesses form opinions, and all facts are gathered and reviewed. You might go to court for preliminary hearings to narrow the contested issues or resolve discovery disputes. Once both sides feel all the relevant information is available, you should begin serious negotiating about whatever is still in dispute in your divorce—issues like who owned what prior to marriage, how you'll divide the marital estate, and how to deal with short- and long-term support needs.

The purpose of discovery is to level the playing field through information sharing. Contrary to what you see on TV, dramatic surprises at trial are rare, because discovery means each side has the opportunity to access the same information. Discovery is intended to encourage settlement and to make cases move more quickly through the system.

Tools of Discovery

The primary tools used in the discovery process are:
- written requests for the production of documents
- written interrogatories (questions answered in writing, under oath), and
- depositions (witnesses appearing in person to answer questions under oath).

Written document requests and interrogatories are the most commonly used tools, because they are less expensive than depositions. Depositions involve attorneys asking questions of a witness (usually one of the parties or a witness with important knowledge), in the presence of a court reporter and possibly a videographer. Between the lawyers' time and the cost of the court reporter, videographer, and transcript, a deposition is an expensive proposition. Make sure there's a good reason to incur the cost, like needing to get the other side to commit to a version of events or a position on an issue, or if there's no other way to follow up on questions asked in written form.

If your divorce is very contentious, it's likely you'll be deposed. If your spouse's attorney wants to depose you, your lawyer will spend significant time helping you prepare.

RESOURCE

Depositions aren't scary if you're prepared. To learn more about depositions and to get prepared if you're going to have your deposition taken, check out *Nolo's Deposition Handbook*, by Albert Moore and Paul Bergman (Nolo).

The Zen of Discovery

Many a divorce client has ranted, raved, and even cried in my office because of the disruption caused by the discovery process. They're frustrated at having to collect all the requested information, frightened by the prospect of a deposition, and angry about things the other spouse is saying. If you find yourself there, all you can do is take a deep breath and know it will end eventually. You must remain focused, be organized, pay attention to deadlines, and—for heaven's sake—do not think it will go away if you just ignore it! Cases have been lost during discovery, simply because of a missed deadline. Cooperate with your attorney and be patient, and you'll get through it.

Stage 4: Pretrial Preparations

There is no clear line between the discovery stage and the pretrial preparation stage. If you have been expecting a contentious fight, then your attorney has been preparing for trial from the time of your first office visit. At some point, though, the energy shifts and you begin preparing in earnest, meaning that the attorney puts together the information gathered in discovery and decides on the theories and themes of your case. If you've consulted expert witnesses on subjects like the value of your home or stock portfolio, those people will become more involved in helping your attorney prepare the case for trial. And the lawyer will line up all of your other witnesses and evidence so that everything is in good order.

Pretrial preparation also includes making efforts to settle the case. At this point, you might participate in a mediation—either voluntarily or because the court orders you to mediate. (See "Mediation," below.) Some judges will require all of you to attend a settlement conference with the judge, who will try to help you to settle before the trial begins. Offers, counteroffers, and settlement proposals might fly back and forth between the attorneys. Some issues might be resolved while others remain in dispute, to be decided in court. Negotiations might continue until the trial begins—and sometimes you'll reach an agreement during the trial.

Stage 5: Trial and Beyond

The final stage in a fully litigated divorce is the trial. In almost all states, divorce cases are decided by a judge, without a jury. A very few states allow a jury to decide certain aspects of a divorce, but the high likelihood is that your case will be decided by a judge alone.

Every court handles trial assignments in its own way. Most commonly, you'll know which judge is assigned to your trial from the very beginning of your case. But in some places, you won't know until you walk into the courtroom on the day the trial is starting. It's helpful to know in advance, because judges have habits, biases, and histories that are useful to know—but you'll just have to take what comes depending on how they do things in your courthouse.

When the trial begins, the person who filed the divorce is the first to present evidence, followed by the other party; the first party then has the opportunity to counter the other party's evidence. Many judges place time limits on the trial, so your lawyer won't necessarily be able to present every piece of evidence that you think is important. Your lawyer should accept input from you, but at this stage of the game you should trust your attorney to put on the best possible case and not try to change the strategy or offer too many unsolicited opinions.

All of the evidence, testimony, and legal arguments are part of an effort to persuade the judge to rule one way or the other. In the end, the judge makes decisions that are reduced to a written order (also called a divorce judgment or divorce decree).

When preparing a client for a trial, I explained that we must paint a simple and clear fact picture for the judge. However, most clients think everything that's happened in their marriage is relevant and important for the judge to know. That is when I reminded them that they were paying me to decide which relevant images would appear on our canvas. After all, we didn't want to overwhelm the judge with a Jackson Pollock look-alike.

Once the judge has announced a final ruling, the prevailing attorney usually drafts the final divorce order. Opposing counsel will have an opportunity to raise any disagreement with the drafted order, and those differences will be presented to the judge for a decision at a post-trial hearing.

Appeals Are Not Appealing

In an appeal, you ask an appellate court to reverse the decision and send everyone back to try the case again. Your claim that the judge didn't evaluate the evidence as you think she should have, and that you got a bad (or even unfair) result, won't win your appeal. An appeal will succeed only when the appellate court concludes that the judge made a serious error in legal reasoning. Appeals in family law cases are rare, because judges have wide discretion to determine the facts and apply the law, and it's very hard to prove that the judge made a legal error. Appeals are extremely expensive, both because you must obtain a full transcript of your original trial, which is very costly, and because appellate lawyers are highly skilled specialists who charge accordingly.

Long-Term Effects of Going to Trial

The idealized picture of a trial is that truth and a fair result will prevail, through an adversarial and evenly-matched presentation of evidence and skillful arguments of counsel. But we all know that is not necessarily what happens, and it's very difficult to predict the outcome of a divorce trial. While the judge is supposed to decide the case just on the facts and the law, other factors influencing the judge could include personal experiences, personal and political beliefs, the personalities and skills of the attorneys, and the demeanor of the parties.

The bottom line is that a trial puts decision-making power into the hands of a stranger who does not have to live with the results. The experience is enormously stressful—divorce litigation could exacerbate health problems, use up vast sums of money, distract you at work, create family tensions that persist for years, and generally create havoc in your life. The effects of a litigated divorce could ripple through the family tree for generations to come. If you can, avoid it. If you can't, accept the outcome, whatever it is, and move on.

Arbitration

Arbitration is similar to litigation in that an arbitrator functions like a judge, making decisions based on evidence presented by the parties. The difference is that the arbitrator is hired (and paid) by the parties. Often, retired judges and experienced lawyers serve as arbitrators in divorce cases.

The arbitration process is quite similar to litigation: You'll engage in discovery, pretrial preparation, and settlement negotiations before the actual arbitration begins. Arbitration might be formal, much like a courtroom where the rules of procedure and evidence apply, or it might be less formal—the parties and the arbitrator will decide together. But either way, the process is adversarial in nature.

> CAUTION
>
> **If you're considering arbitration, check to be sure it's available in your state.** Arbitration is not commonly used in divorce cases, and in fact, some states don't allow arbitration in family law matters.

One advantage to arbitration is that you might schedule an arbitration hearing much more quickly than you could get a court trial, and you have more control over the scheduling. You could choose whether your arbitration is binding, which means that the arbitrator's decision is final and there's no right to appeal the decision or go to a different court, or non-binding, which allows a trial if one party doesn't like the arbitration result. Arbitration could be more expensive than a trial because you are paying for the decision maker's time in addition to the attorney time and costs. Judges, on the other hand, are paid by taxpayers.

If trials and arbitration don't sound appealing to you and if you believe that despite your differences, there is a possibility that with some skilled guidance you and your spouse might reach an agreement without litigation, you have other options.

Mediation and Collaborative Divorce

An increase in the number of divorce filings in the last few decades has clogged court dockets, making it a long, hard wait until a case gets resolved. In addition, the public has an increasing awareness of the negative consequences of highly contested divorces. As a result, professionals in the field have worked to develop other options for resolving divorces. Mediation and collaborative law are two different approaches to negotiating divorce settlements—both far less adversarial than litigation.

Interest-Based Negotiations

The term interest-based negotiations is used in both mediation and collaborative law. Interest-based negotiation is very different from the style used in an adversarial context, which is known as positional bargaining. Before diving into the details of mediation and collaboration, let's take a look at what it means to negotiate from interests rather than positions.

In any negotiation, your fears, desires, goals, and values drive your interests—the outcomes that you want. Your interests, in turn, steer your negotiating positions—what you tell others you want. For example, you might want to stay in your home after the divorce. Thinking there's only one way for that to happen, you might take a strong position that your spouse should accept a certain amount of money as a buyout. That's positional negotiating. To negotiate based on your interests, you would simply state your interest in staying in the house while remaining open to considering a variety of ways you could make that happen.

Positional negotiating involves ultimatums, roadblocks, and barriers that could limit creative problem solving. In contrast, interests are starting points from which you and your spouse identify and try to resolve your differences in ways that meet as many interests as possible. Green-light thinking, brainstorming, suspending judgment, and refraining from negative criticism are all hallmarks of interest-based negotiations.

Interest-based negotiation allows for the exploration of options that otherwise might never see the light of day. Also, it encourages you to hear your spouse's perspective, because you aren't worried that listening means you're going to have to agree with the position your spouse is taking—it just means you're taking in what your spouse's interests are. Understanding what drives your spouse's thinking can open the door for a meeting of the minds.

You're in Charge

One of the advantages of mediation and collaborative divorce is that you and your spouse design the solution that works for you; you are not limited to a settlement structure that is within the boundaries of what a judge could do. Judges do have limits on what facts they can consider and what they can order parties to do. For example:

- Judges do not have the authority to order child support for adult children who aren't disabled; if you design your own solution, you could agree to continue supporting an adult child who's not yet self-supporting.
- Judges do not have the authority to order people to execute wills or trusts that leave certain assets intact for the couple's adult children to inherit, but in many states you could make an agreement to do so.
- In some states, judges can order a spouse to pay alimony only under certain circumstances defined by state law. But you could agree to spousal support regardless of circumstances.
- Judges cannot force parties to delay the divorce until one party becomes eligible for Social Security or Medicare, but you could agree to do so.

After interests are identified in the early stages of mediation or the collaborative process, they become the bedrock of negotiations and settlement proposals. This approach keeps both spouses tuned into what is really important, and avoids the trap of each spouse automatically reacting negatively to positions voiced by the other.

You will not get everything you want in any divorce process. But in a successful mediation or collaborative divorce that is focused on interest-based negotiations, you will likely come away with a well-forged settlement that meets your major interests, concerns, and needs.

Mediation

Mediation is a settlement tool that spouses use together, rather than a decision-making process that they must turn over to someone else, like litigation and arbitration. In mediation, both spouses meet with a neutral third person, the mediator, who helps them try to reach a compromise. In some courts, you're required to go to mediation before your case can go to trial; in others, you must attend a mandatory settlement conference with a judge that is similar to mediation. If mediation is required, then, depending on the rules of your local court, you might have a choice among hiring a private mediator, using a court-appointed mediator, or using the mediation services of a nonprofit dispute resolution center.

What Mediation Looks Like

The mediator, who has special training in negotiation and communication, is selected by agreement of the parties or by a judge. The mediator might be a lawyer or a nonlawyer. The mediator's own style will determine how things proceed, but, in general, everyone involved in the mediation will meet together at the outset. The mediator will go over the process you can expect and make certain agreements that will help things run more smoothly—things like refraining from interrupting, and making sure electronic devices are turned off. The mediator will ask each of you to outline the situation as you see it, in order to learn something about each spouse's interests and ideas and to get a sense of the relationship between you and your spouse.

After that, you might stay in the same room while the mediator works with both of you together, or you might move to separate rooms and speak with the mediator in turn about your interests and ideas for settlement. The mediator will shuttle information and possible solutions back and forth until an agreement is reached or until the mediator thinks it makes sense to get everyone in the same room together again.

Whether you work together or separately depends on what the mediator thinks will be most productive. As long as it's appropriate in the context of the parties' relationship, most mediators prefer to meet together, as it allows for a greater possibility of real understanding. One important benefit of mediation is that it can help spouses understand each other's positions so that they compromise because of that understanding, not just to get things over with. If you hope to have a positive relationship with your ex-spouse in the future, mediation might help you achieve that.

CAUTION

Try not to mediate too early. Most people want to resolve their divorces quickly and economically. But gathering information about assets and other facts is important groundwork that should be completed before serious mediation begins. Do not succumb to pressure to mediate before you have this information. The more informed and prepared the participants are, the more successful the mediation.

Mediators also differ on how often to meet and for how long. One option is to meet for a single mediation session. This assumes that both parties have all the information they need and are prepared to explore settlement. Another style is to break up the negotiations into multiple sessions. The first session might be primarily devoted to information gathering, and you'll be sent away with instructions to think about certain scenarios and to bring back additional information. This is the most common way of conducting divorce mediation, because it's rare for the spouses to have all the information they'll need when they come to the first session. It also limits face-to-face negotiations, which can be emotionally difficult, to shorter periods of time.

Every once in a while, you'll come across a mediator who wants to engage in marathon sessions well into the evening hours. I believe this is a recipe for fatigue and bad decision making, and that agreements signed when the participants are exhausted are suspect. If you are too tired to think straight, tell the mediator or your lawyer and refuse to go on. And while we're on the subject, eat a healthy breakfast on the morning of mediation, and try to resist the candy and sugar-loaded food that often appears on mediation tables. A sugar high is the last thing you need when you're trying to make wise decisions for your future.

Discussions with the mediator are usually confidential. In fact, confidentiality laws often protect everything that happens in mediation. This encourages free and open negotiations because you don't have to worry that things you say and proposals you make will come back to haunt you if you're unable to settle and there's a trial later.

The Role of Lawyers in Mediation

Sometimes lawyers attend mediation with their clients, and sometimes they don't. Mediators might prefer to meet without lawyers present in order to focus on communication and emotional issues before moving on to facts and figures. If you have a lawyer and if your lawyer doesn't come to mediation, you'll consult beforehand to discuss settlement ideas and get prepared. Most mediators allow parties to confer with attorneys by phone during mediation, and you're always free to stop a mediation session if you feel you need advice from your attorney before going further.

There are times when it's important to have your lawyer present in mediation, especially if you and your spouse have settled into "controlling" and "compliant" roles in your marriage. A spouse who is less assertive and who has not participated in decision making during the marriage might find mediation unsettling and overwhelming if not properly prepared and effectively represented, and might revert to acquiescing to the other's demands.

Even when attorneys participate in the mediation, it can be difficult to guide a less-assertive spouse through the pressures of mediation. It is common to revert to a victim role and expect the attorney to make the decisions. If this describes you, try to bring your best and strongest self to the mediation and stand up for what you think is fair. Your lawyer will help and support you, but one of the purposes of mediation is to ensure that parties make their own decisions rather than letting others make them—so take the opportunity to practice doing just that.

Mediating If You're Representing Yourself

Some couples use mediation to resolve their divorce without hiring lawyers to represent them at all. In this situation, you both hire a mediator—usually an attorney—to help you negotiate a resolution and prepare a settlement agreement. The attorney-mediator might give you information about the law, but doesn't represent either of you and isn't allowed to give legal advice to either of you. So, if you don't have a lawyer representing you and your state allows limited legal representation, consider hiring one just for the purposes of coaching you through the mediation and looking over the settlement agreement that the mediator prepares. At the very least, you should absolutely have a lawyer review the settlement agreement before you sign it. Forewarning: In some states, the terms of mediation agreements, signed by both parties, are final and cannot be changed.

Collaborative Divorce

Even when cases are litigated, the vast majority of family law cases settle. So, why not begin with a plan for a more low-key, less stressful, and nonadversarial process that provides each spouse with an advocate while preserving some level of civility between the participants? This is the theory behind the collaborative law model. Collaborative law has been around only since the 1990s, but it has become steadily more popular; for example, over twenty states (including Washington, D.C.) have adopted the Uniform Collaborative Law Act of 2009. It blends the benefits of having an advocate with the nonadversarial approach of mediation, and it's a good option for many people.

A collaborative divorce occurs in a nonadversarial environment where each spouse has an attorney, and together with the attorneys, the spouses negotiate their own divorce decisions in a series of four-way meetings. The collaborative attorneys must withdraw if the process fails. In this event, the parties must hire new litigation lawyers.

Hiring a Collaborative Attorney: Experience Counts

Collaborative law skills are different in many ways from litigation skills, and collaborative practice could be a real change of gears for a lawyer.

Generally, attorneys are taught to debate, argue, challenge, attack, ask tough questions, and trap witnesses. These skills define litigation attorneys (and could make them unpleasant dinner guests). Collaborative training involves a very different set of skills that require training to develop. In collaborative training, attorneys learn to support and encourage nonpositional, interest-based negotiations. Attorneys are encouraged to detach from their usual tendency to exert control over the outcome, instead urging clients to be creative in their thinking about how both spouses could come out of the divorce with their goals met. In addition, collaborative attorneys are trained to understand interpersonal dynamics and to support communication based not solely on financial negotiations, but also on emotional aspects of the process.

Some collaborative attorneys are in the field because collaborative practice comes naturally to them, but many lawyers must be retrained to work in that way. If you're hiring a collaborative attorney, ask how long the lawyer has been practicing collaborative law and ask about the lawyer's training. Just make sure your lawyer has some training and a commitment to continuing to develop a collaborative practice, and isn't doing this one collaborative case as a sideline.

Local bar organizations might maintain lists of collaboratively trained attorneys, and statewide and local collaborative law organizations have referral networks on the Internet. Attorneys who have a collaborative practice will say so on their websites or in lawyer directories, in print or online. You'll find more information about hiring an attorney in Chapter 2, "Getting Guidance—The Professional Side."

The Role of Lawyers in Collaborative Divorce

The most unique characteristic of collaborative divorce is apparent at the outset of the case, when both spouses and their lawyers sign an agreement saying that if the process breaks down and one spouse decides to engage in adversarial litigation, then both collaborative attorneys must withdraw from the case and both spouses must hire new counsel to represent them in litigation. In addition, both spouses and their attorneys agree to share information freely and to cooperate in hiring experts to appraise property or evaluate settlement ideas.

What is behind this rather restrictive structure? The goal of collaborative practice is for attorneys and parties to work together in a nonadversarial style. Instead of trying to give as little information as possible, the collaborative agreement requires the clients and lawyers to share all relevant information so that everyone has equal knowledge about assets, debts, and property. Instead of considering only their own client's advantage, the attorneys evaluate the interests of both spouses. Instead of negotiating outside the presence of the clients, they jointly facilitate their clients' abilities to solve problems themselves.

The goal is to create a safe environment where the best solutions will surface. One spouse might not comfortably sit across the table from the other spouse's attorney and negotiate if the client anticipates being cross- examined by that same attorney in the courtroom some day. Being free of the worry that litigation is looming is a great support for shared problem solving.

All lawyer–client communications are still confidential under the attorney–client privilege. Although your attorney works cooperatively and informally with your spouse's attorney, each lawyer still has a duty to advocate on their client's behalf, to maintain client confidentiality, and share with the other lawyer only information that the client has authorized.

What Collaborative Divorce Looks Like

Other than the initial divorce pleadings and a final divorce order, a collaborative divorce means you agree not to file papers or schedule hearings at the courthouse. This commitment keeps you at the negotiating table. It is not necessary that you agree on any issue at the outset other than to try collaboration. The collaborative process is significantly different from every other resolution method we've looked at so far, including adversarial litigation, arbitration, and mediation. Here are some of the factors that make it unique.

The participation agreement. The collaborative method begins with a participation agreement that both spouses and both attorneys must sign. This written agreement, an enforceable contract, sets out the rules of the road; rules may differ somewhat from state to state and attorney to attorney, but they usually include many of the same provisions, such as:

- Any pending litigation will be suspended and no new litigation will be filed unless each party agrees to file divorce papers.
- The parties commit to a transparent process and the use of interest-based negotiations.
- The parties agree to disclose all relevant information voluntarily, without discovery proceedings.
- What you say and the documents you exchange during the collaborative process are confidential, unless the other side would have a right to get the information in discovery if you weren't collaborating and you were engaged in an adversarial divorce.
- The spouses agree to share the cost of hiring neutral experts.
- You establish procedures for terminating the collaborative process, including a requirement that spouses must hire new attorneys if they don't settle through collaboration.

Joint sessions (four-way meetings). Collaborative negotiations occur in a series of "four-ways" or joint sessions—meetings that you, your spouse, and both attorneys attend. Other neutral professionals might also attend the meetings (see "The Team Model," below). Detailed agendas provide the structure for these meetings; and minutes taken by one of the attorneys or other designated professional provide a written record of any agreements reached, the facts relied upon in reaching those agreements, and lists of tasks for everyone to accomplish between meetings.

The Team Model

An interdisciplinary team approach—in which professionals work together to help resolve a collaborative divorce—is gaining popularity in collaborative circles. Communications experts (also called divorce coaches) who are mental health professionals trained in the collaborative process, might participate in joint meetings or meet with clients outside of the four-way meetings. They help the participants communicate effectively and avoid high conflict. One goal of collaborative law is to help participants develop better communication and problem-solving skills with each other, which will benefit each of them long after the divorce is final.

The collaborative team might also include financial professionals who analyze living expenses, calculate tax consequences, and evaluate the long-term impact of different settlement options. Instead of being immobilized by the vague fear that you will not have enough money to meet your post-divorce living expenses, you'll get accurate budget forecasts and learn the effects of various property division scenarios.

You might also ask for the assistance of appraisers, accounting professionals, and estate planners periodically throughout the process to answer specific "what if" types of questions regarding tax, valuation, and estate planning issues. Specialized attorneys might be brought in so their expertise could be used in negotiating and drafting transfer documents needed to carry out agreements. None of these neutral advisers are hired without the informed consent of both parties. These experts are prohibited from participating in any subsequent litigation unless the participants and adviser agree.

Identifying interests. Each spouse prepares a list of interests (needs, concerns, goals) with the help of that spouse's attorney and the mental health professional on the collaborative team. The parties exchange these lists and might modify them during the collaboration.

Information sharing. The next phase of the collaborative process is similar to the discovery stage in litigation, when information and documents are exchanged and examined. The terms of the participation agreement make full disclosure mandatory, and failure to make all requested records and evidence available might stop the collaborative process and spin the parties into litigation. All financial transactions are available for inspection: Investments gone belly-up, affairs enjoyed, and secret spending will all see the light of day. The process requires truthfulness and openness. It is transparent.

After the parties have disclosed all financial information, they will prepare a sworn inventory, either jointly or individually, of all assets and liabilities. A financial professional (if one participated in the collaboration) or one of the attorneys (with input from the other) will reduce the inventory information to a spreadsheet listing property and debts, current values, and balances.

This spreadsheet is very important because the spouses and their attorneys use it to depict various settlement scenarios and their resulting financial impacts. For this reason, it's important that one attorney not control the process completely.

You'll work through the different elements of your case one by one. Your lawyers might arrange for financial experts, mental health experts, appraisers, and business or estate planning experts to provide additional information that might enlighten the parties and move the process toward resolution (see "The Team Model," above).

Generating options and reaching agreement. During the collaborative meetings, you and your spouse generate settlement options, including those that a judge or attorney might not think of. As you brainstorm about possible outcomes, your attorneys will advise you about the range of possible courthouse outcomes and the law that's relevant to your case. In other words, interest-based negotiations do not occur in a legal vacuum—you'll have all the information you need to assess the case and your options. The best settlements meet many of the interests identified by both spouses.

Upsides of Collaborative Divorce

After hearing about all the professionals who could be involved in a collaborative divorce, you might be surprised to learn that the cost of collaborative divorce is usually significantly less than a full-blown trial. This is because there are no dueling experts, time is not wasted on unnecessary pretrial hearings, and everyone focuses on bridging the gaps meaningfully rather than splitting the difference. Collaborative divorce offers more privacy, too, because less personal information appears in public records.

Many cases are worked out in two to three meetings, while a smaller percentage of cases take months to resolve. Whatever happens, the collaborative case will likely move faster than litigation; the timeline is determined by the participants, not by a judge's docket. Participants' expectations regarding time are discussed at the outset rather than hidden in aggressive paperwork and hearings or passive-aggressive foot-dragging.

One benefit of a collaborative process is difficult to quantify in dollars: the chance to preserve a civil relationship with your ex-spouse. That might not only improve your quality of life in the present and the future (imagine dancing with your ex at your child's wedding), but can also prevent costly post-divorce trips to the courthouse.

Another advantage of using a collaborative divorce process is that it may be a better fit for our aging brains. Research shows that as we age, our capacities to deal with divided attention, novel tasks, recall of new information, and spontaneous verbal fluency diminish. The predictable structure of collaboration—agendas, minutes, ability to schedule meetings for our best times of the day, time to reflect and react to new information and new formats of information like spreadsheets—is more age-friendly than the rigors, unpredictability, and quick decision making that are all required in the courtroom.

Downsides of Collaborative Divorce

If the collaborative process breaks down, you and your spouse will both be facing the cost and time delay involved in hiring new lawyers to pursue litigation. This consequence can actually have an upside because it provides an incentive to hang in there during tough negotiation sessions. But a downside is the possibility of a weaker party being bullied into a settlement that isn't fair or satisfactory, out of fear of the costs of abandoning the process—in other words, the incentive might be too strong. The potential pressure to remain in negotiations that have become unworkable means that collaborative divorce isn't for everyone—especially if you don't think you could stand your ground or walk away from the process if necessary.

When Not to Use Collaborative Divorce

For many people, collaborative divorce offers a welcome alternative to nasty arguing, posturing, and courtroom antics and delays. But collaboration is not the answer to spouses who find themselves in any of the following situations.

Substance and physical abuse. If either spouse is dealing with untreated substance abuse or mental illness, or if you are afraid of sitting across from your spouse because the marriage has a history of physical or mental abuse, collaborative divorce is not the right choice for you. You will need dedicated, sometimes aggressive people on your side to manage the process.

You really don't want to make the call. If you want to delegate your responsibility for significant life choices to someone else (a judge), you should consider the trial route instead. For example, you or someone advising you might be firmly convinced that a judge will rule in your favor no matter what.

You suspect your spouse has agreed to collaboration in hopes that its informal nature will allow that spouse to take advantage of you. The bedrock of collaborative law is that the parties enter the process in good faith. Nevertheless, some spouses want to use collaborative law because they think it is easier to control the other spouse in that kind of environment. In other words, the occasional spouse uses the process in bad faith, thinking that it might be easier to stall for time while gathering information and engaging in machinations in the background. If you believe this is your spouse's intention, think twice before investing your time and money in a collaborative process.

If collaboration isn't successful in reaching a settlement, all is not lost. Much of what you learn in the collaborative process is useful in the litigation context, and the confidentiality rules only prevent you from disclosing offers, counteroffers, options, and opinions—but not actual facts about your marital estate. For example, if you learned in a collaborative process that your spouse was hiding assets or engaging in other financial skullduggery, this discoverable evidence could still be used as evidence at trial.

RESOURCE

Learn even more about mediation and collaboration. For much more detail about these ways of resolving your divorce, along with worksheets and examples, take a look at *Divorce Without Court: A Guide to Mediation & Collaborative Divorce,* by Katherine E. Stoner (Nolo).

Marital Property: Steps to a Fair Division

You're probably vaguely aware that dividing assets and debts is one of the biggest challenges of negotiating a divorce. But did you know that Social Security retirement benefits are not a marital asset? Are you aware that some public retirement plans do not allow a former spouse to receive survivor benefits? Is it true that individual retirement accounts in the name of one spouse can be awarded to the other spouse without tax consequences in a divorce? You might never have thought about any of these questions, but understanding your options and your rights with regard to marital property is probably one of the main reasons you're reading this book—and for good reason.

The upcoming chapters are designed to help you gather the knowledge you need. In this chapter, you'll get an overview of the steps to a fair division. In Chapter 6, we'll cover the most valuable items in your marital estate, and in Chapter 7, we'll look at the rest of your assets. Chapter 8 is all about the bad news: debts and taxes. Chapter 9 sorts out the puzzle of health care, and Chapter 10 addresses how you will move forward financially after your divorce. With all that ahead of you, let's get started.

Four Steps in Analyzing Marital Property

Even if you have a lawyer for your divorce, it's crucial that you educate yourself about your financial situation and how divorce and money fit together. Family lawyers represent several clients at once, while you, the client, have only one divorce. Certainly, your attorney will ask you questions. But the lawyer could not possibly ask every question necessary to elicit all of the relevant facts. If you understand how the facts of your situation fit into the divorce process, your communication with your attorney—and your outcome—are likely to be greatly improved. Plus, you will feel and actually be more in control of your future.

Four simple verbs describe how we assess assets and debts in any divorce:
- Identify: List assets you own and debts you owe.
- Characterize: Determine whether property is marital or separate.
- Value: Evaluate what your property is worth.
- Divide: Decide who gets what.

These actions occur in the order they're listed here, so you might have to curb your tendency, which is very common, to jump right in and start dividing assets. Sometimes my clients arrived at our first meeting with a property division plan already sketched out. They asked, "What do you think? Is this fair?" My usual response was: "Before I can answer, I have some questions." My questions always followed the four steps above, and usually resulted in the client remembering forgotten assets, learning something new about how assets could be divided, or reconsidering some part of the proposal. Here's how each of the four steps works.

Identify

You could start identifying your property by making a list of all that you own and all that you owe. Your attorney will probably give you an inventory form to fill out, but if that isn't the case you can use the form in Appendix A. This is a big task, so give yourself plenty of time to complete it. It might seem overwhelming, too, but the time you devote to accurately identifying your assets and liabilities is one of the most important contributions you will make to your case. Rest assured that every minute you spend gathering this information will save you many dollars you otherwise would spend on having your attorney or the attorney's staff collect and organize your records.

Remember that you have a right to access all of the financial records related to your marital estate. In this context, the word "estate" doesn't mean an opulent English manor house; it just means all of the property and debts that either you or your spouse owns or owes. Even if you own only the shirt on your back and one credit card in your wallet, you have an estate.

The chart below is intended to prompt your memory about property categories. The list is long for a reason: The biggest mistake clients make is to overlook an asset or debt. They do this not because they are hiding anything, but because their memory bank was not tapped in an effective way.

The left-hand column of the chart lists the asset categories (and after those, debt categories). The right-hand column lists the types of documents you should look for in the category, and notes other reminders that are relevant.

Even if you think that an item is not worth very much, include it in your list. I suggest you use file folders to organize your search-and-find mission—create one folder for each asset (or category of assets if there's not much in the category). Slip a blank page of paper in the front of each folder, on which you can capture random thoughts, questions, and information about the asset. Remember that being thorough now will pay big dividends later.

It's important to document both assets and debts that you know about and those you might not be sure about. For example, if you have a vague memory that your spouse has a money market account, but you haven't heard anything about it for a long time, add it to your inventory list. If it turns out not to exist, fine. But don't cheat yourself out of assets you might be able to locate with just a bit of effort.

Despite its length, this list is not all-inclusive. In addition to these items, you might find that you need historical financial documents that will prove separate property claims or help you expose a spouse who's hiding assets. The list also does not include the financial records needed for business valuations; if you're dividing a business, your attorney will tell you what documents are needed.

Finding the Records

You'll be looking for a lot of information, and you might be wondering where you are going to find it all—especially if your spouse has maintained the financial records during your marriage. You have every right to see all of these records, so unless you think your spouse is hiding assets or will refuse to turn things over, ask where the documents and records are kept. If you don't think you'll get everything you need that way, be methodical and thorough in your search. Look through household file cabinets, desk drawers, storage areas, and computer files. Check safe deposit boxes. If financial records are not in your house, are they being kept off premises at your spouse's office? Even if they are, you have the right to see and copy them.

ASSETS	
Asset or Asset Category	**Documents to Collect**
Financial Accounts	
Checking Savings Money market Brokerage Cash management accounts Mutual funds Credit union accounts Employment-related savings accounts (nonretirement) Certificates of deposit Health Savings Accounts (HSAs) Flex Savings Accounts	Latest statement for each account Photocopy of certificates of deposit NOTES: Include a memo of any noteworthy activity regarding the accounts. For example, at the time of marriage, did you or your spouse have an account that still exists or from which funds were transferred into a joint account? Were the names on an account changed during marriage? Did you or your spouse inherit money? Do you suspect that other accounts exist? Were accounts closed or consolidated?
Bonds	
Savings bonds Other bond certificates not held by a brokerage company	Photocopy of bond certificates
Stocks	
Held outside of a brokerage account	Photocopy of stock certificates
Real Estate	
Residence Vacation home Rental property Unimproved real estate Time-share properties Commercial property Leases (lessor or lessee) Oil, gas, and other mineral interests Cemetery plots	Deeds Latest mortgage statement (including any equity loans) Loan security agreements Lease documents Appraisals and other valuations Homeowners' insurance (and endorsements) NOTES: List the source of money used for purchasing property and for major remodeling projects, especially if separate funds were used. If separate funds were used to purchase real estate, include a copy of the settlement statement received when you closed the property purchase.

ASSETS (continued)	
Asset or Asset Category	**Documents to Collect**
Motor Vehicles	
Automobiles	Title documents
Boats	Appraisals and valuation documents
Motorcycles	Latest periodic loan statement
Jet skis	
ATVs	
Trailers	
Travel vehicles	
Livestock trailers	
Scooters	
Airplanes	
Employee Retirement Accounts	
Pension	Summary plan descriptions (SPDs)
401(k) and other retirement plans	Paycheck stubs and W-2s if contributions are made through payroll deductions
Profit-sharing	NOTES: Contact the plan administrator for copies of your SPDs. If these assets already existed as of the date of marriage, try to obtain information as to the value or account balance on that date.
Individual Retirement Accounts	
IRAs	Latest statements
SEP IRAs	
Roth IRAs	
Business Interests	
Sole proprietorships	Partnership agreements
Corporations	Corporate charters or articles of incorporation
Partnerships (general and limited)	Bylaws
	Buy–sell agreements
Joint ventures	Entity tax returns for last five years
Other business interests	The entity's most recent financial statements including balance sheet and profit and loss statements

ASSETS (continued)	
Asset or Asset Category	**Documents to Collect**
Employment-Related Benefits	
Stock options	Stock grant agreements or instruments
Restricted stock	Employee handbooks and correspondence describing benefits
Employee stock purchase plans	Documents reflecting current balances in health savings accounts, flexible spending accounts, and other plans
Deferred compensation	
Accrued vacation benefits	Pay stubs showing accrued vacation leave
Bonuses	Summary plan descriptions for medical, dental, and vision plans
Life and disability insurance acquired through employment	Summary plan description for long-term disability insurance
Health savings and Flex plans	
Medical, dental, vision insurance	
Long-term disability insurance	
Life Insurance and Annuities	
Term life	Copies of policies
Whole life	Beneficiary designation forms
Universal life	Annuity contracts
Annuities	Statements reflecting status and value of insurance policies or annuities
Trusts	
Of which you are a beneficiary	Trust creation documents describing terms of the trust
Of which you are the settlor (i.e., you created the trust)	Statement of assets held in the trust
Season Tickets or Charters	
Sporting events	Documents showing ownership
Cultural events	Tickets for future events

ASSETS (continued)	
Asset or Asset Category	**Documents to Collect**
Livestock and Pets	
	Livestock inventories
	Livestock purchase agreements
	Pedigree documents
Club Memberships	
Country club	Membership purchase contract
Social clubs	Documentation about rights to sell or transfer
Dinner clubs	membership
Sports clubs	
Health and fitness clubs	
Frequent Flyer Accounts and Reward Programs	
Credit card	Current statement of miles, points, rewards,
Airline	or credits
Hotel	
Collectibles and Collections	
Stamps	Purchase documents
Guns	Appraisals
Art	Other information about value (e.g. online sales
Antiques	or auction comparables)
Coins	NOTES: Write down the location of all
Rare books	collections.
Cars	
Equipment	
Sports, recreational, and physical fitness	Receipts
	Other information about value (for example,
Electronics	eBay offers)
Computers	
Gardening	
Hobbies	

ASSETS (continued)	
Asset or Asset Category	**Documents to Collect**
Accounts Receivable (Money owed to you)	
Loans/promissory notes Business accounts receivable	Loan agreements Payment records on live loans Receivables report from business
Safe Deposit Boxes	
	Photograph or list of the contents. If items aren't identified in any other category on this list, write down value and obtain any documents related to the item.
Jewelry	
	Receipts Appraisals Notes about how item was purchased or received, especially if it was a gift NOTES: Write down the location of jewelry.
Household Items	
Furnishings Appliances	Receipts Appraisals Photographs of contents of home, including garage and storage areas
Intellectual Property	
Patents, copyrights, and trademarks Creative works—completed Creative works—in progress	Documents identifying patent, copyright, or trademark List of creative works, including status and value, if known, or potential value
Legal Actions	
Pending lawsuits against you Pending lawsuits by you against someone else Potential claims not yet filed	NOTES: Describe situation and identify any pending lawsuits by court, case number, and attorney contact information

ASSETS (continued)	
Asset or Asset Category	**Documents to Collect**
Taxes	
	Federal and state returns for past five years
	Status of returns, if on extension
	Notes about taxes owed
Social Security	
	Most recent benefit statements
Premarital or Postmarital Agreements	
	Copies of agreements and any amendments made to agreements since signing
Separate Property Claims	
	For inherited property, a copy of will or correspondence describing property
	For other property, notes about why you believe it is separate property
DEBTS (Secured and Unsecured)	
Debt Category	**Documents to Collect**
Mortgage	Loan documents
Auto	Current statements reflecting balance owed
Margin loans in brokerage accounts	Photocopies of both sides of credit cards
Personal loans	If debt existed on date of marriage, balance of loan on that date
Credit card debts	
Student loans	
Loans against retirement accounts	
Business-related debts	

Identifying assets and liabilities and gathering related records could feel like the most arduous task you have ever undertaken, but it has many benefits. It educates you, makes you an informed negotiator, and puts you in a better position to manage your estate after the divorce.

If You Lack Information or Suspect Hidden Assets

What if you are in the dark about your financial situation? What if you do not know whether certain types of assets or liabilities exist? What if you think your spouse has been hiding assets or other financial information from you? Unfortunately, all these scenarios do happen—especially the one in which one spouse is sadly uninformed about the couple's finances.

The vast majority of divorcing spouses voluntarily provide the information necessary to complete the divorce fairly and equitably. But some people will go to great lengths to hide money and assets, either to keep them from the other spouse or to avoid having to pay support.

Common Ways of Hiding Assets

Some common ways people try to hide assets are by:
- transferring cash into accounts held in someone else's name
- opening offshore accounts
- stashing cash in hidey holes (rather than in financial institutions)
- overpaying credit card accounts to create credit balances
- overpaying estimated tax payments in order to create refunds in the future
- delaying distribution of income from trusts
- in business, hiding money by using fake employees, writing off or understating accounts receivable, overstating accounts payable, and delaying bonuses or other forms of compensation, and
- moving personal property to undisclosed locations.

I'm sure that there are additional ploys, including new ones being developed all the time as technology marches along.

What Can You Do?

If you have a strong suspicion, or you know, that your spouse is hiding assets, your lawyer will use the discovery process to gather all the information that could help you ferret out what's going on. But depending on how sophisticated the scams are, you might not be able to find the hidden money. If things look complicated, you might want to hire a forensic accountant. These professionals have many, many tricks of the trade that will help you find hidden assets—legally— and these accountants are trained to review financial records with an eye toward shenanigans, including analyzing computers for hidden data. You can also hire a private investigator to search for assets. The sophistication of the world of private investigators and forensic experts is astounding.

Finding Gold

I once had a client who described how secretive her husband was, hiding things and keeping information from her. She vaguely remembered his purchase of Krugerrands years earlier, but she could find no trace of them in any of the usual places—safe deposit box, chest of drawers, their home study. Early in the divorce process she moved out of the family home due to fears for her safety, but her husband still lived there, and I asked and got the court's permission to return to the house to take an inventory and look for missing records. My client insisted that the Krugerrands had to be in the house somewhere. It was a long day, and eventually I had to visit the bathroom. On a sudden instinct, I lifted the lid on the toilet tank. There, glistening in the bottom of the tank, were the Krugerrands! Moral of the story: Persistence (and a little luck) pays off in the end.

> ⓘ **CAUTION**
> **Play by the rules.** There are also shady ways to look for hidden information, and you might have friends or family encouraging you to use these methods. Do not do this. It's important that you approach the search and carry it out with clean hands. For one thing, it's the right thing to do from an ethical standpoint—and even if your spouse isn't playing by the rules, you are answerable to your own conscience. On a practical level, too, you do not want to taint any information you find. Make sure you discuss your plans with your attorney before hiring an investigator or investigating on your own. If you play fast and loose, you might not be able to use the information as evidence.

Characterize

All of the property in your marital estate falls into one of two categories:

- marital property (also called community or joint property), meaning it's owned by the two of you in equal or unequal shares, or
- separate property (also called sole or nonmarital property), meaning only one of you owns it.

In some community property states, there's also a category of property called quasi-community, which is treated as community property for purposes of division.

Characterizing property is the process of determining whether a given asset or debt is marital or separate.

Impact of Characterization

Characterization could have a significant impact on how you (or the judge) will divide and allocate property. Characterization is most important when you are in a contested court case, because whether property is marital or separate determines who takes it home after the divorce. Most states have rules that marital property is divided and each spouse keeps that spouse's separate property—so each spouse wants to characterize as much property as possible as separate, in order to keep it.

Characterization might be less important to you if your divorce is amicable and you and your spouse intend to agree on how to divide your property without going to court (or if you live in one of the states that allow judges to take all property into consideration irrespective of characterization). In that case, you might want to simply skip ahead to the section on "Value." We'll also return to the impact of characterization on asset division in "Divide," below.

General Rules of Characterization

Here are the general characterization rules about which most states agree:

Marital property. Marital property is property that you or your spouse acquired during the marriage. The most common examples are money that either of you earned through your labor and effort (for example, at a job) and assets purchased with that earned income.

Separate property. Each person's separate property is property that person brought into the marriage, inherited or received by gift during the marriage. In most states, personal injury awards that compensate for pain and suffering are also separate property. If one spouse uses separate funds to acquire an asset during marriage, then that asset will also be characterized as separate, as long as that spouse continues to hold title as a sole owner.

Exceptions to the General Rules

As is the case with most legal concepts, nuances and exceptions affect the above rules. Explaining all of them could easily fill the remaining pages of this book. But for our purposes, you just need to be aware of a few of the common ways that states vary the general rules.

Income produced by separate property during marriage might be marital property in some states. Examples include rental income from separate property real estate, interest income on financial accounts (including retirement accounts), dividend income, and income produced by separate business entities. Some states characterize such income as marital property; others, as separate.

Name changes on assets might create a marital interest in the property. If one spouse adds the other's name to a separate property bank account or real estate deed, questions arise about its character and about whether a gift to the other spouse was intended.

Time and energy expended by a spouse on separate property might create a marital interest. For example, a spouse inherits investment accounts and then devotes a significant amount of time and effort to managing those accounts, resulting in earnings. Because a person's time is considered to belong to the marital community and the person otherwise might have been generating community earnings, the time spent managing separate accounts might create a marital interest in their increased value in some states.

A professional education might be an asset. If a spouse earns a professional degree during marriage and then divorces, a minority of states consider that degree or license a marital asset, meaning that the marital estate will include a value placed on the degree (the degree itself, of course, is awarded to the professional spouse). Once the value is assigned, the professional spouse must pay the other spouse a share. Valuation is very difficult, requiring economic and accounting experts to measure things like (1) the present value of future earnings both with and without the professional degree or license, or (2) the cost to the marital estate of the education and training.

Even if it's not considered an asset, as is true in a majority of states, the supporting spouse may receive compensation in other ways, such as reimbursement for the cost of the education, an award of spousal support, or a property division that affords the nonprofessional spouse an opportunity for higher education after the divorce or provides a larger share of the marital estate.

Co-ownership of property between the marital and separate estates might mean the property is shared. For example, you and your spouse purchase a house during marriage, using one spouse's inherited funds for part of the down payment and using marital savings for the other part. In this case, you'll have to identify which portion of the property is marital and which is separate. In many states, the rule is that the spouse who contributed separate property must be reimbursed for the down payment money before the property—which is considered marital property—is divided. In other places, the mixed contribution means that the property itself is part separate and part marital.

Commingling of assets creates confusion. Commingling means that different types of money have become so mixed up that it's difficult to characterize any portion as one spouse's separate property, even though you know there's some separate property involved. Commingling frequently occurs in bank or brokerage accounts. For example, imagine the very common scenario where you and your spouse have a joint money market savings account and you inherit $10,000 and deposit the inheritance into that money market account. Years pass, during which you and your spouse contribute additional marital funds into the money market account, and spend some on major purchases. Then you decide to divorce; at the time the money market account balance is $25,000. Tracing the value of your contribution versus the marital contributions could be very difficult, because of the different deposit and withdrawal dates and the accrual of interest at different rates at different times.

Tracing Can Be Challenging

Tracing is the term for determining what portions of commingled property are joint and what portions are separate. Tracing can be tedious, time-consuming, and expensive, depending upon the period of time, the number of transactions involved, and the availability of financial records. Some states presume that if the character of funds is mixed, then the funds remaining at the time of divorce are marital property and subject to division. But in states that don't have that presumption, you might need to hire a forensic accountant. Unfortunately, banks are required to hold onto records (checks, deposit slips, and statements) for only five years, making records availability a problem. (Some banks will retain records for longer, so be sure you check with the financial institution about their retention policies.) All you can do is your best—and at a certain point, it might serve your interests better to compromise on ownership of the amounts rather than spending enormous sums of money trying to trace the funds. Of course, you might be someone who keeps all of your own records, as one of my clients was—she had all of her banking records throughout the entire 23 years of her marriage, and it saved her hundreds of thousands of dollars when it came time to resolve the divorce.

Some states will conclude that you gave the separate inheritance money to the marital estate when you deposited it into the joint account; but others will say you can trace back, calculate the interest on each type of contribution, allocate the withdrawals between estates, and be reimbursed.

Changing Characterization

Your state's law determines the character of property, but you can take steps that will override state law. For example, a premarital agreement might change the character of property—in fact, that is one of the primary purposes of such agreements. Some states allow spouses to change characterization during marriage—generally by written agreements called partition and exchange agreements, postmarital agreements, or transmutation agreements. It's also possible to change the character of property unwittingly, as in the example above where one spouse deposits a separate property inheritance into a joint account, possibly rendering the inheritance marital property.

Reimbursement

Financial interactions between the marital estate and each spouse's separate property are fairly common and could create the potential for reimbursement claims at divorce (sometimes called claims for economic contributions).

Reimbursement might arise when one estate (separate or marital) suffers a loss, while another estate benefits from that loss. The result is that one estate might owe money to another estate, as an adjustment.

Two common examples are when one spouse uses inherited funds (separate property) to pay for improvements to the family home (marital property), and when one spouse uses separate property funds to pay off the mortgage debt on the marital residence. Reimbursement theory says that such contributions should be paid back to that spouse at time of divorce. It could go the other way, too—for example, when spouses use joint money to make improvements to separately owned property, the separate property owner might be required to pay back the marital estate at divorce.

Many states have mechanisms for reimbursement in these circumstances, though states vary as to how you measure the amount of reimbursement. These adjustments could have quite an effect on the final division of the marital estate.

Value

The third stage in dealing with assets and liabilities is valuation: what a given asset is worth. Your first inclination is probably to think in terms of what an asset is worth to you. That type of value is called intrinsic value and is different from the measure of value most frequently used in divorce, which is fair market value (FMV). FMV is based on what a willing buyer would pay a willing seller for an asset under circumstances that do not involve a forced sale (as a divorce might). An asset might not be worth its FMV to you, or it could be worth more to you.

It's fairly simple to value certain assets, like bank accounts: The value is the balance on a specific date (though you might argue about whether the date is the separation date or the date of the final division of property). Stock exchanges set the values of stocks and mutual funds on any given date. Other types of assets might require experts to calculate value. In the case of a business valuation, there is gross value, net value, book value, and adjusted net value. Retirement assets have a pretax and posttax value. We'll deal more with some of these details later. For now, we'll look at value in general terms.

Two Aspects of Value

In a divorce, two points are primary in valuing property:

- **At what point in time the value is set.** Is the value of property for purposes of division set on the date you and your spouse separate, the date you agree on who gets what, the date the divorce is final, or some other date? Inflation, market conditions, and accumulated income could all affect the value of an asset during the divorce process. States vary on the point in time when valuation is calculated, and it could be a significant negotiating point in settling a divorce.

• **The relationship of value to the division of the marital estate.** If you are looking at a marital estate worth $100,000, it seems obvious that an equal division means that each spouse ends up with net assets worth $50,000. Assume there are two assets in this marital estate—a house with equity of $50,000, awarded to Spouse A, and a retirement account valued (before adjustment for taxes due in the future) at $50,000, awarded to Spouse B. Once taxes are factored in, the retirement account actually has a posttax value of $35,000, and its funds are not accessible for five more years, while Spouse A has the house equity available much sooner. This means that Spouse B's share is less than 50% of the marital estate. An asset's value affects the overall net value of the marital estate, and also influences the fairness of the allocation of marital assets. A value that's too high or too low could skew a final property division unjustly.

Games People Play

It's very easy to try playing games in the valuation arena. I encourage you to refrain from this, as it often backfires. Here are some of the most common manipulations:

• overvaluing an asset you want your spouse to have and undervaluing an asset you want

• deliberately failing to take known tax consequences into account when valuing real estate and retirement assets

• lowballing the cumulative value of low-value items for the sake of convenience (household furnishings or sporting equipment, for example), and

• purposely decreasing the value of a business in order to achieve a lower value during a divorce.

Each of these strategies could work against you; it's much easier to play it straight and make sure the division of property is fair.

Expert Opinions

Spouses frequently agree on how to value most of their assets. But for certain big-ticket items—such as the marital home, a business, or a pension—an independent third-party valuation might be necessary. In a contested divorce, each side might hire an expert for a ridiculously expensive Duel of the Experts, with the judge deciding the victor. Sometimes this is necessary, but it's much less expensive and time-consuming for divorcing spouses to jointly hire an expert and agree to abide by that person's valuation. (Even fighting over who the expert is will be much less expensive than hiring two and fighting over their conclusions.)

An attorney could guide you through the valuation techniques accepted in your local courts, and your lawyer should be familiar with experts who are respected by your local judges, as well as which ones to stay away from because they are known "hired guns" whose conclusions are driven by what their client wants, not by their profession's directives.

Sometimes the valuation stage feels like one big guessing game. But negotiating carefully over value could have a tremendous impact on how well you come out at the end of your property division. Professional valuations might offer you peace of mind that your own estimates would not provide.

Divide

The last stage of dealing with your property during divorce is to divide it. You might think it all gets automatically split down the middle, but that's not always so.

Equally or Equitably?

States differ as to whether they divide marital property equally or equitably, meaning one person may get more than half of the marital assets on the basis of fairness. California, for example, is a community property state that divides marital property equally, but Texas is a community property state that has adopted the concept of equitable division (or equitable distribution).

An equitable division refers to a result that is fair and just—not just an automatic 50/50 division between the spouses. A multitude of factors might be taken into consideration to justify an unequal division.

Equitable Factors

The laws in equitable distribution states give divorce judges wide discretion in dividing property, and there are a number of factors the judge will consider.

Disparate earning capacity. If one spouse's earning capacity is greater than the other's, a court might factor this in, especially if one spouse put a career on the back burner to raise children, with a resulting loss in earning capability. Of course, if a spouse is at the end of the income- generating years, this factor loses steam.

Supporting a spouse through school. If one spouse put the other through school, especially a professional school, that effort might be rewarded through equity.

Health condition of both spouses. If one spouse is disabled or has serious health problems, that person might need more property (or alimony).

Fault. Although fault doesn't factor into whether a spouse can get a divorce in the first place, if one spouse has been cruel in the marriage, the effects might be factored into the division of property. If a spouse has committed adultery, or is otherwise at fault in the breakup of the marriage, that also might be taken into consideration.

Separate property owned by spouses. If one spouse has a substantial separate estate in comparison to a smaller marital estate, those outside resources might be an equitable factor.

Other factors include the length of the marriage (judges view short-term marriages differently from long-term marriages) and the size of the marital estate (as when there is so much property that there's plenty to go around with a 50/50 division). Usually, both sides of a case present equitable considerations, and the judge pulls out the scales of justice to balance one against the other.

If you are negotiating a settlement rather than letting a judge decide, equitable factors are still relevant, and some knowledge of the propensities of local family court judges is helpful. When negotiating and mediating property settlements, and even in the context of a collaborative family law divorce, knowing what might happen in the courthouse could affect negotiations.

The Spreadsheet

How do you start the division of a marital estate? First, you create a spreadsheet of assets and liabilities. An example is below. This format allows you to move assets and liabilities around to determine the bottom line of different allocation scenarios. The net value of the total marital estate is the value of the pie you are slicing. If you know you are trying to reach a 50/50 division, for example, then you want to put enough assets and liabilities in each column that each spouse ends up with 50% of the net estate value.

The sample spreadsheet highlights the relationship between valuation and the allocation of property and debt. It also underscores the relevance of all the time and attention you give to creating a thorough inventory and organizing your records. You want a true figure for the net value of your marital estate. Omitting a debt or failing to capture the character of property can skew the eventual division— possibly to your detriment.

Market Value	Debt Balance	Net Value	Description	To Spouse A	To Spouse B
			Asset and Debt Spreadsheet		
Real Property					
$450,000	$(200,000)	$250,000	Residence on Olive Street	$250,000	
Accounts					
3,000		3,000	ABC Bank checking account—joint	1,500	1,500
10,000		10,000	XYZ Investment account—joint	9,500	500
5,000		5,000	Certificate of deposit at ABC Bank	3,000	2,000
Vehicles					
20,000	(15,000)	5,000	2018 Subaru Outback	5,000	
14,000		14,000	2015 Toyota Camry		14,000
Life Insurance					
500		500	Long-life Ins. Co.: SpB is insured for $25,000. Cash surrender value		500
Retirement					
2,500		2,500	IRA—in SpA's name	2,500	
260,000		260,000	401(k)—in SpB's name		260,000
Miscellaneous Assets					
1,000		1,000	Sporting equipment		1,000
Household Furnishings					
10,000		10,000	Items in SpA's possession	10,000	
5,000		5,000	Items in SpB's possession		5,000
Debt					
	(5,000)	(5,000)	SpB's credit card		(5,000)
	(2,000)	(2,000)	SpA's loan from her parents	(2,000)	
$781,000	$(222,000)	$559,000	TOTALS	$279,500	$279,500
			PROPERTY DIVISION	50%	50%

Basic Financial Principles

In addition to understanding the four steps to a fair division of your marital property, you'll be better prepared for dividing your property if you also understand certain financial principles. To assess what assets best serve your needs, keep the following three concerns in mind: the value of a mixed portfolio, your level of tolerance for risk, and the time value of your money.

At the end of this divorce you will have assets, no matter how small, to build on for your future well-being. Even if you do not get all that you want, you will know clearly your limitations and how to adjust to them.

The Value of a Mixed Portfolio

A standard financial investment strategy is to diversify your investment assets when possible—the opposite of putting all your eggs in one basket. Having a mixed portfolio is a goal worthy of your serious consideration, even if only one or two major assets are in your marital estate.

> EXAMPLE: Spouse A wants the marital residence. Its value is $150,000 with a $100,000 mortgage balance. Based upon projected income at the time of divorce, Spouse A can just afford the house and is willing to let Spouse B keep B's pension plan, estimated to be worth $25,000. Spouse B wants something out of the house whenever it is sold, so they agree that Spouse A will pay Spouse B $15,000 at time of sale. There is no fixed date by which the house is to be sold. Spouse A feels like the winner. However, Spouse B wisely secures the $15,000 future payment with a second lien on the house, which means that after the first lienholder (the mortgage company), Spouse B is next in line to have what Spouse A owes to Spouse B paid from the proceeds of sale.
>
> Six months later, the housing market crashes and recession is in full swing. Spouse A still has a job but takes a pay cut and can no longer afford to make payments on the mortgage. The house is now worth $110,000

and Spouse A must sell it. After paying $5,000 in closing costs incurred at the time of sale, Spouse A expects to net about $5,000 from the sale. But Spouse B's second lien funnels that $5,000 to Spouse B—and in addition, Spouse B could sue Spouse A for the $10,000 balance on Spouse B's second lien. Spouse B still has the retirement asset; Spouse A has nothing except a $10,000 debt to Spouse B. Why? Spouse A's future was risked for one asset, failing to spread Spouse A's risk by keeping a joint interest in the home plus a percentage of Spouse B's retirement plan. Spouse A's eggs were all put in one basket.

Stories like this are not rare, especially in difficult economic times. I include it not to scare you but to remind you that divorce is a financial crossroads, especially in the second half of life. At any financial intersection, you need to consider the impact of the curves outside your field of vision. You might decide to take a risk like Spouse A in this example did. But before you make the decision, know your tolerance for risk.

Risk Tolerance Levels

The concept of risk tolerance levels—the amount of risk that an investor is willing to live with, or, in other words, the amount the investor is willing to lose if things go badly—is usually associated with purchasing investments like stocks or bonds. But the concept of risk tolerance is relevant to bargaining in a divorce as well.

Every investment carries a number of risks, including the risk that asset prices, interest rates, exchange rates, or commodity prices will change. Whether you are willing to bear those risks with regard to any given asset depends on certain factors specific to you.

Age. The younger you are, the more risk you could take. Time is your ally. For example, younger investors could have a stock-heavy portfolio because they have more time to recover from short-term setbacks.

Diversification. If your portfolio is diversified, meaning that you have a wide variety of investments, your overall risk is lower and you might be willing to take on a riskier investment.

Knowledge. The more you know, the more confident you will be in making decisions, including decisions that involve higher risk. If you follow markets and feel confident investing, or if you have a trusted professional guiding you, that will be a factor in your decision making.

All of these factors combine to create your own risk tolerance level. Below are the standard categories of tolerance levels that investment professionals use. As you read them, consider which one best describes your risk tolerance:

- **Conservative.** Conservative investors want investments that will keep up with inflation and pay living expenses; they cannot tolerate much market fluctuation.
- **Moderately Conservative.** These investors want income, not just to keep up with inflation, but also want to be protected from large downside market fluctuations. They are willing to limit their market participation in up markets.
- **Moderate.** Those with moderate risk tolerance want good returns and know some risk is involved. A balanced portfolio will go up less than the market and go down less than the market as a whole.
- **Moderately Aggressive.** Investors in this risk level want to accumulate significant wealth in the future and are willing to wait a reasonable amount of time and take more than average risk to achieve it. They take more downside risk than the market but expect to do better than the market on the upside.
- **Aggressive.** Aggressive investors want to outperform the markets and know they are exposed to high levels of risk. Usually they have enough income from other sources to fund their living expenses, or are in a hurry to accumulate substantial wealth, or have not personally experienced significant losses in the market. They easily could lose significant value in a short time frame and take years to recoup the loss.

Where do you see yourself in these descriptions? Think about your marital assets and the potential risks and rewards offered by each. Once you know your risk tolerance, you could examine the investment choices offered by your marital assets as you balance each asset's potential risk and reward.

The Time Value of Money

The value of money in relation to time is based on the assumption that money available now, in the present, is worth more than the same amount in the future, because money has earning capacity that begins immediately.

Think of money on deposit in a savings account. It is earning interest. If we assume a 5% interest rate, $100 today invested will be worth $105.00 in one year ($100 multiplied by 1.05); conversely, $100 received one year from now is worth $95.24 today ($100 divided by 1.05), assuming the same interest rate.

The time value of money is also related to a concept called opportunity cost. For example, your spouse agrees to pay you $1,000 over the next couple years, and in the meantime you have the opportunity to travel with friends to Mexico for $1,000. You have to pass up the invitation because you do not have the extra funds for travel. By taking money over time, rather than now, you not only lose the interest on this investment but also the opportunity to spend it on something you would have enjoyed.

Future Value

Future value is the growth of an investment over a specific period of time at a specific interest rate. Back to our prior example: If you put $100 in a savings account and it is earning 5% interest, in a year you will have $105, so $105 is the future value of $100 invested for one year at 5%.

If you stretch this example using $100 and compound your 5% interest daily for three years, the future value of your $100 is $116.18. Numerous websites will do this calculation for you, including www.investopedia.com, which I used for this example. Use a search engine and enter "future value." Note that this example does not take into consideration any inflation that might influence the future value.

What About Inflation?

When you calculate the present and future values of money, do not overlook inflation—the loss of purchasing power. Inflation is the increase in the prices paid for items from one year to the next. When you calculate future value, subtract an inflation rate from the interest rate, because your money's growth is being negatively affected by inflation.

We have enjoyed low inflation rates for years, but economists suggest that might substantially change in the near future. Stay alert to this likely trend. The Bureau of Labor Statistics publishes annual inflation rates at www.bls.gov/data/#prices. Another inflation calculation website is www.smartasset.com/investing inflation-calculator.

Present Value

Whenever a sum of money is going to be paid in the future (such as a promised future payout for alimony or to equalize a property division), you want to know what that money is worth in today's dollars. After all, you are negotiating your property division today, based on the value of the assets today.

When calculating present value, you will need to determine the rate of return that your money could have earned if it had been paid now, then invested—this is called the "discount rate." The higher the rate of return, the greater your risk of loss if you accept a promise of future payment.

> EXAMPLE: Your spouse owes you $10,000. Your spouse will pay you that sum in three years. How much is that worth in today's dollars? It depends on the discount rate used. If we use a 5% discount rate, the present value of what you receive at the end of three years will be $8,607.17. If we use a 3% discount rate, the present value is $9,139.35. Either way, you could easily see that time ate into the value of your money! The money you are promised in the future is not worth $10,000 today. You now want to point that out to your spouse, and either increase the $10,000 to an amount that will equal $10,000 in three years, or use the discounted figure in the marital property spreadsheet when analyzing and negotiating proposed property divisions.

One source for calculations of future benefits is the U.S. Office of Management and Budget. The OMB publishes an annual projection of interest rates in January of each year. Other sources are the IRS and the U.S. Securities and Exchange Commission websites. The Internet also has present value calculators. Just enter "calculate present value" into a search engine and you will have plenty to choose from. One that I have used is www.calculator.net/present-value-calculator.html.

Picking a Discount Rate

How do you select the discount rate to use when calculating present value? The U.S. government bond rate is usually the lowest interest rate you will consider. But remember that the rate of return on government bonds reflects no risk of delayed payment or nonpayment. In the real world there is a risk associated with a promise to pay money in the future. You should probably consider a higher interest rate than the U.S. government bond rate so you take risk into consideration. Another factor to consider is whether you have collateral for the promise of future payment—like a lien on your spouse's house that backs up the promise to pay you later. The discount rate is lower when you have good collateral because it minimizes some of the risk of nonpayment or late payment. If this is confusing, just remember that the higher your discount rate, the lower the present value.

How Long Will My Assets Last?

You might want to know how long an investment asset will last, especially if its value is providing you with a stream of income.

> **EXAMPLE:** Let's assume that you receive $100,000 as a cash settlement. You put it in a savings account that earns 3% per year. You have some income, but need an additional $2,000 per month to cover your living expenses. You know that the source of that $2,000 will be your cash settlement. How long do you have until your $100,000 savings is exhausted? Just 53 months or 4.4 years. And this calculation does not take inflation or taxes on earnings into account.

You could do your own calculation. Enter "calculate how long my money will last" into a search engine for calculation websites. Some ask for your marginal federal income tax rate to make a more precise calculation. The site I used for the above calculation is www.calcxml.com/do/how-long-will-my-money-last.

Financial Planning

Financial planning is no longer a perk only for the wealthy. Independent financial advisers could help you avoid serious obstacles and irrevocable mistakes during your divorce, by offering tax advice, investment advice, and advice on selecting insurance.

Financial advisers go by many titles: financial planner, financial adviser, financial consultant, money manager, investment manager, divorce financial analyst, divorce financial planner. If you are looking for assistance with a broad range of financial matters (for example, retirement planning, insurance planning, and budgeting), a certified financial planner (CFP), a chartered financial consultant (ChFC), or a certified public accountant-personal financial specialist (CPA-PFS) are good bets. Their qualifications and designations are explained further at these websites: www.cfp.net, www.theamericancollege.edu, and www.aicpa.org.

A certified divorce financial analyst (CDFA) is a type of financial professional specializing in financial issues surrounding divorce. The Institute for Divorce Financial Analysts provides training and examinations; to become a CDFA, a person must have two years of financial planning or legal experience. A CDFA can offer advice on issues such as asset distribution, short- and long-term financial planning, and evaluation of settlement options. (See Chapter 10, "Your Financial Survival," for more on financial planning.)

Whatever type of professional you choose, check out credentials and ask whether the person ever faced disciplinary action from a professional licensing agency. Also ask whether you'll be charged by the job, based on a percentage of your estate, or on an hourly basis, so you'll know what to expect.

The Next Phase

You might think you know right now what assets you want to walk away with. But let's be sure. You might discover that an asset you think you want might not serve your interests well in the future. And there might be options you have not considered. You need to determine the advantages and disadvantages of specific assets in the context of your age, situation, and future expectations. How you measure value now might be quite different from how you perceived value in your twenties, thirties, and forties—and you will surely make different decisions now than you would have if you had divorced earlier. The next step in understanding marital property is to take an in-depth look at the assets in your case, and the next three chapters will help you to do that.

The Big-Ticket Items: Your Home, Your Retirement, and Your Family Business

T his chapter deals with the items of property that, for most people who own them, account for the bulk of their marital estate—the family house, pensions and other retirement accounts, and the family business. (Chapter 7, "More About Assets—And What They're Worth to You," covers the rest of the asset categories that we identified back in Chapter 5.)

Of course, if you don't have any of these three major assets, you can skip ahead. Just use what's useful to you. We'll start with what is most people's biggest asset—the family home.

Your Home

Your home probably has more layers of attachment than any other asset in your marital estate. Your home has the emotional attachments of your family history, your bonds with neighbors, and the comfort of familiarity, not to mention your reliance on it as a major investment. Often, the older you are, the harder it is to imagine relocating, and you might be very fearful of losing the house. On the other hand, you might be ready to part with it, downsize, and put the memories behind you. Either way, it's one of the most emotional elements of the divorce for many people. It's important to acknowledge these feelings and recognize the ways they might drive your decision making, because you must examine your options as objectively as you can.

Options for Dealing With the Family Home

You have numerous choices about what to do with your house at divorce. Your decision will depend in part on your emotional attachments and, in part, on financial considerations. Even if you think you know what your plans are, review each of these options so that you're sure you've considered each one carefully.

Award All Interest in the Marital Home to One Spouse (Buyout)

A very common way for divorcing couples to deal with the family home is for one spouse to buy out the other's interest. This means that one spouse pays the other for the right to continue to own the house alone—the selling spouse no longer has any interest in the property or any responsibility for the mortgage or other loans. The buying spouse might pay cash or trade other property in the divorce negotiations to compensate the selling spouse for the selling spouse's share of the net value of the house. Net value means the fair market value (FMV) minus any debt secured by the property (and minus estimated closing costs if the residence will be sold soon).

Assuming there is a mortgage, a buyout usually requires that the spouse keeping the house qualify for a new loan. The mortgage lender will charge transfer fees and closing costs when title changes hands, costs that you should factor into the negotiations about net value. If the buying spouse does not qualify for a new loan and the departing spouse is willing, the spouses could continue co-owning the home. See the sections on continuing co-ownership, below.

The buyout option places a premium on determining the fair market value of the house, discussed in "Fair Market Value," below.

Place the House on the Market for Immediate Sale and Divide the Sale Proceeds

Many couples decide to sell the marital home and divide the proceeds. This option places the least weight on estimating FMV because the market will set the value of the house. You and your spouse will have to work together to determine the asking price, the listing realtor, and what happens while waiting for the sale. For example, will one spouse remain in the house while it's on the market? If so, is that spouse responsible for making the house presentable for buyer showings? Who pays the mortgage, insurance, taxes, and maintenance while the house is on the market? You'll also need to decide what to do if the home does not sell as expected. Finally, you'll negotiate about whether the division of the sale proceeds will be equal or whether you'll split it another way, perhaps to compensate one spouse for giving up other assets, such as a share of a pension.

Award One Spouse the Home in Exchange for Future Payment

Sometimes one spouse wants to remain in the home but cannot afford to buy out the other spouse at the time of the divorce. The spouses could agree to payment in the future, either in an amount set when they negotiate the divorce settlement, or in the form of a percentage of future sale proceeds. Often, spouses will agree that one of them may stay in the house as sole owner for a certain period of time before making a buyout payment, with a provision that if the staying spouse cannot come up with the money by that date, the house must be sold.

Sometimes, when one spouse wants to stay in the home but cannot qualify for a loan to buy the other spouse out at the time of the divorce, the couple will agree between themselves that the staying spouse will be responsible for paying the mortgage (even though both of them will continue to be jointly liable per the original mortgage document). The other spouse will receive an agreed-upon percentage or value when the buyout finally occurs, or when they sell the house in the future, and will be released from any further liability on the home loan. This scenario requires special real estate documents drafted by an attorney to avoid triggering a "due on sale" clause in the original mortgage documents. Don't try to write this agreement by yourself.

The risk to both partners is that if the real estate market drops, the spouse in residence may be "upside down" with the property—that is, owing more money to the other spouse than the house is worth. In that case, the staying spouse might not only be unable to pay, but selling the house won't solve the problem.

TIP
You can keep your house agreements private. If your settlement agreement provides for a future sale, and especially if it contains details about things like how long you'll keep the house before selling or what the price reductions will be if it doesn't sell, you can keep these details out of the public records by making a side agreement that you do not file with your final judgment (though the final judgment must reference the document to make it enforceable). You do not want a potential future buyer to have access to your settlement agreement with those details.

Continue Joint Ownership Temporarily While One Spouse Remains, Then Sell

Another option for dealing with your home is for both spouses to remain owners of the home while one continues living there and the other moves out. You might choose this option if:

- You have minor children and want them to stay in the house until they graduate from high school.
- You want to sell the property but the real estate market is bad and you expect it to improve.
- One spouse wants to buy the other out but can't qualify for a loan and needs more time to get financing together.
- One spouse wants to remain in the house until some other event occurs, like making a career change or receiving an expected inheritance.

In most of these circumstances, the spouse remaining in the house generally pays most or all of the monthly mortgage, insurance, and tax expenses, or pays a monthly amount based on the fair rental value of the home. All the triggering events and contingencies must be spelled out in either the divorce decree or a separate document referenced in the decree.

Continue Joint Ownership as Rental Property

In a variation on the previous option, you could continue owning your house jointly and rent it out rather than one spouse remaining there. It's a good option in a depressed real estate market and offers the benefits of an income stream and tax deductions. In a rising market, this option allows both spouses the opportunity to reap higher sale values in the future. Because you'll continue to own the house after the divorce settlement is final, how you split rental income will be negotiated in your overall settlement. You'll also need to figure out how long you'll continue owning the property and what events would cause you to sell it. Renting your home mighty risk some of the tax benefits when you sell the home, so be sure to review "Your Home's Value to You," below, and "Taxes and the Family Home" in Chapter 8.

> **TIP**
> **Renting the property is one way to keep it for a while if your intention is to sell it in the future and put all or part of the proceeds into a trust for the benefit of children.** This assumes that neither spouse needs home equity for future support, and it provides a guaranteed source of inheritance for the children.

Fair Market Value

You can learn the FMV of your home in several ways. The easiest way, of course, is to put it on the market and see what someone will pay. But if you're not ready to do that, or if you aren't intending to sell it, you'll need to use another method to estimate what would have happened if you had sold it that way. And even if you are planning to sell, you need to know enough to estimate the FMV so that you can set an asking price. (If you have a vacation home, rental property, or unimproved acreage, the same methods apply.) Here are the valuation methods available to you.

Appraisals

Certified real estate appraisers are in the business of determining the value of real estate. An appraiser will prepare an analysis of your home's value that takes into account recent sales of comparable properties, overall market conditions in your area, the replacement cost of your home, and the house's potential rental value. A professional appraisal is the most comprehensive and useful valuation method available. An appraiser might be a more convincing trial expert than a real estate agent, which is why many family law attorneys rely on formal appraisals in contested cases. An appraisal is especially important if the real estate market is very high or very low, if the property is uniquely designed or situated, or if the divorcing parties have significantly different opinions of value.

An appraisal could be expensive. If you and your spouse are working together collaboratively (see "Collaborative Divorce" in Chapter 4), it's likely that you will agree to use one independent appraiser and share the cost. If you're working with an attorney, your attorney will be able to recommend an appraiser. States usually license and certify appraisers, so you could check with two professional organizations for member listings: the Appraisal Institute at www.appraisalinstitute.org, or the American Society of Appraisers at www.appraisers.org.

Real Estate Broker Evaluation

A real estate broker will give you a general idea of your home's FMV by reviewing comparable properties and preparing a market analysis on that basis. Using a broker is a much less expensive option than using an appraiser, especially because some realtors do not charge for providing these comps if they expect (or hope) to list the property for sale.

Consider a licensed broker who has sales experience in your neighborhood, rather than a nonbroker agent. Licensed brokers in most states are required to have more extensive training, experience, and continuing education than agents. They supervise agents and might also own and operate a real estate business. Hire someone with whom you do not have a personal connection—although you might have a friend who also happens to be a realtor, it's important that the broker be truly objective, and you want to avoid the appearance that one spouse has a leg up because of a personal relationship with the broker. When dealing with this major component of your marital estate, it's extra important to get an accurate and objective valuation.

Your Role in the Valuation Process

Whether you use an appraiser or a realtor, that person will conduct an on-site inspection of the property. You and your spouse, or representatives, should be present. Having both sides attend avoids the concern that someone will influence the appraiser or broker toward a value that benefits that person most (for example, in a buyout situation where the buying spouse wants a lower number and the selling spouse wants a higher value). After you receive the appraisal or analysis of comparative properties, examine it closely. Are the comparable properties really comparable? Are the details about the house correct? Are recent improvements referenced in the report? When an evaluation isn't complete or correct, these problems are typically present. It pays to look at more than the report's bottom line.

Government Valuation

Government taxing authorities—usually, county assessors—value real estate for the purpose of setting property taxes. Some county appraisal offices provide up-to-date fair market values, but others use values that lag behind current market conditions because the agencies are short staffed and do not review all property annually. Your annual property tax statement might show more than one value for your home—a market value and a taxable value. You do not want to use the taxable value because it is discounted by age or disability deductions or exemptions, so it is almost always less than the actual FMV.

Adjustments to Fair Market Value

Figuring out the fair market value of your home isn't the end of the road as far as setting the value you'll use in your divorce. If the house is going to be sold right away, it makes sense to use an adjusted fair market value for the house on the marital property spreadsheet. The adjusted value is the FMV reduced by anticipated closing expenses that will reduce your profits, such as appraisal and inspection fees, escrow fees, recording fees, loan discount points, and the like. (A realtor could provide estimates of charges and fees related to the sale of your home.) You would use an adjusted FMV on the spreadsheet if, for example, one spouse receives the house in the property division and intends to sell it to a third party immediately. In that case, the adjusted FMV more accurately represents the property's value to that spouse, because the spouse must pay the closing costs and other expenses. The same thing would be true if one spouse incurs closing expenses to refinance the loan in order to buy out the other spouse.

In addition to closing costs, other costs, such as repairs, maintenance, and remodeling, will also reduce the FMV. Don't forget prepaid premiums for homeowners' insurance or prepaid property taxes, which should be added to the property's FMV or treated as a separate asset on the marital estate spreadsheet.

If you are not intending to sell your home as part of the divorce or soon after the divorce is final, future costs of sale might be too speculative to justify an adjustment.

Your Home's Value to You

Fair market value is only one of the things you will need to factor in when you consider what will happen to your house in your divorce settlement. For one thing, your home's value to you includes elements of intrinsic value that are not quantifiable in dollars. Subjective benefits to home ownership can be especially relevant in late-life divorces, as well as financial benefits that could be valuable to you depending upon your age, health, and financial circumstances.

Local property tax exemptions. Local taxing authorities often grant property tax breaks to older homeowners—those older than 60 or 65. Property values may be frozen or reduced for a specified period of time or even indefinitely once the owner reaches a specific age. Check with your local taxing authority for details on these age-related benefits that reduce your property taxes.

Federal tax benefits. The Tax Cuts & Jobs Act of 2017, in effect until 2025, brought changes to the tax deduction arena. If you itemize deductions because your expenses are greater than the standard deduction, you could deduct mortgage interest and property taxes from ordinary income. The value of this benefit depends on your tax bracket and the value of your qualified home loans. When you sell your primary residence, you might exclude gain up to $250,000 ($500,000 total for both spouses). After paying off closing costs and any debts, up to $250,000 of your equity is tax free. Capital gains rates, which are lower than tax rates on ordinary income, apply to gains above the exclusion amount. There are many ins and outs regarding this tax exclusion; for example, you must live in the house as a primary residence for two of the five years prior to sale. So be sure to consult with a tax specialist to learn how the exclusion applies in your circumstances.

The federal income tax exclusion could be significant, depending on when the property is sold. If you plan on selling your residence in the near future, the fact that you or your spouse will shelter up to $250,000 from taxation could be a bargaining chip in your overall property settlement.

There's more about taxes in "Taxes and the Family Home" in Chapter 8.

> **TIP**
>
> **Document your spending.** If you're keeping your house for now, be sure you also keep the records of all improvements, as you might need them later to document the tax basis for the home to reduce taxes.

Rental income. Right now, you might want to keep your home so that you could live in it. However, if you need income, renting out your house, or just a room, might be an attractive option. You could rent a room to a college student or family member in order to supplement income in retirement years. Short-term rentals through online rental companies like HomeAway, VRBO, or Airbnb, are becoming a major source of income for homeowners. Be sure to consult with a tax specialist before doing this, especially if you decide to rent out the entire house and live somewhere else. You might not want to jeopardize the tax exclusion, which applies only to a principal residence, should you later sell your home.

Reverse mortgages. If you have significant equity built up in your home and you need income later in life, you might be eligible to take an advance on your equity with a reverse mortgage (RM). The advance is basically a loan to you, but you don't pay back the loan as long as you live in the house; instead, you begin making payments when you sell the house or stop living there. If you die after tapping into an RM, your heirs can repay the loan and keep the house. The lender does not own the house—you do or your heirs do.

An RM could be paid to you in tax-free monthly increments, a lump sum, or a line of credit that you use only when you need money. The advantage of the line of credit is that you pay interest only on money you actually borrow. A key attraction of RMs is if the real estate market tanks, and the RM balance due is larger than the house equity when it is sold, the RM lender is limited to collecting only what is generated by the house sale.

You could obtain an RM even if you have a conventional mortgage loan on your residence. If you need income to pay the primary mortgage, an RM might relieve the stress of monthly mortgage payments or fear of potential foreclosure.

The United States Department of Housing and Urban Development (HUD) is the source for 90% of RMs. Others are provided by private lenders or government-controlled agencies such as Fannie Mae. The federal reverse mortgage program, which might offer access to larger sums than other state or private lender resources, is called the Home Equity Conversion Mortgage (HECM) program.

RMs have age requirements—usually you must be 62 or older. The older you are, the more you can borrow because your life expectancy is shorter and there is less chance for the loan to exceed the value of the equity in the home. An RM calculator is available online at www.rmaarp.com; you can use it to get an idea of available options where you live.

I recommend that you begin your research on RMs with the Federal Trade Commission's Consumer Information website: www.consumer.ftc.gov/articles/pdf-0058-reverse-mortgages.pdf. It provides a good summary of the pros and cons of RMs. Then check the AARP.org website for current news about RMs.

Special treatment for public benefits. As long as you live in your house, it will often be treated differently from other assets when you are trying to qualify for public benefits. An example is Medicaid. Your home, regardless of its value, is exempt from being counted as a resource when determining your Medicaid eligibility. However, the equity interest in your principal place of residence is relevant to eligibility for Medicaid's long-term care benefits. The term "equity interest" depends on whether you own your home jointly, with a spouse or someone else. You are not eligible for long-term care benefits if your equity interest in your home exceeds $603,000, but states can raise this ceiling up to $906,000; these limits are subject to adjustments based on inflation.

For more information on how your home's value and equity might affect Medicaid benefits, check the Department of Health and Human Services websites, www.medicaid.gov.

Bankruptcy. If you must file for bankruptcy, equity in your personal residence might be exempt, in whole or in part, from the reach of creditors. The amount of the exemption depends on whether federal or state bankruptcy exemption laws apply, and you'll need a lawyer to advise you about which apply to you. For more details about bankruptcy and its two common forms, Chapter 7 and Chapter 13, also see this book's Chapter 8, "The Bad News: Debts and Taxes."

Subjective value. All of the items listed above are measurable, verifiable ways that your house might return value to you in the future if you decide to keep it in the divorce. But you might also have layers of attachment that make up the emotional value of your home. These subjective factors include your relationships with neighbors, feelings of safety, pride in decorating and design, comforting familiarity, and lifelong memories. Your home might provide you social status that you feel is slipping in the divorce. Your adult children might retain a strong attachment to the house. Only you can weigh these elements of value— just make sure you weigh them alongside the financial elements (you won't attempt to enter them on your asset worksheet).

Final Thoughts About Your House

No matter how your home equity is allocated in your divorce, the key to a satisfactory result is a written property agreement that spells out how you will handle the what-ifs. These include fluctuating real estate markets, unexpected repair expenses, disagreements over realtor choices, asking price and offers, and other details. You will prevent costly misunderstandings in the future if you can anticipate these what-ifs and agree now how you are going to resolve them.

Demystifying Retirement Plans and QDROs

Along with the family home, retirement benefits are the other bedrock asset for most people. And like the house, they are particularly important in late-life divorce, with the importance increasing the closer you are to retirement.

Trying to understand these assets could leave you glassy-eyed. You will begin to think you are submerged in an alphabet soup of COLA, QDRO, ERISA, QJSA, QPSA, DFAS, MPDO, SBP, and more. It is likely that your marital estate does not include more than one or two of the types of retirement plans described in this section. But you want to be certain of that, so make sure you review everything here that could be relevant to you.

> **RELATED TOPIC**
>
> **Social Security benefits are also a major component of retirement income.** Details about Social Security retirement benefits are covered in Chapter 10, "Your Financial Survival."

Let's begin with basics. Employment-based retirement plans fall into one of two general categories—defined benefit and defined contribution plans. We'll start with those and then move on to discuss individual (nonemployment) retirement assets.

Defined Benefit Plans

Defined benefit plans are commonly referred to as pension plans, in which the retired employee periodically receives a certain amount of money. In the last few decades, American employers have trended away from these plans and toward defined contribution plans (like 401(k)s, discussed in "Defined Contribution Plans," below). In 1983, 62% of private industry employees with retirement coverage had a pension only, while just 12% had 401(k)s. As of March 2020, the U.S. Bureau of Labor Statistics reports that approximately 12% have access to a pension and 79% have access only to 401(k)s. The change is a result of employers' efforts to cut costs and shift responsibility for retirement planning onto employees. Pensions do still flourish in the public sectors of military, federal, state, and local governmental employment.

Traditional defined benefit plans required the employer to make all the contributions, but employees later began to participate by paying a portion of each month's salary into the pension fund to be added to the employer contribution. Upon retirement, the employee receives a monthly retirement payment, sometimes called an annuity. Each defined benefit plan has a formula that determines the amount of the annuity. The complicated calculation takes into consideration the participant's life expectancy, length of employment, compensation upon retirement, and retirement age.

To receive benefits, an employee must be "vested" in the plan, meaning the employee has met the plan's requirements for how long a person must work before the benefit becomes payable, even if the person leaves the company before retirement. If an employee is terminated and has unvested employer contributions, the employee simply leaves them behind, to be allocated among the remaining participants in the plan.

Valuing Interests in Defined Benefit Plans

Valuing an interest in a defined benefit plan is challenging, might be somewhat speculative, and often requires the services of an actuary. A number of variables affect the value of a defined benefit plan in the context of a divorce.

Pension funds are not distributed until the participant qualifies for retirement, so there's no possibility for a cash distribution at divorce. In other words, the nonemployee spouse has an interest in an asset that won't be available until a later date. At the time of the divorce, the spouses have a choice:

- The participant (employee) spouse could buy out the nonparticipant spouse by way of a lump sum payment or by giving the nonparticipant spouse other property of equal value. Equal value means equal to the present value of the marital share of the pension, which is determined by complex calculations that are best left to an actuary.

- The spouses could agree that the nonparticipant spouse will receive a share of the benefits when they are paid later, usually when the participant spouse retires.
- If the participant spouse earned some of the pension benefits before marriage or will continue to do so after divorce, some portion of the benefits might be separate property.

Whichever option you choose, the calculations will include figuring out what share of the pension belongs to the marital estate.

Whether you choose a lump sum or a future payout depends on a number of things. If you're concerned about income flow in your later years, waiting for the pension payout might work for you. On the other hand, a lump sum payment is the proverbial bird in the hand and relieves you of the risk that the pension plan could become insolvent. (See "Future Value," in Chapter 5.)

Defined Contribution Plans

With defined contribution plans, employees contribute a specific amount or percentage of wages each pay period, and the contributions go into a segregated account in the name of the employee. The employer might also contribute to the account. A participant could access the account starting at retirement age, and it's always clear how much is in the account because it is specific to the employee, rather than part of a general fund. Most defined contribution plans are in vehicles that depend to some extent on market forces, so the value will fluctuate over time.

If an employee with a defined contribution plan leaves a job, it's usually possible to roll the account assets into an individual retirement account that's no longer associated with the employer. Some plans don't allow that, though, and in those cases the account balance remains with the employer. At retirement, employees receive a lump sum or take distributions in the form of an annuity.

There are many types of defined contribution plans; they differ with regard to the type of employer involved (large or small, public or private), whether contributions are mandatory for either employee or employer, annual limits imposed on contributions, and the complexity of the plan administration.

401(k) plan. This is the most common type of retirement vehicle. Employees contribute pretax dollars by way of payroll deduction. Employers could make tax-deferred contributions, too. The employee pays tax not when contributions are made, but when benefits are distributed.

Thrift Savings Plan. Federal civil service employees (and members of uniformed services) are offered benefits through the Thrift Savings Plan, which is similar to 401(k) plans. A participant's contributions are tax deferred and contributions might be matched by the federal agency.

403(b) plans and TSA plans. 403(b) plans are available to some employees of educational institutions and nonprofit organizations. As with 401(k) plans, payroll deduction contributions are made from pretax dollars, and ordinary income tax is paid upon withdrawal. A tax sheltered annuity (TSA) plan is a type of 403(b) plan where contributions purchase an annuity (making the plan more like a defined benefit plan, with periodic payments beginning at a specified time in the future).

Profit sharing plans. An employer might contribute (voluntarily) to a profit sharing plan each year the company is profitable. Contributions are based on a percentage of the employee's compensation and involve pretax dollars.

Money purchase pension plans. Unlike profit sharing plans, contributions to money purchase plans by employers are mandatory each year. The pretax contributions are based on a percentage of the employee's compensation and are not taxed until the money is withdrawn.

Employee Stock Ownership Plans (ESOP). Employees and employers make contributions toward the purchase of stock in the company; each plan has its own rules for when and how the employee may exercise the rights to purchase and sell the stock.

Simplified Employee Pension Plans (SEP IRA). A SEP plan is a simple method for employers to contribute toward their employees' retirement and, if self-employed, their own retirement. Each employee has an IRA account or annuity to which the employer contributes directly. Any time there's a contribution to the employer's own account, it must be matched by an equivalent contribution to the employees' accounts. A major benefit of a SEP IRA is that the employer's contribution vests immediately.

Simple IRA. As its name reflects, a simple IRA gives small employers a simplified method to make contributions directly to an employee's individual retirement account or individual retirement annuity. Employees might choose to contribute through salary reduction with the employer matching the contribution, or by paying a mandatory smaller percentage contribution.

Salary Reduction Simplified Employee Pension plan (SARSEP). These plans are no longer being offered (as of January 1, 1997), but old ones continue to operate. Employee contributions fund the retirement accounts, and employers may contribute even if employees elect not to contribute themselves.

Valuing Interests in a Defined Contribution Plan

It's much easier to determine the present value of defined contribution plans than defined benefit plans—all you have to do is look at the value of the assets held in the employee's account. However, in a divorce, you might need to make some adjustments.

Marital versus separate portion. If the employee spouse earned some of the retirement benefits before marriage (or after separation in some states), these benefits are generally considered that spouse's separate property. Some states measure the separate property share by the value of the account on the date of marriage. Others start with that amount, estimate the interest and growth that the amount would have earned between the date of marriage and the date of divorce, and attribute that to the earning spouse's separate property as well. Still other states include in a spouse's separate estate only the premarital income and dividends that were actually reinvested, based on tracing the account from its inception. Each approach can lead to some really complex tracing to tease out the marital and separate portions.

Regardless of how it's calculated, once you determine what share of the account is the separate property of the participant spouse, that amount is subtracted from the total account value as of the date of divorce (or date of separation, in some states). The balance is the marital estate's portion that is divided between the spouses—equally or unequally, depending on the terms of the settlement or judgment.

Pretax versus posttax. Another adjustment hinges on whether income and contributions were made with tax-deferred or taxed dollars, and on when you expect to take the money out of the account. When money in a tax-deferred account is withdrawn, ordinary income taxes are due. If withdrawals are made before age 59½, the IRS assesses a 10% penalty on top of the ordinary income tax due on those funds. So if you intend to withdraw funds immediately, the estimated taxes and penalty should be reflected on the spreadsheet. You could reduce the value of the retirement account by the amount of penalties and taxes, reduce the value of some other account that will be used to pay the penalties and taxes, or as a separate line item on the spreadsheet identify the taxes and penalty as a debt to be paid by the withdrawing spouse in the near future. But if you don't know when money will be withdrawn, then from a fairness perspective, it doesn't make as much sense to consider tax consequences, because a person's tax bracket now might be quite different in the future.

There is an exception, in 401(k) plans only, to the 59½ age requirement. Employees who retire, quit, or are fired at age 55 can withdraw from their 401(k) without penalty. (See IRS Publication 575, *Pension and Annuity Income*, for more important details about this Rule of 55 option.)

Dividing Private Retirement Plans

Whether they're defined benefit plans or defined contribution plans, all private benefit plans are subject to division at divorce. We've already seen that retirement funds could be divided at the time of divorce through a lump sum payout or, in the case of pensions, at the time of distribution. This section explains the details of division.

The Role of ERISA

A federal law known as ERISA (short for the Employment Retirement Income Security Act of 1974) is an important factor in how private retirement plans are divided at divorce. You might be wondering, "What does this federal law have to do with my divorce?" The answer is, "More than you can imagine!"

ERISA governs all qualified private retirement plans, including rules for participation, funding, accrual of benefits, vesting, identifying participants, and information that must be provided to employees. To be "qualified" and thus governed by ERISA, a plan must meet certain minimum IRS requirements. Qualification means that plan contributions are tax deductible.

ERISA requires people who are dividing certain kinds of retirement benefits at divorce to use a document called a qualified domestic relations order (QDRO, often pronounced "quadro"). A QDRO is an order that is separate from your final judgment but that you'll file with the court as part of your divorce along with your judgment. It enforces the right of someone other than the participant to receive benefits under a participant's retirement plan. This other person is called an "alternate payee." An alternate payee is any spouse, former spouse, child, or other dependent of a participant; a participant is any employee or former employee who is or might become eligible to receive a benefit from an employee benefit plan.

A QDRO requires careful drafting and is definitely not something you want to try on your own. It must specify the names of the plan, the participant, and the alternate payee, and identify the benefits to be paid to the alternate payee. A QDRO must be accepted by the plan administrator—the person who takes care of the administrative details of the plan for the employer. The administrator is responsible for determining whether the domestic relations order submitted to them is "qualified," thus meets the legal requirements of a QDRO. Plan administrators do not represent either spouse's interests. Their job is just to make sure the language in the QDRO meets the requirements of federal law and the specific plan.

A QDRO is always necessary when you're dividing a defined benefit (pension) plan, and sometimes necessary when you're dividing a defined contribution plan—in the latter case, the plan administrator will let you know whether a QDRO is required to accomplish the distribution.

Limitations on the Reach of ERISA

ERISA does not govern public retirement plans such as state, federal, military, and local governmental units. These plans might have their own sets of laws addressing some of the same issues as ERISA. In fact, many states modeled their government retirement plans on the language of ERISA, as did the Civil Service Retirement and the Federal Employees Retirement Systems. Many of these government plans require QDRO-type orders to be used at divorce. If your case involves public retirement plans, it is imperative that you consult an attorney with experience in that area. As with QDROs, government plans present drafting pitfalls that you must avoid.

Tax Consequences

The tax consequences of distributing retirement funds at divorce will depend on which type of plan is involved.

Defined benefit plan. If the nonemployee spouse will wait until the employee spouse retires before taking a share of the retirement benefits, each spouse will pay tax on that spouse's share of the benefits when they're paid (assuming contributions were pretax, as is usually the case). If the employee spouse is buying out the nonemployee spouse by trading cash or other property for the right to keep the entire retirement, the fact that the employee spouse must pay taxes later while the nonemployee spouse gets a tax-free lump sum at the time of the divorce should be considered in the negotiations.

Defined contribution plan. Distribution from a defined contribution plan to a nonemployee spouse is a nontaxable event as long as the distribution is made pursuant to a properly drafted QDRO, and as long as the transfer is what's called a trustee-to-trustee transfer. This means that the funds never go directly into the hands of the alternate payee, but transfer directly into an individual retirement account (IRA) that the payee opens for the purpose of receiving these funds. If the employee pays the money out of the employee's 401(k) directly to the divorcing spouse, taxes will likely be due, along with penalties if age requirements aren't met.

Survivor Benefits

ERISA requires all qualified pension plans to provide survivor benefits. Typically, this benefit comes in the form of a qualified joint and survivor annuity (QJSA), under which the participant receives retirement benefits during life, and, upon the participant's death, the surviving spouse receives a periodic payment for the rest of the survivor's life in an amount that's equal to at least half of the participant's payment (the plan determines the precise amount). If the participant dies before receiving the first retirement payment, in most cases the plan must pay the surviving spouse a monthly survivor benefit, called a qualified preretirement survivor annuity (QPSA).

How does divorce fit into this death benefit scenario? Generally, if your spouse dies while your divorce is pending but not final, you'll probably still get the benefit. But if the divorce is final before the participant's annuity starting date, the divorced spouse generally loses all right to survivor benefit protections. If the divorced participant marries again, the new spouse acquires a right in these survivor benefits. That's a pretty harsh consequence, but fortunately, an exception to these general rules can help: A properly drafted QDRO can require that a former spouse be treated as the surviving spouse and receive survivor benefits after the death of the participant.

If your QDRO includes this provision, any subsequent spouse will not be treated as the participant's surviving spouse for purposes of these benefits. You might be surprised at how many arguments arise about which spouse is entitled to survivor benefits, but lawsuits result when there's a failure to plan ahead or to state clearly what the plan participant has agreed to. If you or your spouse has a defined benefit plan with a survivor benefit, make sure to talk to your lawyer about putting the appropriate orders and beneficiary designations in place so that your wishes—and your agreements—are followed.

CAUTION
Make sure you get a copy of the summary plan description. Before you sign a QDRO or finalize your divorce, make sure you've seen the summary plan description (SPD) for every retirement plan that's part of your marital estate. The SPD describes the terms of the plan and summarizes the rights and benefits of participants and alternate payees. Obtain a copy from the plan administrator, who must provide the SPD to any interested person who requests it.

Nonqualified Retirement Plans

Nonqualified retirement plans are not governed by ERISA. They usually coexist with qualified plans at the same company, providing additional benefits (which receive less favorable tax treatment) to highly compensated executives. Two common types of nonqualified retirement plans are the excess benefit plan and the supplemental executive retirement program (SERP). The distribution rules for nonqualified plans are different than those for ERISA plans, and a nonemployee spouse can't receive benefits directly from the plan. But the plan is still part of the marital estate, and the nonemployee spouse should receive something of equal value in the settlement. Alternatively, the employee spouse could pay benefits directly to the nonemployee spouse when the retired employee spouse receives them.

Additional Issues When Dividing Retirement Benefits

At this point, you might not want to know anything else about QDROs or any other part of this alphabet soup. But hang in there—here are a few additional points you should discuss with your attorney in the name of securing your retirement income.

COLAs. Cost-of-living adjustments (COLAs) are valuable features of defined benefit plans. If the alternate payee is to share in COLAs, the QDRO must say so, and the nonemployee spouse's interest in the plan must be stated as a percentage, not as a dollar amount.

401(k) loans. Some defined contribution plans, such as 401(k) plans, allow participants to borrow against the assets. Be sure you check with the plan to see whether your spouse took out any loans that need to be accounted for when the account balance is divided. (Chapter 10, "Your Financial Survival," has more about loans.)

When benefits are paid. The alternate payee's benefits should not be tied to the participant's actual commencement of benefits, but should be payable at the earliest point at which either spouse could become eligible (check the plan to see if this setup is possible). An early payout is especially important when the alternate payee is older than the participant or is in need of the benefits before the participant-spouse. Your QDRO should include an early payout agreement.

Earnings on defined contribution plans. Defined contribution accounts might accrue earnings between the time the QDRO was drafted and the time a distribution is made to the alternate payee. The alternate payee does not receive increases in value unless that is spelled out in the QDRO, so make sure your QDRO addresses this.

Accounting for all contributions. Sometimes employers make contributions to profit sharing plans and ESOPs after the close of the plan's year. These earned, but not-yet-distributed, sums should be accounted for if the intent is to divide future contributions based on marital employment.

Using model QDROs. Employers frequently draft model QDROs that they make available to divorcing spouses. You might think that using a canned QDRO would be a great cost-saving option, but think twice before using it. For one thing, many QDRO models are biased in favor of the participant spouse.

Second, some important elements might not be addressed in the model QDRO—such as those mentioned in this section. Third, provisions relevant to state laws (such as the ability to modify QDROs post-divorce) might need to be added to the model if the employer operates nationally.

Individual Retirement Accounts

Individual retirement accounts (IRAs) are retirement vehicles created outside of employment by an individual's contributions or by rollovers from a qualified retirement plan (in the case of a divorce or change of employment). Spouses who are not in the workforce and do not have employment retirement plans often have IRAs, which could be liquid assets invested in bank or brokerage accounts or in an annuity purchased from an insurance company. (Liquidity is explained more in Chapter 7.) Contributions might be made with tax-deferred or already-taxed monies.

These are the primary characteristics of IRA accounts:

- There's a limit on the total amount you can contribute each year.
- Withdrawals before age 59½ are subject to a 10% penalty.
- After age 72, minimum distributions must begin.
- Hardship distributions might be allowed, but you can't get a loan.

Types of IRAs

There are different types of IRAs, and it's possible to have more than one at a time. Their differences might be significant to you in planning your financial future.

Traditional IRA. A traditional IRA is a personal savings plan through which you set aside money for retirement and receive tax advantages. Contributions are usually made with tax-deferred dollars, but not always. You don't pay tax on increases in value (earnings and gains) until funds are distributed. You must start withdrawing money from a traditional IRA at age 72. Now you can contribute to a traditional IRA with no age limitations if you are working or have earned income.

Roth IRA. Unlike a traditional IRA, Roth contributions must be made with already-taxed dollars and are not tax deductible. However, earnings accumulate free of tax until you withdraw them. If you satisfy certain requirements for qualified distributions, earnings might be distributed tax free; examples are a first-time home purchase, college expenses, and to deal with permanent disabilities. You could make contributions to your Roth IRA indefinitely, and there is no mandatory withdrawal age. Generally, you could maintain funds in your Roth IRA as long as you live.

Rollover IRA. A nonemployee spouse could receive a portion of an employee spouse's qualified retirement plan by way of a rollover pursuant to a QDRO. Usually, rollovers are into traditional IRAs, but you could convert the traditional IRA into a Roth IRA if it's better for you to pay the taxes at the time of the rollover.

Dividing IRAs

Dividing an IRA is similar to dividing a defined contribution plan. A QDRO is not required. However, the trustee (financial institution) holding the IRA might ask for a document containing language similar to that in a QDRO, before it will authorize the transfer of IRA assets to the nonowner spouse. The transfer of a spouse's interest in an IRA to a former spouse under a divorce decree is not a taxable transfer, as long it's a trustee-to- trustee transfer with the money going directly into another IRA account.

Some IRAs resemble an annuity (meaning it's paid out periodically pursuant to a specified schedule). You'll find valuation and division issues addressed in "Annuities" in Chapter 7.

Military Retirement

Former spouses of military personnel might receive a portion of the military spouse's disposable retired pay. Disposable retired pay is gross monthly retired pay minus any sums owed to the government (such as overpayments or forfeitures) and any deductions for annuities paid to a spouse or former spouse pursuant to a court order.

A number of different issues can arise when one spouse is in the military. Here are a few notes for your consideration:

- If the military spouse is retired at the time of divorce, it is much easier to determine how much the civilian spouse should receive, because retirement benefits are set.
- If the military spouse is not yet retired at the time of divorce, an actuary should value the military pension, especially if the nonmilitary spouse is going to receive assets of comparable value instead of sharing in the pension when the military spouse is eligible for retirement.

- If a retired military spouse is receiving medical disability pay or veteran's disability compensation, those payments are generally not subject to division in the divorce. After a divorce, a military spouse could elect to take disability pay in such a way as to eliminate the retirement pay altogether, leaving the former spouse out in the cold with an unenforceable divorce division of benefits. (In 2017, the U.S. Supreme Court ruled that a court could not order a vet to make up the loss to an ex-spouse should the vet elect to convert some retirement pay to disability pay.)

Payment Through the DFAS

If you are the non-military spouse who has at least 10 years of marriage overlapping 10 years of your military spouse's creditable service (years served), you can receive your share of retirement benefits directly from the Defense Finance and Accounting Service (DFAS), as long as the payment is no more than 50% of the monthly pension. If the civilian spouse is awarded more than 50% of the pension, the amount in excess of 50% must be paid by the military spouse directly to the civilian spouse. Direct payments from DFAS require that a military pension division order (MPDO) be in place. This is similar to a QDRO. (Helpful information is provided on the DFAS website at www.dfas.mil.)

CAUTION

Make sure you get your COLA. Former spouses could receive a proportionate amount of future cost of living allowances (COLAs), but the DFAS sometimes disallows COLAs to former spouses if court orders aren't worded just right. The details are beyond our scope, but you should discuss the COLA issue with your attorney.

If your marriage has lasted for less than 10 years, you can't receive direct payment through DFAS. However, a state court might still order your military spouse to share the pension, in which case the military member would be required to forward the benefits to you within a specific time period after receiving them.

Get the Pay Stub

Whatever the retirement status of the military spouse, you'll need to know what the spouse is receiving each pay period (and what's being taken out). Non-retired military personnel receive a Leave and Earnings Statement (LES), the military payroll voucher that explains what the service member is paid, what deductions are made, and what elective allotments apply. For retired military, the voucher is called the Retiree Account Statement (RAS). Each of these statements provides important information for valuing and dividing military retirement, so be sure to get a copy of the most recent voucher.

The Survivor Benefit Plan

The Survivor Benefit Plan (SBP) is an annuity that helps retired military members provide for their survivors; beneficiaries could include a spouse, former spouse, children, or a combination of these. Premiums differ for each category. The election of a beneficiary does not happen until the military member is eligible to retire.

In divorce situations, timing regarding the SBP is crucial. State courts have the authority to order a military member to designate a former spouse as a beneficiary, as part of the divorce judgment. But even with a signed divorce decree ordering the designation of a "former spouse beneficiary," the former spouse must take additional steps *within one year from the date of the divorce, or be forever barred from "former spouse" SBP coverage.* It's probably best to have a lawyer help you with this, even if you aren't using an attorney for your divorce in general.

The former spouse must file or register the divorce decree with the DFAS. You must inform DFAS that the purpose of filing the divorce decree is to activate the "deemed election" for survivor benefits as a former spouse at the time the military member is eligible to retire. Just submitting the divorce decree to the DFAS is *not* an adequate election for survivor benefits. Once made, the election is irrevocable for the duration of the former spouse's life; a service member is entitled to designate only one category or class of beneficiaries. If the service member (or the court) has properly deemed an election of a former spouse beneficiary, the military member cannot designate another category as a SBP beneficiary (for instance, a subsequent spouse could not become a beneficiary and bump the former spouse's status).

Businesses and Professions

If you and your spouse don't own your own business and neither of you is a self-employed professional, you can skip this section and move on to Chapter 7. But if you do have a family business or a professional practice, then characterizing, valuing, and dividing these important assets might be especially challenging tasks in your divorce. Business valuations can evolve into one of the most heated and expensive aspects of a divorce, because the differences in spouses' perceptions of value can be huge—especially when one spouse is involved in the daily business operations and the other is not.

This is an area where a lawyer's guidance will surely benefit you— as well as the input of a business appraiser, accountant, and possibly other professionals who could help you establish value and decide on a division or buyout scenario. My goal here is to give you a quick course in the basics of business structures, valuation issues, and the questions that might arise about your business or profession in the course of your divorce.

Types of Business Entities

We'll start with a brief review of the different types of business entities, because the type and size of the business often dictates the best method for valuing it.

Sole Proprietorship

A sole proprietorship is an unincorporated business owned and run by one person with no distinction between the owner and business, often operating under a business name or DBA (doing business as).

The owners pay taxes on the business earnings on their personal returns. Sole proprietors are personally liable for the debts and other financial obligations of the business. Some sole proprietors create corporate structures, such as limited liability corporations (see below), which protect the owner from liability and might also have tax advantages. In the nine community property states (Arizona, California, Idaho, Louisiana, Nevada, New Mexico, Texas, Washington, and Wisconsin), married couples who work in their business might qualify to be treated as a sole proprietorship (see the IRS Revenue Procedure 2002-69).

Partnership

A partnership is a voluntary association of two or more people (or business entities) who jointly own and carry on a business, usually under a written partnership agreement that provides, among other things, how the participants will share in profits and losses. For legal and tax purposes, a partnership is usually considered an entity separate from the partners. A partnership might be general or limited.

General Partnership. In a general partnership, all partners participate in the daily work of running the business. The partners share in the risk of the liabilities and share in the profits and losses according to the terms of the partnership agreement (or in equal shares if there's no specific agreement).

Limited Partnership. A limited partnership means there are two classes of partners: general and limited. The general partner(s) operate the business and have personal liability for the partnership debts. Limited partners are not involved in the business operations and are not liable for the partnership debts beyond the amount of their capital contributions (the money they paid to own a piece of the action).

Limited Liability Companies (LLCs)

Limited liability companies are legal entities that are distinct from their owners, and offer business owners a way to shield their personal assets from the obligations of the business. Owners pay taxes on their personal returns, or they may elect to file a separate business return. LLCs are popular because they offer flexibility and personal protection.

Corporation

A corporation is an entity distinct from the shareholders who own it—a legal being separate from its stockholders. This separation protects stockholders from corporate liabilities—one of the attractive features of incorporating. Unlike general partners, stockholders could be far removed from the company's daily management and operation. A corporation has the right to issue stock and to exist indefinitely, even through changes in stockholders and directors. Stock certificates provide evidence of shares of ownership and show any restrictions placed on the stock. There are a number of corporate forms, including C corporations, S corporations, and limited liability, professional, and closely held corporations. Each has its own details, rules, and restrictions.

Professional Entities

Doctors, lawyers, accountants, and other professionals often practice in a group called a professional association, professional partnership, or professional corporation. Such a group is formed because it could be more economical for a practice. You must be a licensed professional, of the type comprising the group, to be a member-owner of the group.

Valuing Business Interests

You can take one of two paths through the complex terrain of a business valuation. One is the path of least resistance: You skip this section and rely on the conclusions of the business valuation expert you hire and your attorney's advice, trusting that these experts will come up with a value for the business that will protect your interests. This path acknowledges the common assumption made by clients, especially those who are not actively involved in the business, that they will not understand the valuation and will contribute nothing to the report.

I believe that assumption is wrong and that if you are willing and able to take a more active role in the valuation process, you should consider taking the second path. On that path, you will first plow through the rest of this chapter for a basic introduction to business appraisals, then ask your attorney to schedule a three-way meeting— you, your attorney, and your business valuation expert—to discuss the expert's preliminary report when it is ready.

This meeting serves several important functions. First, it gives you an opportunity to ask questions about the report and have the valuator explain the report in simple terms. Next, preparing for the meeting nudges your attorney to examine the report closely.

Unfortunately, many family law attorneys, due to their own aversion to numbers, accept expert valuation reports without question and fail to question the experts. Many lawyers also do not prepare the valuators to advocate for their conclusions in plain English (the language preferred by judges and parties alike). And when this happens, you are the one who suffers. The three-way meeting is a crucial opportunity for you to be an active participant in your case. Time and again I've seen clients leave these conferences with a better understanding of the valuation report they paid dearly for, as well as more confidence in the numbers that land on their spreadsheets.

TIP

Don't give up on reviewing the report just because you're not the businessperson. Often, clients who aren't involved in the business will ask a crucial question, or remember an important fact, which improves the accuracy or completeness of the business valuation report. One client of mine asked a question about her husband's practice of running cattle on a cousin's pasture, a side operation that had escaped the attention of the valuator hired to value a ranching operation. Another client remembered that his spouse had bragged about a potential merger and business buyout—a tidbit that led to a fruitful revision of the valuator's final report.

Approaches to Value

The concept of fair market value (FMV)—the amount that a willing buyer would pay in cash to a willing seller—applies to a business just as it does to a house. But it's even more difficult to apply this hypothetical definition of FMV to a business than to a residence, which is why we have alternative methods to estimate the value of a business. Three broad approaches: cost/asset, market, and income are at your disposal.

Cost/asset approach: The cost/asset approach starts with the cost of the underlying business assets. The current value of each asset is determined, then all asset values are subtotaled. The current value of each liability is determined, then all liability values are subtotaled. The subtotal liability value is subtracted from the subtotal asset value, and that produces a total value of the business. Total value is frequently called book value, or adjusted book value, or liquidation value. You might use this approach when the business value depends primarily on the value of tangible assets. If intangible assets exist, like goodwill, they will be another part of the calculation. The asset approach often produces the lowest number for value. It is usually not the best method to use when the business is a going concern—one that has a viable workforce, inventory, and the intent to continue operating.

Market approach: The market approach uses a comparison with similar businesses. Market information—the buying and selling of similar businesses in the public and private sectors—is a resource for the valuator. The history and trends in these markets are also important to this valuation approach. If you have a small or unique family business, the market approach might not be a useful way to value your business.

Income approach: Often used for businesses with an established track record, this approach converts anticipated economic benefits into a present value. In other words, the value of the business is equal to the present value of its future economic benefits, including cash flow and net income. The income approach offers three major variations: capitalization of earnings, discounted cash flow, and excess earnings method. The nature of the business determines the appropriate choice. The income approach is probably the most difficult approach to understand, and it is often the one that produces the highest value. It's also the approach most frequently used to value an ongoing business at divorce.

Adjustments to Value

Once an appraiser arrives at a valuation for the business, several factors might lead to adjusting that value. Some of the most common are described here.

"Normalizing" adjustments for nonrecurring fees, nonoperating assets, and nonbusiness expenses. Things that aren't going to happen regularly shouldn't generally be included in an assessment of value.

The historical collectability rate of accounts receivable. Not everyone pays their bills, and some businesses have a higher collection rate than others. If collection rates are poor, the appraiser might need to discount accounts receivable.

Adjustments in compensation. It is not unusual for compensation of a controlling shareholder of a private company to be higher than market rate compensation. A buyer is likely to employ a manager to operate the business at a lower salary, so it is appropriate to add back the above-market portion of the compensation.

Calculations for goodwill. Goodwill is relevant in some states, but not all. There are wide differences in what constitutes goodwill and what type of goodwill is divisible on divorce. (See "Commercial and Personal Goodwill," below.)

Valuing Specific Types of Business Interests

If you're valuing a partnership or corporation, you will want to consider some additional issues.

Partnerships. If a partnership is merely a way to jointly own an asset, such as a piece of real estate, then valuation is easy—you value just the asset. But if the partnership is a going concern, such as a medical practice, what is valued is called the partnership interest. This interest is more than simply a percentage of ownership in a specific partnership asset. It is an interest in the collective effort that makes up an ongoing business concern, and includes such things as tangible and intangible assets and the value of income streams.

Commercial and Personal Goodwill

Business or commercial goodwill is generally regarded as the sum total of all the special advantages, not otherwise identified and valued, related to a going concern. These include such things as a good name, capable staff, high credit standing, reputation, expectations of continued patronage, and favorable location. Business goodwill is measured by a formula: the amount by which the cost of the acquired company is greater than the sum of the assets less liabilities.

Personal goodwill is a different animal. It is an asset that relies on a particular individual whose presence generates cash profits that would be lost if the individual were not present. Many states do not consider personal goodwill a marital asset, and in business valuations, that type of goodwill might not be included in the entity's total goodwill, because it is too closely identified with the person and isn't inherent to the business. Personal goodwill is often an issue in the type of long-lived businesses commonly seen in late-life divorces.

As your divorce gets going, the first documents you want to see are the partnership agreement and any buy-sell agreements related to the partnership (a buy-sell agreement describes the terms under which a partner's interest is valued, then bought or sold, under specific circumstances such as termination of a partner's employment or death of a partner). The partnership agreement might control which valuation method must be used when a partner divorces. In that case, the issue is whether such a term is binding on a spouse who never agreed to such a provision or who might have consented to the provision without independent legal advice. And the real question is whether a judge is bound to use the partnership's valuation method. States vary on these matters. Even though divorce might not be mentioned, these documents might describe methods for valuing the entity when a partner dies or withdraws from the partnership, and you can extrapolate from those for purposes of the divorce.

Corporations. If your business is a corporation that has issued stock but hasn't generated adequate stock sales to establish a value (very common in small, closely held corporations), then you have to use factors other than stock sales to establish a market price, including the following:

- the nature and history of the business
- the general economic outlook and the outlook of the relevant industry
- the book value of the stock and the financial condition of the business
- the company's capacity to earn income and pay dividends
- whether the enterprise has goodwill or other intangible assets
- sales of stock and the size of the block of stock to be valued, and
- the market price of stock in corporations engaged in the same or similar line of business, and whose stocks are actively traded in a free and open market, either on an exchange or over the counter.

Other aspects of valuing corporate stock involve reductions in value, called discounts. One discount is for lack of control: If the shareholder spouse is a minority shareholder, then that person's stock is worth less than stock held by a majority shareholder. Another discount is for lack of marketability. For a closely-held corporation whose stock isn't traded publicly, not only is there no open market on which to trade shares, but the corporation might have placed restrictions on the transfer of shares and prices to be paid for those shares. (Organizational documents will give you this information.)

Business Appraisers

It should be apparent how complex it is to value an ongoing business and why business appraisers could be very helpful in a divorce. A business appraiser is an objective third-party expert who investigates all aspects of a business and offers an opinion about its value, usually in the form of a written valuation report. If you're in a collaborative divorce process, you'll likely hire one agreed-upon appraiser and accept the valuation (but you'll still have a chance to offer the input described above in the discussion about three-way meetings). In a contested process, each spouse might hire an appraiser and the two experts' reports will both be considered (and argued over).

It's a good idea to use a professional appraiser rather than the business's accountant—or the family accountant—to avoid questions about objectivity and expertise.

RESOURCE

Find a business appraiser. Check the websites of the American Institute of Certified Public Accountants (AICPA), which offers a special credential for business valuation called Accredited in Business Valuation (ABV); the National Association of Certified Valuation Analysts (NACVA), which certifies valuation analysts (CVA); the Institute of Business Appraisers (IBA), which focuses on small to medium-sized businesses and offers certifications as certified business appraiser (CBA) and business valuator accredited in litigation (BVAL); or the American Society of Appraisers, which trains and certifies real estate and personal property appraisers.

The Value of Value

One of the side benefits of going through a business valuation is that you will learn a great deal. Whether my clients were the business operators or their spouses, time and again they comment on how much they learn from reading an outsider's valuation of their businesses. It could be a sobering experience, either rewarding or disappointing. Either way, it will allow you to understand what you're dealing with when it's time to make decisions about dividing the business.

Dividing Business Interests

Having worked through the complicated issue of value, the next thing you will consider is how you are going to divide the business that might constitute a big part of your marital estate. Business entities, and certainly professional practices, are almost always awarded to the spouse who operates the business. It's unusual for a court to order sale or liquidation of a business. The uninvolved spouse receives property of value similar to the businessperson's share of the business or a cash buyout from the spouse keeping the business.

What about a business in which both spouses are very involved? Former spouses have been known to continue working side by side after a divorce. When that happens, it is wise to engage the services of a business transaction attorney to prepare arm's-length management agreements. These agreements can go a long way toward avoiding problems when one former spouse wants to buy out the other one, or when management duties need to be clearly delineated.

Buyout Issues
A business can be a high-value item, and sometimes a spouse whose interest is being bought out will agree to have the buyout completed over time. The business-owning spouse must provide the other with a promissory note for the balance of the purchase price. If you're the person being bought out, get security for the note (in the form of a lien on business assets or another piece of property awarded to your spouse), so that you don't find yourself in line with other business creditors should the business run into hard times. While we are on the subject of buyouts, another issue of concern is called redemption—when the business itself, rather than the owner-spouse, redeems (buys) the non-owner spouse's interest. Chapter 8 describes the potential tax problems with redemption.

Characterizing Business Interests

Businesses, like other assets, must be characterized as marital property, separate property, or a mix of the two. If a business originates during marriage, it is marital property. But a business could be a spouse's separate property if it was created or incorporated prior to marriage.

Separate property businesses create some interesting issues at divorce, depending on the characterization laws of your state. The stream of income generated by a separate property business during the marriage is usually considered marital property. But at time of divorce, all of that income might have been spent on living expenses, leaving nothing to divide. If the income was used to purchase nonbusiness assets, then those marital assets would be part of the marital estate, but the business entity itself would not be. If part of the business income was reinvested back into the business—which is customary in well-run businesses— then that reinvestment, and any resulting increase in the business's value, could remain separate as well.

Another issue is whether the marital estate was fairly compensated by a separate business for the businessperson's time and effort. Remember that the marital estate is entitled to the time, toil, and talent of the spouses. If a spouse spends 100% of his or her time working for a separate property corporation and enhancing its value without the marital estate receiving adequate compensation, the marital estate might have a claim for reimbursement.

A business could also be part separate and part marital property, such as when a spouse acquires additional stock in a separate corporation after marriage or a spouse's ownership percentage of a separate property partnership increases during marriage as a result of the spouse's efforts. In those cases, the additional stock or partnership interests might be characterized as marital property because they were acquired during the marriage. The result is a business with dual citizenship in the marital and separate estates.

How a sole proprietorship is characterized also depends on when the business began, but that might not be as clear-cut as it is when you have partnership agreements and corporate charters evidencing a definite start date. Take a business with an inventory, for example. If the inventory of a separate sole proprietorship business was sold long ago and the current inventory was acquired with income produced during marriage, the current inventory might be marital property.

If you have a separate or mixed estate business at issue in your divorce, you definitely want the guidance of an attorney, as well as a skilled accountant or business evaluator, to unravel the characterization questions.

Managing the Business in the Interim

If you are not involved in the day-to-day operations of your spouse's business, ask to receive monthly business financial statements and other reports so that you and your attorney can monitor changes and detect red flags during your divorce proceedings. If your spouse doesn't provide this information voluntarily, ask a court to order it. Judges can also prohibit spouses from certain actions in order to preserve a company's status quo—for example, making sure that neither party makes unusual purchases or incurs unnecessary indebtedness that might undermine the business operations.

What if both you and your spouse are employed in the family business? If your divorce is fairly amicable you might continue running the business together, perhaps with new written documents that make your relationship a business one only. But if your divorce is acrimonious, the judge might help you to preserve the value and operational integrity of the business, by ordering a delineation of duties and responsibilities— possibly right down to setting your respective work hours. In very high-conflict cases, I've known judges to place the business in a temporary receivership and name a person (called a receiver) to manage the business until the divorce is complete and the parties' rights have been determined. This is an extreme remedy—and a costly one—but it could happen if spouses prove themselves unable to work together for the good of their business.

More About Assets—
And What They're Worth to You

E verything that belongs to your marital estate must be divided between you and your spouse in your divorce. It will be simple to divide some of the assets covered in this chapter, as you and your spouse will each have ideas of what you want to keep and the other person might agree easily. For example, you might have two cars of relatively equal value and decide that each of you will keep the car that you regularly drive. Your checking and savings accounts might be simple to divide. Other assets are more complicated because valuation isn't simple, or a dispute arises over who gets the actual item, or an asset is difficult to divide.

Liquid Assets

When you hear the word liquidity, you think of cash or assets that are relatively easy to convert into cash, like bank accounts and certificates of deposit (CDs), or publicly traded stocks and bonds. Assigning a value to liquid assets is not tricky—the value is the amount in the account or the amount you can raise by selling the asset. Nor is dividing them very complicated in most cases. On the other hand, identifying these assets can be trickier than you might think.

Cash

You know you have thirty bucks in your wallet, but do you know what you have put aside or forgotten in places like safe deposit boxes, piggy banks, out-of-season purses, the desk where you keep foreign coins collected from travels, and home safes? The sums you find might not be great, but everything counts—and you might be surprised what you find.

Checking, Savings, and Money Market Accounts

The most recent statements from your bank, credit union, or investment firm reflect your current balances in checking, savings, and money market accounts. Be sure you take into consideration all outstanding checks and withdrawals and that you review your accounts online to get the most up-to-date balance when you make your marital estate spreadsheet (see Chapter 5, "Marital Property: Steps to a Fair Division").

This is the time to check who has authority to sign on all of your accounts. Check the features that attach to each, like overdraft protection or a payable-on-death (POD) feature, which transfers the account directly (without probate) to your designated beneficiary upon your death (more about that in Chapter 11, "Estate Planning and Divorce").

Certificates of Deposit

Certificates of deposit are savings vehicles that have a fixed interest rate and time limit: They last anywhere from three months to as long as 10 years. CDs usually earn more interest than savings accounts because the bank has the use of your money for a defined period. At the end of the specified time period, the CD matures and you can withdraw your money plus the accrued interest. (You could also withdraw interest as it is earned, but you'll earn more if you leave it to be compounded.) The bank imposes a penalty (usually forfeited interest) if you cash in the CD before its maturity date.

At one time actual certificates were issued; these days, you'll just get a simple notation of the CD's existence on a statement from the bank that holds it. For your divorce, you need to know the owner's name, the face amount, the maturity date, the interest rate, and whether the CD will automatically renew. Also check whether your spouse has used the CD as collateral for a loan, without your knowledge. If you discover a loan, learn as much as possible about it (amount, date, and terms), by asking the lender or your spouse, and ask for a copy of the loan documents.

Brokerage Accounts

A brokerage account is an account in which you hold, buy, and sell stocks, bonds, mutual funds, and other investments. You can manage your brokerage account yourself or have a professional broker manage it.

Brokerage accounts include subaccounts for holding cash from sales of assets. The value of the brokerage account is the current fair market value of all the assets held in the account, minus any indebtedness. Due to the volatility of the market, it is best to check online for current values when you're at the point of negotiating a final settlement or preparing a marital estate spreadsheet. You should also find out whether the account has outstanding margin loans (debts incurred to purchase assets) that your spouse incurred without your knowledge.

As with bank accounts, you want to know who has signatory authority over each brokerage account and whether the accounts have a "payment on death" (POD) feature. If you don't have previous statements, it's very important to get a history of transactions. Transaction history is evidence of asset acquisition dates (you'll need acquisition dates so you can calculate holding periods for capital gains taxes). The account history will also give you purchase prices (the purchase price becomes the tax basis of each asset, again necessary for calculating capital gains). These tax consequences can have a major effect on how you value the assets in the account, especially if you need to liquidate stocks and bonds quickly to generate income. Knowing the capital gains hit that such a sale will entail might influence the choices you make about which assets you want to keep and which you want distributed to your spouse.

Evaluating the Value of Brokerage Account Assets to You

When deciding whether and how to negotiate for assets in your brokerage accounts, consider the following factors that apply to stocks, bonds, mutual funds, and ETFs.

Stocks. If you have held stock for more than a year, long-term capital gains rates apply. (The difference between the purchase price and the sale price, minus brokerage fees and commissions, is the taxable gain.) Otherwise you'll pay the slightly higher tax rates for ordinary income. Keeping an asset that qualifies for the capital gains tax rate is better than keeping assets that will be taxed at ordinary income rates when you sell them. When you contemplate whether you want to negotiate for specific stock in your marital estate, ask for advice about its investment value from a reputable stock investment broker or other financial adviser, who can advise you about the likelihood that the stock will increase in value and that you will receive dividends. The value of stocks to you also depends on how long you want to hold them and that, in turn, depends on the totality of your financial circumstances. (You will learn more about this in Chapter 10, "Your Financial Survival.")

Bonds. When you buy a bond, you are making a loan to the issuer. If you buy a U.S. Treasury Bond, you are lending money to the federal government; if you buy a municipal bond, you are lending to a local government. A corporate bond is a loan to a corporation (including utility companies that might be a combination of public and private ownership). Bonds produce either tax-free income (such as municipal bonds) or taxable income.

The risk associated with bonds depends on the stability of the borrowing entity and on interest rates. Usually bond prices go down when interest rates go up, and vice versa. Bonds could provide a steady source of income from interest, and at the end of the loan period you should receive your principal.

Bonds are valued in terms of their yield—how much you'll receive in interest as compared to the bond's current market price. The present value of a bond is its cash flow (interest and principal) discounted at a suitable interest rate. Various formulas compute these measures of bond value, and a full explanation of them is beyond our scope. That is why I recommend you consult with a bond broker to get a better idea of the value of your bonds, their current market ratings, and the solvency of the issuing entity. This big picture will help you know how highly to value the asset in negotiating the divorce.

Mutual funds. When you own a mutual fund, you're invested in a fund operated by portfolio managers who, in turn, invest in assets —stocks, bonds, or both, as well as commodities and real estate investment funds.

You receive a share in the fund in exchange for your investment—in other words, a percentage of the total value of the securities contained in the fund. Investors earn money from dividends on stocks and interest on bonds.

An index fund is a type of mutual fund, with a portfolio constructed to track the components of a market index, such as the Standard & Poor's 500 Index. Index funds typically have lower management expenses and historically have outperformed other types of mutual funds.

It's easy to determine current values of shares in mutual funds by checking the Internet. Taxable gain is calculated as with stock: the difference between the purchase price and the sale price, less brokerage fees and commissions. Unless you are an experienced investor, you should consider reviewing your mutual fund holdings with a financial adviser experienced in the mutual fund market before you decide which of these assets you might want to have at the end of your divorce.

ETFs. An ETF (exchange traded fund) is bought and traded, like stocks, on a market exchange. But unlike a stock, which focuses on one company, an ETF focuses on a group of several companies' securities. While ETFs might be cheaper and more tax efficient than mutual funds, they do carry risks. As with the other brokerage account assets, consult with a brokerage professional to determine the pros and cons of selling or maintaining ETFs in a divorce scenario.

When you're ready to make decisions about which of the investments discussed above to keep and which ones to let go, keep in mind that not only should you work with current values, but the precise time of day at which you check is important. Stocks and ETFs trade throughout the day, while mutual funds trade only at the end of the day.

Dividing Brokerage Accounts

Dividing brokerage accounts isn't difficult, but it's important to avoid making the mistake of assigning dollar values to each spouse's share. During the period between that assignment of dollar values and the actual signing of the final divorce paperwork, values in brokerage accounts could fluctuate significantly.

EXAMPLE: On the day you negotiate a settlement with your spouse, the mutual funds may be worth $30,000, and to equalize other assets one spouse is assigned $12,000 and the other $18,000. But on the day you go to transfer the funds to each spouse's separate account, the funds may be worth more or less, throwing off your spreadsheet.

To avoid this problem, it's simpler to assign each spouse a percentage of the account, so that both spouses share proportionally in all assets and also in market fluctuations. Percentage divisions also put spouses on equal footing with regard to gains, losses, and taxes. If you do decide to use dollar amounts, make sure your written settlement agreement addresses what happens if those accounts experience increases or decreases in value. One solution is to agree that the two of you will recalculate the division only if there is a 10% or more swing in market values.

U.S. Savings Bonds

U.S. Savings Bonds identify the owner and have a series identifier (E, EE, or I, for example) and a face value. You may hold the bonds in either paper or electronic format. When a U.S. Savings Bond matures, the entire face amount (or face amount plus interest earned) is redeemable.

Determine who owns the bonds in your estate, whether any beneficiaries are named, and whether the bond series is still accumulating interest.

Some EE bonds stop accumulating interest at maturity, so you could decide to redeem those mature bonds in the course of the divorce, pay taxes on the interest, and divide the remaining proceeds. You can also award the bond to the individual who is designated as the owner, or transfer owner- ship between spouses as long as the divorce decree authorizes the transfer. Generally, any transfer of assets between spouses pursuant to a divorce decree is a nontaxable event. However, U.S. Savings Bonds are an exception. The transferring spouse must report and pay taxes on all interest that the bond has earned up to the date of the transfer, and the receiving spouse will be taxed on interest earned after the transfer when the bond is cashed or matures.

It's easy to calculate the value of U.S. Savings Bonds, even if the series designation is no longer issued. The U.S. Treasury Department has a calculator site for savings bonds: www.treasurydirect.gov/indiv/tools/tools_savingsbondcalc.htm. You can calculate value, earned interest, and final maturity dates using their on-site tools. Remember to keep paper bonds in a safe place.

Nonliquid Assets

Nonliquid assets are those you can't turn into cash with ease, though many of them have significant value.

Life Insurance

Insurers offer various types of life insurance, and they have different values—both in terms of their cash surrender value and in terms of their intrinsic value to you. A policy's intrinsic value refers to the insured's inability to obtain new, alternate insurance. For example, someone might have a medical condition that arose after the original policy was written, but that now renders that person uninsurable by a new carrier. In that event, the old policy is extremely valuable—a common scenario in late-life divorces.

Term Insurance

Term life insurance is considered "pure" insurance, where the premium buys protection in the event of death and the policy has no other features. In exchange for your premiums, the insurance company promises to pay a sum of money to designated beneficiaries in the event you die within a given period of time (the policy term). Term insurance does not accumulate cash value, so you pay less for it than for other types of life insurance.

In divorce, spouses can use term insurance to provide security for future obligations, such as alimony, spousal support, or divorce property buyouts. Spouses also might bargain to retain status as the beneficiary, especially after a long-term marriage, either in exchange for the insured spouse's receiving something else or based on a moral obligation that represents consideration for sacrifices made during the marriage, such as putting a career on the back burner in order to raise a family.

Permanent Life Insurance

The distinguishing characteristic of permanent life insurance is that a portion of your premiums is invested in a fund that earns tax-deferred interest, so the policy accumulates a cash value that you can borrow against or use to pay future premiums. The policy remains in force until the insured person dies, as long as premiums are paid. Permanent life insurance policies are more expensive than term policies, and if you cancel them, a surrender charge will be due. There are three types of permanent life insurance policies.

Whole Life. The premium is fixed, and the future cash value is guaranteed. You can access accumulated cash values through policy loans, on which you pay interest.

Be Careful With Beneficiary Designations

Many states have laws that automatically revoke spousal beneficiary designations after a divorce is final. At the same time, it's not uncommon for one spouse to agree to keep the other as a life insurance beneficiary as part of the divorce settlement. In this case, the insured spouse must redesignate the beneficiary after the divorce is final. Otherwise, the security you bargained for will be worth nothing. You will also need to bird-dog the beneficiary issue after the divorce, by including a provision in your agreement that gives you access to information about the policy so you can periodically check to be sure you're still the beneficiary and premiums are current.

Universal Life Insurance. Universal life insurance provides flexibility in the amount and timing of premium payments and has the potential for a higher rate of return. You can permanently withdraw accumulated cash without the interest charged on whole life loans. It also includes a cash account that is increased by premium payments.

Universal Life Insurance comes in two varieties. First, Indexed Universal Life is similar to Universal Life, but interest credited to the policy is linked to an external index (such as the S&P 500) and thus carries more risk. The second type, Variable Universal Life, gives the owner more investment choices in sub-accounts for potentially greater returns (but, again, more risk than Universal Life).

Endowment. An endowment policy pays a lump sum after a specified period of time (usually 10, 15, or 20 years), or on death, whichever is sooner. It also builds up a cash value, but you must surrender the policy to access the cash.

Cash Values

Cash value grows slowly in the first few years, then faster in later years. You don't pay taxes on interest earned until you withdraw it. Withdrawing cash could reduce the death benefit by the amount withdrawn or more, depending on the terms of the policy. All of that assumes you keep the policy: The proceeds of a loan against cash value might be taxed if you surrender the policy or let it lapse before paying off the loan.

At divorce, the cash surrender value is the most common number used as the value of a permanent life insurance policy. Many policies include charts with estimates of cash value, but the best way to determine the current cash value is get it directly from the company. This gives you a more accurate figure and reveals any outstanding policy loans you might not know about.

Viatical and Life Settlements

A viatical settlement is a way to use insurance, allowing the insured person to obtain cash by selling the policy for a portion of its face amount. Viatical settlements began when insurance companies started purchasing policies from people who were terminally ill and needed money. The market has broadened to include elderly policyholders from whom the company purchases policies at rates ranging from 5% to 80% of the face amount. The terms "life settlements" or "senior settlements" typically refer to older people (65+) wanting to cash in their policy to cover retirement or long-term care expenses. A policy rider called "accelerated death benefits" is in most life insurance policies, and this allows the policy owner to tap into the death benefit and use the money tax free.

You can check with the insurance provider or contact a "life-settlement broker" for options available to you. If you're interested in turning an insurance policy into cash that you could divide as part of your divorce, consider some caveats. For example, there might be tax consequences; doing so might affect one's ability to qualify for Medicaid; and commissions could be high. Ask your lawyer or insurance agent to find out whether the company offers this type of settlement and whether you qualify based on your age or health conditions. Check with your state's insurance agency to determine if the buyer-company is licensed and has any consumer complaints.

Annuities

An annuity is a contract between an annuitant and an insurance company, but it's not insurance per se. The annuitant pays money in exchange for the insurance company's promise to pay back a specific sum in the future, over a specified period of time. The annuitant can name a beneficiary in case the annuity doesn't start paying before the annuitant dies. Annuities can be fixed or variable:

- **Fixed Annuity.** The insurance company guarantees a minimum rate of interest during a set period of time and guarantees that periodic payments will be a specified dollar amount. The periodic payments might last for a definite period (for example, 20 years) or an indefinite period (like your lifetime or your spouse's lifetime).
- **Variable Annuity.** You can choose whether your payments are invested in mutual funds, stocks, bonds, or a combination. The return on your payments and the amount of the periodic payments you receive in the future depend on the performance of the investment vehicle(s).

Valuing Annuities

Private annuities are valued in a two-step process. First, the lump sum value of the annuity payments is determined using actuarial assumptions. Second, the value of the lump sum is discounted to ascertain present value. Present value is explained further in Chapter 10, "Your Financial Survival."

Dividing Annuities

One way to divide annuities at divorce is to cash them in and divide the proceeds between the spouses, but this can be very costly. Cashing in an annuity before maturity results in a penalty, assessed by the annuity provider, as high as 7% if you withdraw in the first year. The penalty decreases each year until you reach the scheduled distribution point. In addition, if you are under 59½ and you want to withdraw any of the gain on a variable annuity, the IRS will penalize you 10% on the withdrawal (unless at the time of withdrawal you are permanently disabled). Be sure you know all the costs before you calculate the annuity's present value—especially if you want to access your money before the annuity matures or if you want to negotiate for property of equal value.

To provide greater benefit to both spouses, it's common to negotiate for a court order that calls for dividing annuity payments between spouses when they're received. If you're still paying premiums, the post-divorce premiums are factored into the annuity's lump sum present value. Another point of negotiation is whether spouses will remain as beneficiaries on the annuity after divorce.

Intellectual Property

Intellectual property (IP) assets involve creative work of any kind: inventions, artistic creations, written works, music, and many other categories of creations. If a divorcing spouse is a published author, Grammy-winning songwriter, collected artist, or inventor of a successful product, intellectual property is visible and clearly valuable. But intellectual property comes into play in more subtle ways in many other scenarios. Consider these: a spouse whose Great American Novel is still in draft stage on the household computer; a spouse who tinkers in the garage inventing new gardening tools; a weekend photographer; a playwright producing works for the local church pageant; and the spouse who uses desktop printing to publish recipes in a cookbook.

All of these situations involve intellectual property. IP is an intangible right, granted by law to the author or originator of the creative product, who has the exclusive use and control over it. Creative types protect their intellectual property in one of three common ways:

- **Copyrights.** Copyrights protect original works of authorship, including literary and dramatic works, music and lyrics, choreography, sculptural works, artwork, sound recordings, and audiovisual works. Copyrights are a federal protection and they generally endure for the life of the author plus 70 years or longer, depending on the type of authorship.

- **Patents.** A patent means the United States Patent Office grants an inventor the right to exclude others from making, using, and selling one's invention; as well as the right to license (allow) others to produce, use, or sell it. In essence, patents grant a monopoly to the inventor to produce the invention. If a patent is developed through employment, the employer usually owns the patent.
- **Trademarks.** A trademark distinguishes a particular merchant from others. It might be a symbol or phrase, or a distinctive mark, motto, device, or emblem that is affixed to goods. While trademarks are referred to as a type of IP, they are more accurately described as intangible commercial property and are a business asset. For that reason, our discussion about IP focuses on copyrights and patents.

Valuing Intellectual Property

In most states, a copyright or patent is marital property if the underlying work was created during the marriage. In general, revenue or potential revenue from a patent or copyright, in the form of royalties and licensing fees, is the major component of value. If there is already a stream of royalty or licensing revenue, it will be discounted to present value, depending upon the remaining useful life of the asset. Useful life could mean legal, contractual, physical, functional, technological, or economic life.

If the IP doesn't yet produce revenues but is likely to in the future, then you'll need the services of an expert to establish value by examining industry-related royalty rates and licensing agreements. It's challenging to characterize income generated by IP when the creative work was produced during marriage but the income stream doesn't begin until after the divorce; or when the creative work was produced partly before and partly during marriage. States are all over the map on this issue, so you'll have to ask your attorney how your state deals with it.

Dividing Intellectual Property

You have a number of options for dividing intellectual property, and the challenges that make valuing IP difficult affect division as well:

- The actual property right could remain the creating spouse's asset, with future income divided between the spouses according to percentages negotiated as part of the overall divorce settlement.
- The copyright or patent ownership could be transferred in part to the noncreating spouse. (The creating spouse might not be too keen on this, because it could adversely affect future licensing transactions.)
- If the IP is artwork, the artist spouse could share the actual works with the other spouse, possibly with conditions on the transfer— for example, the artist could retain a right of reasonable access to the artwork for exhibits and reproductions, or a right of first refusal to purchase the artwork back.

Don't Undervalue Creative Work

Perhaps the intellectual property in your marital estate is similar to the examples cited above, and the creative endeavor has not yet produced income and is viewed by both spouses as a hobby. In that case, either spouse might be tempted to just award the fruits of creative labors to the ingenious spouse. Right now, you think, "Gee, there are other worthwhile assets I need to focus on in this divorce rather than cluttering up my head worrying about my silly hobbies (or my spouse's)!" But just because a creative effort has nominal present value is no reason to totally ignore it. Include the fruits of your creativity in your divorce decree or agreement. You might have written a future bestseller! And if so, you will be eternally grateful to *this* author.

If an inventor or writer has done significant work during the marriage but needs to do more to complete a project or to maximize future royalties, the question arises whether that work is merely a continuation of the IP that is a marital asset, or whether the creative spouse has a separate property interest in the portion completed after the marriage ends. If the postdivorce creative effort could be quantified, spouses could agree to deduct an amount or percentage from royalties before the royalties are divided. The divorce decree could also include ways to measure future efforts or mechanisms (such as using an arbitrator) to determine the value of future creative efforts.

Employment Benefits: Beyond Retirement

A spouse's employment history is fertile ground for discovering assets besides the various retirement plans discussed in Chapter 6. Some are obvious and appear on pay stubs. Some are not so obvious—you will find them in employee manuals, correspondence with the employer, and contracts. Examples of the latter are severance agreements, leave pay, and stock options. Not all of these assets have a determinable fair market value, but they all have potential value. First, their availability to the employee spouse might influence the judge's calculation of fairness in equitable distribution states. Second, they might be considered a category of income when measuring a spouse's ability to pay alimony. Third, they might provide security for divorce obligations.

The Obvious

We'll start with the assets that you've probably already identified and that don't take much searching to locate.

Insurance

Many employers provide one or more types of insurance to employees—and, often, their families—as a benefit.

Health insurance. No one doubts that employer-provided health insurance is an invaluable asset, even though it does not appear on the marital estate spreadsheet. The loss of medical insurance for the nonemployee spouse might be eased after the divorce through COBRA coverage, or through health care exchanges created by the Affordable Care Act, both discussed in detail in Chapter 9, "The Health Care Puzzle."

Flexible–cafeteria plans. Cafeteria plans are also known as flexible spending arrangements (FSAs) or 125 plans (because they are defined in Section 125 of the Tax Code). Flex plans allow employees to use before-tax dollars to pay for uninsured care, out-of-pocket prescription drug costs, and qualified over-the-counter items for the employee or a dependent, for health insurance copays or deductibles, or for dependent care for a child or other dependent. The downside to most FSAs is that they're use-it-or-lose-it plans. At the beginning of each year the employee must decide how much should be withheld (up to the maximum allowed), based on an estimate of what will be needed in that year. If you overestimate your needs, you lose any balance left in the account at the end of the year (as a result of the COVID-19 pandemic, however, some carriers extended their use-it-up period).

But if an FSA account has a balance at the time of divorce, it's an asset of the marital estate. Generally, the employee spouse will pay the other spouse cash as a buyout of the amount remaining in the account.

Life insurance. Life insurance policies through employment are term insurance, which does not accumulate a cash surrender value. Nevertheless, such policies could be used to provide security for postdivorce payment obligations, including alimony and property settlement buyouts. Even if the employer doesn't pay the premiums on the employee's behalf, premiums are usually much less than those on the private insurance market, and if coverage needs to be increased to provide the security for obligations, it's less expensive through employment-based policies.

Disability insurance. Employer-provided group disability insurance is much less expensive than insurance on the open market. As with life insurance, disability insurance doesn't have its own value, but could be used to secure payments for postdivorce obligations in case the paying spouse loses earning capacity as a result of disability.

If an employee is receiving disability insurance payments (or workers' compensation benefits) due to illness or injury that occurred after the date of marriage, payments during marriage are usually considered marital property as long as they replace income that would have been earned during the marriage. If the illness or injury occurred before the date of marriage, disability payments received after the date of marriage might be characterized as either separate or community property, depending on your state's laws. Most states consider postdivorce disability payments to be the sole property of the spouse receiving the income, but the amount of the payments might be taken into consideration—for example, in establishing support obligations.

Deferred Compensation

Deferred compensation plans are used when a highly compensated employee wants to defer base salary or a bonus to a future tax year in order to spread tax consequences over time. Employers usually place deferred payments in an account that the employee could access at a later time. It's difficult to transfer these accounts at divorce because of antiassignment provisions, so they are usually awarded to the employee spouse, who must then pay a share to the nonemployee spouse or offset the value with other property to be awarded to the nonemployee spouse.

The Not So Obvious

Some employment benefits can be easily overlooked during a divorce, giving an advantage to the employee spouse who gets to keep them. A little bit of attention to detail can pay off when you take the time to evaluate work-related benefits beyond salary and insurance. Below are some of the commonly overlooked benefits.

Severance Pay

Whether severance pay is an asset of the marital estate depends on when the employee received it, what its purpose is, and whether it relates to the period of marriage.

- **Marital asset.** If a severance payment compensates for past years of service, and those years fall within the marriage, the payment is a marital asset. For example, an employer might reward a retiring employee with a bonus, meant to thank the employee for past work, in which case the payment would be part of the marital estate.

- **Mixed marital and separate.** But severance that an employer pays to induce an employee to retire early might be considered compensation for a future time period—defined as the years (or months) between the receipt of the severance payment and the earliest possible retirement date (per the terms of the severance agreement). If some of those years fall during marriage and some fall after the date of divorce, the severance pay should be apportioned between the marital estate and the employee's separate estate.

The bottom line is that if you think your spouse could receive a severance payment after your divorce, the settlement agreement should address how will be divided. And if you're expecting severance yourself, don't hide it. It might be a marital asset that you have an obligation to disclose.

Leave Pay

Employees who leave a job might be able to cash out accrued vacation leave (and, in rare cases, unused sick leave). If the benefit is payable upon termination, it is often considered a marital asset; basically, it's like a savings account earned during the marriage, and the employee spouse must compensate the nonemployee spouse for the latter's share of the accrued leave (the part that was earned during the marriage). If it is not "cashable," but only available as a way to take time away from employment, leave pay does not have asset value.

Bonuses

Bonuses are linked either to employee performance or company performance, and either way, if they were earned during the marriage, they're part of the marital estate. If you're anticipating a bonus at the time of divorce, you should include a provision in your settlement that says, if either spouse receives a bonus that could be part of the marital estate, that spouse must notify the other spouse, provide written verification of the amount, and divide the money by whatever method the parties agree to (or the judge orders).

Bonuses might be called performance awards, signing bonuses, retention bonuses, or even loans made with an expectation that the debt will be forgiven in the future. If performance rewards are part of employment agreements entered into during marriage, they are likely to be considered marital property, unless they are actually earned in whole or in part through work done after divorce, in which case the bonus might be apportioned between the marital estate and the employee's separate estate.

Expense Reimbursements

Employers who pay for employee educational expenses usually do so on a reimbursement basis. If a spouse has paid out of pocket for expenses but hasn't yet received reimbursement, the future reimbursement is akin to an account receivable and should be considered an asset owed to the marital estate. The same is true for other types of reimbursable expenses, like travel or entertainment.

Stock Options and Restricted Stock

Courts mostly agree that employee stock options and restricted stock represent something of value to an employee and thus to the marital estate—but the questions of how to value them and whether they should be considered assets or future income are subject to much debate.

An employee stock option is a contract that grants the employee a right to buy stock at a specific price (the exercise price) during a specific period of time. The stock is typically that of a publicly traded company or a company anticipating an initial public offering (IPO). The employee is usually required to stay with the employer for a minimum length of time before the options can be exercised ("vest"), at which point the employee could exercise the right to purchase stock. Restricted stock is a share of stock that is granted to an employee with certain limitations, like keeping the employee from selling until a certain period of time has passed.

Vesting

The term "vesting period" refers to the time that must pass before a stock option can be exercised or before the issuing company lifts any stock restrictions. If an employee leaves the company before the vesting period ends, unvested options and restricted shares revert to the employer. Vested options are usually considered marital property, in whole or in part, if they are granted during marriage, or if the vesting period falls during the marriage.

A stock option has no initial value; it simply allows the employee the future right to purchase a share at the exercise price, based on the theory that as the employee's performance contributes to the increased value of company stock, the value of the option increases.

EXAMPLE: Company grants Employee 100 stock options at the exercise price of $5.00 per share. The vesting period is five years, and five years later the stock is worth $8.00 per share. Once vested, Employee has the right to buy shares worth $8.00 for only $5.00. Employee does so, then sells 50 shares for $8.00 each, gaining $150.00, and keeps 50 shares in the belief that the stock will continue to rise in value.

Valuing employee stock options is an imperfect science, because if they're not vested, they have no value at all, and they might never have any value—but on the other hand, they might be worth a great deal in the future. To assign them a value, analysts must speculate on the likely future value of the stock, an estimate under any circumstances.

Dividing these assets is also difficult. If a spouse anticipates receiving stock options or restricted stock soon after the divorce as compensation for work done in whole or in part during the marriage, those options are at least partially marital property. You must also determine how much of the vesting period took place during marriage; if some part of the vesting period was outside of marriage, then there's a separate property interest. The most challenging question is how to factor in postdivorce employment that is part of the vesting period—for example, if the option was granted in 2020 and vests in 2025, and the employee divorces in 2023, then part of the vesting period occurs during the marriage and part after the divorce, and it's difficult to separate out the value of the work done before and after the divorce as contributing to the ownership of the stock options (and, later, of the stock).

For all of these reasons, especially the hazards of second-guessing the stock markets, courts tend to divide the options themselves, giving each spouse a certain number of options to deal with as that spouse chooses. This spreads both the risk and potential gain. However, most employers will not create a separate stock option account for a former spouse, so the employee spouse must manage the stock options on behalf of the former spouse. The marital settlement agreement or judgment will set the terms for the employee spouse's management of the options, including requirements that the employee spouse must keep the nonemployee spouse informed of all exercise dates, provide copies of all relevant communications from the employer, and respond in a timely way to the nonemployee spouse's directions regarding purchase or sale of stock.

Once again, the clearer the details regarding the postdivorce relationships between spouses, the fewer potential conflicts down the road. If your marital estate contains stock options or restricted stock, you should consult an attorney before negotiating about how to divide them.

Military Benefits

The world of military employment also contains some not-so-obvious marital assets. (Military retirement is discussed in Chapter 6, "The Big-Ticket Items: Your Home, Your Retirement, and Your Family Business.")

Medical and commissary benefits for military divorcees. A former spouse who has not remarried is entitled to commissary and military exchange privileges when the marriage to the military spouse lasted 20 years during which at least 20 years of military service occurs. This is sometimes referred to as the 20-20-20 Rule—20 years of qualifying military service, 20 years of marriage, and 20 years of overlap between the two. For those spouses who do not meet the 20-20-20 requirement, a COBRA-type of continuation health insurance known as the Continued Health Care Benefit Program (CHCBP) offers up to 36 months of coverage and indefinite ongoing coverage for some who qualify. The Continued Health Care Benefit Program has eligibility requirements, so go to one of the following websites and look at the CHCBP handbook: www.tricare.mil or www.humanamilitary.com.

Accrued leave. A military service member can accrue up to 30 days of paid leave each year, not to exceed 60 days total. State laws differ as to whether the value of paid military leave is a marital asset in a divorce, but if your spouse is in the military and has accrued leave, let your lawyer know and make sure you don't leave it on the table.

Personal Property

Personal property is pretty much anything that is not real estate. In this section, the term refers to automobiles, household furniture and furnishings, clothing, jewelry, and other personal effects accumulated during the marriage. (Intellectual property, such as copyrights, is also personal property, but we deal with that above.) Pets are usually considered personal property, but that approach might be changing, as discussed later in this chapter. Property that is affixed to real estate—in most cases, appliances—is included in the real estate value as a fixture and isn't considered personal property.

Because of the sheer number of objects that most people own, especially late in life, determining value and dividing things up could feel like a nightmare. If it's at all possible, you and your spouse should try to agree on how to divide personal property without bringing it into court. This will save you time and money and, if you do go to court on more important items, it will keep the judge from being frustrated with you—judges do not like spending their time deciding who gets to keep the Calphalon cookware. You might be able to divide your property without even having to agree on the value of many items. Here are a few methods:

- Toss a coin to decide who goes first and begin selecting contested items in an alternating drawing until all the items are chosen.
- Agree on what you can and then toss a coin to decide who gets disputed items.
- Assign each item a number, put the numbers on pieces of paper in a container, and alternate drawings.
- Use an informal arbitrator to listen to your reasons for wanting the property, and have them determine the fate of disputed items.

If you do need to determine value, your valuation can be based on replacement cost, garage sale value, and even online auction values. If an item is particularly valuable, it might require an appraisal. And some items are a little more complex and require particular mention.

Club Memberships

The club memberships most often in dispute are country clubs and athletic clubs. You might think that after a divorce, spouses wouldn't want to keep going to the same club, but that's not always the case, and often, resolving club memberships is difficult. One option for dividing a membership is for each spouse to create a separate membership, but when the initial membership fee is significant, this could be complicated. In that case, the initial investment made by the marital estate is considered marital property and the spouse not keeping the membership should be reimbursed for the marital share. If the initial fee has increased since it was purchased, the current initial fee is an indicator of fair market value.

In friendly divorces, I've seen spouses agree that the nonmember spouse could continue to use the member-spouse's country club membership, with the nonmember reimbursing the former spouse for charges incurred at the clubhouse.

Frequent-Flier Miles

The value of a frequent-flier mile depends upon the value of the ticket purchased with it. How much it's worth in exchange for a ticket, in turn, is determined by the distance, date and time of travel, and destination, so the monetary value can vary from 1 cent per mile to 5 cents per mile.

More and more airlines are starting to divide frequent-flier accounts, but many still won't, which means that the miles stay with the spouse whose name is on the account. Remember that the account holder can usually use miles to obtain travel for someone else. So, the non-account spouse could be awarded a certain number of airline tickets or a certain number of miles that the account-holder spouse must purchase or redeem for the other spouse when asked to do so. If the account-holder spouse doesn't want to deal with these future transactions, you could try to figure out a monetary value, but it will have to be a fairly arbitrary amount, and it will be hard for the buying spouse to keep from overpaying. One online resource for valuing miles is www.cashformymiles.com.

Credit Card Rewards, Points, Cash-Back Benefits

Credit card companies offer a variety of benefit programs, usually involving rewards, points, or cash-back features. The starting place is to look at the most recent credit card statement, which usually displays the balance of such benefits. Cash-back balances are easy to determine from the statement. The value of points or rewards is tricky. They can be hard to value, and some companies will not divide them in a divorce situation, which leaves you to agree upon a method to allocate them between you and your spouse. Some couples even agree to use the benefits solely for their children or to contribute them, when possible, to a charity.

Your starting point is to contact the card company to find out if their policies allow for splitting the benefits between you and your spouse. If that is a no-go, check out www.thepointsguy.com or search for other current online resources for online valuations of various rewards and points.

Season Tickets to Cultural or Sporting Events

You might divide season tickets by each taking a certain number of tickets for the games or concerts, or by having one spouse buy out the other's interest. You might assume that the face value of a ticket determines its value at divorce, but that's not always the case. Many season tickets for college and professional sporting events include fees and contributions far in excess of actual ticket prices. For example, some sports teams require a buyer to pay for charters, licenses, premiums, or hefty membership fees before being eligible to purchase season tickets. These buy-in costs should be included in calculating value, and the spouse not keeping the original seats should be reimbursed for the value of the initial or current seasonal outlay, either dollar for dollar or on a prorated event basis.

Art, Antiques, and Collectibles

By the time they are 50 or older, many people have amassed collections of something or other along the way. This includes collections of art, Dickens Christmas villages, guns, cars, vintage clothing, baseball cards, antique furniture, stamps, or coins—even LPs and 8-track tapes. The value of collectibles often escapes serious consideration in divorce, but I encourage you to consider the items that might be in your glass display case, garage, or safe deposit box.

Valuing Art and Collections

The popularity of eBay, Etsy, Craigslist, and the Antiques Roadshow can give you an idea of the value of collectibles and how many willing buyers are out there. The Internet offers a wide range of sites that will provide suggestions of value, and for some items, like commercially viable art or antiques, it is easy to research value that way. Art commanding large price tags should have a provenance—a written history of ownership—that confirms its authenticity. If you receive valuable art in the divorce, be sure you also get each work's provenance and purchase receipt.

Homeowners' insurance policies with endorsements for valuable items, especially when they're based on appraisals done when the owner purchased the insurance, can sometimes provide indicators of value.

If you don't have any of these helpful sources of information, another way to approach valuation is to start with the original cost of the item and then increase the value by the average inflation rate since it was acquired. You can find inflation rates at www.usinflationcalculator.com. These calculations might not reflect current value, but this type of calculation could be a starting point for negotiations. Depending on how valuable the items are, you're sometimes better off compromising, even if you think you lose a little, because the loss will likely be less than the cost of hiring an appraiser.

Finding an Appraiser

If you need a personal property appraisal during your divorce, check any of these established appraisal associations and organizations:

American Society of Appraisers (ASA)—represents all disciplines of appraisers, not just artwork. www.appraisers.org

Appraisers Association of America (AAA)—the oldest nonprofit association of personal property appraisers, recognized as the authority for setting standards and regulation of the profession. Members are certified and appraise fine and decorative arts, jewelry, and household contents. www.appraisersassoc.org, and

Art Dealers Association of America Art Appraisals (ADAA)—used by collectors and museums to value important works of art. ADAA appraisals are known for their acceptance record with IRS and their professional quality. www.artdealers.org.

Consider segregating items that have extraordinary value and for which a market might exist.

One more way to estimate the value of art, antiques, and collectibles is to have a commercial establishment estimate values for jewelry, stamps, coins, and so on. They might charge fees for doing so, but the cost might be less than you'd pay a certified appraiser.

Dividing Collections

High-end personal property in these categories is usually awarded to the spouse who is the collector or who has the greatest attachment to the items. If you're the noncollector spouse, you can negotiate to receive cash or other assets in exchange for your share of the value. The burden will probably fall on you to establish value, so take the time to gather the information and ensure you get full value on your share of collectible items.

Pets

Don't forget the pets. Our furry family members are technically personal property under the law, even though their value is personal and subjective (unless your pet is a valuable breed). If you think pets escape the conflicts of division, let me set you straight. Pets often play an outsized role in the divorce tug-of-war more often than you might assume. My office parking lot was frequently the exchange location for a number of ugly dogs and grouchy cats, and my clients always came up to my office to cry about the situation or to thank me.

According to a 2014 survey of the American Academy of Matrimonial Lawyers, 27% of the lawyers surveyed noted an increase in pet custody cases during the preceding five years; 88% of those disputed cases involved dogs. With many Americans adopting pets during the pandemic, pet custody cases will likely increase during these stressful times.

Because pets have been treated as personal property in the divorce context, judges would not determine their custody in contested divorce cases until recently. Since 2017, four states have enacted laws that allow a judge to rule on pet custody: Alaska, California, Illinois, and New Hampshire. Similar legislation is pending in Rhode Island,

Pennsylvania, and Washington, D.C. In other states, some judges treat pets differently from material possessions and acknowledged the intrinsic emotional value of pets. Still, despite this progress, these "enlightened" states' courts do not have authority to order "petimony," to order or supervise visitation, or to enforce custody orders. And if the pet were brought into the marriage by one spouse, the court will likely award the pet to that spouse as that spouse's separate property.

The relevant evidence of a pet custody case includes the following factors: who cares for the pet's daily needs, nutrition, training, grooming, and exercise; the home environment of each party; each party's financial ability to provide for the pet; who acquired the pet; and other factors involving the creature's best interests. This approach to determining custody is a hybrid of traditional "best interests" standards for children and the "best for all concerned" equitable standard for some forms of property.

Divorced spouses have been known to share custody of their pets, settling issues concerning custody, visitation schedules, and even pet support. While you won't get a judge to order pet support, you and your spouse could reach such an agreement (sometimes called a "petimony contract") as part of the divorce settlement. But if you and your spouse don't agree on who will keep a pet, you might not get much help from the judge. Some judges simply won't spend their time making decisions about animals, and instead order the parties to figure it out.

Special Treatment for Pets

Protecting the rights to and of pets is also apparent in other legal arenas related to family law:

- A type of premarital agreement called a "pup nup" is a contract addressing what happens to the pet if the couple divorces.
- Pet owners who are planning their estate (writing wills or trusts) may specify that a trust be established at the death of the survivor, which will provide for the care of a pet and its offspring. This practice is validated by the Uniform Probate Code.

While pets might be considered property, no other form of property has laws that protect it against cruelty or has public advocates such as humane societies. Other living beings—slaves, women, children—were also considered to be property at one time, and those views were slow to change, too. Nevertheless, our pets are the only assets that provide us longtime companionship during and after the dismantling of a marriage—a value that defies a spreadsheet.

A Major Accomplishment

Having assessed all of their property, it was common for clients to tell me, "I didn't know I had so much stuff!" Some clients even started to look forward to downsizing. Others focused on what they could and could not live without. Completing an inventory of assets and determining what you want to negotiate for is a major accomplishment, so pat yourself on the back, but not for too long. Now that the asset side of the ledger is filled in, we will forge ahead through debts and taxes.

The Bad News: Debts and Taxes

Until now, we've dealt with the plus side of the spreadsheet—your assets. But the spreadsheet has a negative side, and liabilities are equally important to an analysis of the marital estate. Debts, obligations, and liabilities are simply three words to describe the same thing: Your marital estate owes somebody money.

Just like marital assets, every marital debt must be identified, characterized, valued, and divided. But your control over what happens in the area is more limited. Your divorce is between you and your spouse—from a legal perspective, no other parties are involved. This means other parties aren't controlled by agreements you make in your divorce. The Internal Revenue Service, your mortgage company, the lender on your automobile, your landlord, and other creditors are not parties; the court doesn't have control over them, and they don't sign on to your settlement agreement or court decree.

As a result, no matter how a marital debt is assigned in the divorce, if the spouse who takes on the debt doesn't pay it, the creditor could look to the other spouse for payment. Yes, even if that person isn't supposed to be responsible for the debt.

You can try to mitigate this possibility by making sure your divorce decree includes an indemnity provision (also called a hold harmless clause) that gives you the right to sue your former spouse to get back money you paid on a debt that was not supposed to be yours. The downside, of course, is that between attorneys' fees and costs, not to mention personal aggravation, suing is an expensive proposition. And if your former spouse did not pay the debt in the first place, what makes you think that you will be paid later? It's far better to divide your debts in ways that minimize the chances of this undesirable scenario.

Identifying and Characterizing Debts

The chart in Chapter 5 alerted you to the categories of debts that you should be sure to identify when you're preparing a complete list of your obligations. If your spouse has incurred debts that you're not aware of, you might learn about those from your credit report (see "Credit Reports," below). It's important to be sure you've captured all of your obligations, so that nothing comes out of the woodwork after the divorce is final.

The next question is whether the debts are part of the marital estate or are the separate debt of one spouse. Whether the debts were incurred during the marriage is only the beginning of the analysis. In some states, just being married to someone who incurs debt during the marriage isn't enough to make you automatically liable for that debt. Only if you sign onto the obligation will you be held responsible for paying it back.

Other states assume joint liability for certain kinds of debts, usually for "necessaries"—housing, food, health care, and clothing—regardless of whose name is on the dotted line. And some community property states regard all obligations incurred during marriage to be each spouse's obligation, even when the debt was incurred without one spouse's knowledge or consent and regardless of its purpose. In these states, marital property could be seized to pay one spouse's debts regardless of when the debts were incurred, so you might even be held responsible for debts that your spouse incurred before you were married.

Credit Reports

Even if you think you know about all of your debts, it is worth obtaining credit reports for you and your spouse. If your spouse resists, talk with your attorney. Everyone is entitled to one free credit report each year, available at www.annualcreditreport.com. (If you want your credit score, however, you might have to pay for a report from one of the three major credit bureaus.) Credit reports provide important information, including how current your bills are, the identities of your creditors, and whether your spouse has applied for credit recently (evidence of a recent application could lead to an eye-opening discovery that a spouse has a "secret" credit card).

The marital estate could also become responsible for one spouse's premarriage debts if you use joint funds to pay part of the debt during the marriage, or if the debt is mixed between premarital and postmarital expenses (for example, when you have a credit card balance before marriage and you use the card for expenses during marriage). The bottom line is that how liabilities are treated in your jurisdiction will seriously affect how you negotiate the division of your marital estate. A lawyer's advice on this topic is essential.

Types of Debts and How to Divide Them

There are different types of debts, and it's likely your marital estate includes more than one.

Secured Debts

Secured debts are attached to a specific asset that serves as collateral for the debt and that the lender can retrieve if the borrower doesn't make good on the debt. Real estate mortgages and auto loans are the most common examples of secured debts; business entities often secure debt with equipment and inventory.

Problems brew when the underlying asset is awarded to one spouse and the secured debt is awarded to the other.

> **EXAMPLE:** Spouse A gets the car and Spouse B is ordered to pay the car loan. B does so for a year; then falls on hard times and stops paying. The lender is entitled to repossesses the vehicle parked in A's driveway—a year after A thought the divorce was settled and done with.

The best way to avoid this situation is to rework the property division spreadsheet so that the person who gets the car also gets the attendant debt, along with other assets that will equalize the division. If you are getting the car, for example, you could either refinance the debt in your own name, or leave it as a joint debt but take responsibility for the payments. Either way, you are responsible for it and don't have to worry about what your ex-spouse does or doesn't do. Another option is for you to take on the car note while your ex pays alimony, so you could afford to make your payments; a third is to have your spouse pay you the amount of the payment each month so you could then send it to the lender. If your spouse fails to send the money to you, you still have the option of making the payment and then recovering the money from your ex. But none of these options guarantees that you won't end up footing the bill for a debt your spouse was supposed to pay—only refinancing or keeping the debt yourself will do that.

The other most common secured debt is a mortgage on real estate; the issues of the family home and its mortgage are covered in detail in Chapter 6, "The Big-Ticket Items: Your Home, Your Retirement, and Your Family Business."

Unsecured Debt

Most of your marital debts are unsecured—things like personal loans both spouses signed for, credit cards, and miscellaneous debts like the bill from your dentist. When it comes to credit card debts and loans, the same considerations discussed in "Secured Debts," above, apply. The very best way to protect yourself is to retire the debts at the time of divorce. If you are selling your home or another high-value asset, you and your spouse could use some of the cash to pay off these joint debts, or you could use other available cash. That way you both walk away from the divorce secure that you are free of joint obligations.

If you don't have adequate funds for that and you have joint credit card accounts on which each of you is liable, what can you do? First, close the accounts so no more charges can be made. (Closing the account not only avoids unwelcome charges by the other spouse, but keeps the bookkeeping cleaner.) Credit card companies will not remove a spouse from the account if that spouse has liability for the charges, but they will allow you to put a "hard close" on the account so that neither of you can make new charges. If you want to retain your own credit card with that company, they will require you to open a new account in your name alone.

Next, divide the joint accounts between you, with one person taking the VISA and the other the Discover card, and so on. Assigning each account to one or the other means you'll at least have full control over the accounts that are yours. Your divorce decree must clearly state that you are liable for paying certain accounts and that you will hold your spouse "harmless" from having to pay those debts; and vice versa for the accounts assigned to your spouse.

Dividing and isolating credit accounts is important for several reasons. First, you are protecting yourself should your spouse file bankruptcy, because this decree language makes the debts nondischargeable "domestic support obligations." The importance of this is covered below in "Bankruptcy." Second, even if there's no bankruptcy crisis, if a creditor for whom your spouse is responsible comes knocking on your door for payment, you could show them the decree language providing for a separation of liability. This evidence of your lack of involvement in—lack of control over—the account since the divorce might give you some leverage and work in your favor.

Do not share responsibility for paying on the same account (for example, alternating payment months or sharing each monthly payment). Doing so keeps you entangled with the account (and with your former spouse) and takes away any leverage you might otherwise have to resist the creditors if they come after you. And if your spouse doesn't pay, you'll be stuck with paying the whole bill.

Finally, when dividing your debts make sure that your divorce decree includes the specific dollar amount still owed on the card at the time of the divorce, as well as a requirement that each of you will remain entitled to receive copies of all statements. This way, you can monitor the account.

Households often use their credit cards to "auto pay" periodic bills for utilities and insurance. Be sure you have identified all "auto-pays" that are charged to credit cards.

The reality of marriage is that you've tied your financial future to another person; the reality of divorce is that it's not easy to sever those ties. Once you've protected yourself as described in this section, you just have to hope that your spouse will be responsible and meet all assigned obligations.

Make Sure You Know Who's Responsible

Some states recognize a difference between being a signatory on a card and being jointly liable for charges made with the card, so make sure you learn who's actually liable for the card's debt. If the credit card company issued the card based on the income of both spouses, then it is a joint debt. If a credit card was issued in one spouse's name, based solely on that spouse's income, the second spouse might not be jointly liable even if a secondary card was issued in that second spouse's name. Depending on which spouse you are, this could work in your favor or against you—but either way, it's important to know the answer.

Contingent Debts and Guarantees

Contingent debts and guarantees are "sleeper" debts, often flying under the radar at divorce. These are debts you promise to take on only if the primary borrower defaults—you are not the borrower, but a cosigner or guarantor. Student loans are a typical example. You might have signed as a guarantor of the loan, and if your child does not pay the debt, the lender could look to you for payment: You are second in line. This type of debt is also common in the business context. When a new business partnership lacks a credit history, the bank will require all the general partners to sign personally on the debt as guarantors before providing a line of credit. Another sleeper obligation is agreeing to be a guarantor on a residential or commercial lease—if the tenant doesn't pay rent or cover other financial obligations, you're on the hook.

Debts that are contingent hinge on events that have not yet occurred and might never occur. In the case of a guarantee, the event would be the default of the primary borrower. Or, assume you were at fault in an auto accident and your auto insurance coverage did not cover all of the other driver's damage claim. That other driver might decide to come after you for the balance. Your liability is contingent upon your insurance carrier not paying and also contingent upon the other driver deciding to pursue collection from you. Even though you might not owe any money on them now, these liabilities should be identified and allocated in the divorce decree.

Bankruptcy

The prospect of you, your spouse, or both of you having to jointly declare bankruptcy is one you should discuss with your attorney as soon as you consider it a real possibility. Your lawyer will probably give you the wise advice to consult a bankruptcy attorney who can help you assess your options. This assessment might influence how you resolve your divorce. It's not pleasant to think about, but proactive bankruptcy planning is worth every penny you spend on it.

Personal bankruptcy can take one of two paths: Chapter 13, known as payment plan bankruptcy, allows for both secured and unsecured debts to be discharged (wiped out) after the debtor has made regular payments under an approved plan for three to five years. Another type, Chapter 7, allows for complete discharge of most debts right away. Chapter 7 was used more often by individuals before the Reform Act passed. Now, Chapter 13 is the most commonly used form of bankruptcy for individual debtors.

All is not bad news in the bankruptcy legislation, at least if you are getting a divorce. The Reform Act reinforces rules that prevent an ex-spouse from escaping divorce-related support obligations through bankruptcy. While a bankruptcy discharge keeps creditors from attempting to collect debts at a later time, the new bankruptcy law makes it harder to discharge debts that arise from a family law case, including alimony and, in some cases, promises to repay marital debts.

Below are examples of how the new bankruptcy rules affect divorcing spouses:

Families first, creditors later. Domestic support obligations have the status of a first priority claim and must be paid under a bankruptcy plan before the court will grant a discharge. These priority obligations must be part of a court order or separation agreement; they include alimony, maintenance, and support payable to a spouse, former spouse, parent, or child (or someone on behalf of the child, including a government agency).

Changes in Bankruptcy Laws

Before 2005, bankruptcy courts began with a presumption in favor of granting the relief requested by the debtor, consistent with the notion that bankruptcy was intended to provide a fresh start to honest debtors. Then Congress passed the Bankruptcy Abuse Prevention and Consumer Protection Act (the "Reform Act"), removing the presumption and requiring the court to inquire into the appropriateness of the relief requested in every case. The bottom line is that although it is harder to receive a bankruptcy discharge now, it is not at all impossible if you qualify. Major bankruptcy reform legislation, more favorable to the consumer, has been introduced in Congress but, as of the publication of this edition, it has not gained traction.

Support also includes a third-party debt when a spouse is ordered to pay it and not hold the other spouse liable—so if your final judgment orders your spouse to pay certain debts, such as credit cards, that obligation can't be discharged in bankruptcy.

Support payments must continue. Normally, creditors must suspend their efforts at collection while the bankruptcy case is ongoing. Known as the "automatic stay," this pause does not apply to domestic support obligations, which can be collected even during the bankruptcy.

If not for this rule, the automatic stay that is created upon the filing of a bankruptcy action would immediately protect the debtor-spouse from collection efforts by the recipient-spouse. The recipient-spouse would remain unsupported until the bankruptcy is closed, dismissed, or the debtor is discharged.

Exempt property might be fair game for support obligations. Each state and federal law has a list of assets or items that a debtor gets to keep in bankruptcy, such as tools needed to perform a trade, motor vehicle (up to a certain value), some household appliances and furnishings, and retirement accounts. However, even property that state or federal law says is exempt from being used to satisfy most bankruptcy debts could be used to satisfy domestic support obligations.

RESOURCE

The New Bankruptcy: Will It Work for You? By Cara O'Neill (Nolo).

Don't Forget the Tax Consequences

Tax law permeates almost every aspect of a divorce. It influences the value of assets and can create formidable liabilities. Although your divorce attorney will advise you on the tax issues that are important in your divorce—and help you find a CPA or divorce financial professional if need be—in the end, you are the one who signs the tax return and the one who negotiates for assets and the tax consequences that come with them. So it's important that you have at least a basic understanding of the far-reaching role tax laws could play in your divorce.

On December 22, 2017, the U.S. Congress passed the extensive Tax Cuts and Jobs Act. Most of it was in effect beginning tax year 2018; however, many provisions go into effect later, while others automatically terminate after a period of time. Gone are personal exemptions, alimony deductions, and local and state tax deductions over $10,000, while the individual standard deduction is increased to $12,400—just to identify a few changes.

CAUTION

You cannot assume that because you relied on the advice of a divorce attorney you will be relieved of responsibility for taxes, specifically tax penalties. In fact, federal tax court decisions in the past few years have made it clear that reliance on a divorce attorney might not be a defense to assessment of a penalty, especially if the attorney doesn't have specialized knowledge about tax consequences.

The discussion here is limited to federal taxation, because state tax laws vary a great deal. Be sure to check with your CPA or attorney about state tax laws that might have a bearing on your case in addition to the rules discussed below.

Joint or Separate Liability?

The vast majority of married couples file joint returns, which each spouse signs. Joint returns often result in the couple's paying lower taxes than they would if each spouse filed a separate return. But there's also an advantage for the IRS: Filing a joint tax return means that both filers are on the hook—you and your spouse are jointly and severally liable, meaning that the IRS can hold either or both of you responsible for taxes owed, and if one spouse doesn't pay, the other is responsible for the full amount.

Past Tax Liability

If you owe back taxes and you're aware of the amount owed, then the back taxes are treated as just another debt and assigned to one spouse or the other, or split between the spouses. But there's also the possibility that you could have additional tax liability in the future for tax returns you filed when you were married. Although you must file your income taxes on time, the IRS has three years to audit a tax return and 10 years to collect any taxes that are deemed owed after the audit. (If fraud is involved, there's no time limit at all.)

Some couples know at the time of divorce that a potential tax bill is hovering in the background, because an audit is in process or has been threatened. Others might believe there is no exposure. But the IRS could come knocking with an audit as many as three years after the divorce. Then what happens?

It's common for a divorce decree to say which spouse is responsible for federal income taxes incurred during the marriage, and to indemnify the other spouse. This is not binding on the IRS, but it means that if the spouse released from liability ends up paying, that spouse could sue the one who was supposed to pay. However, as with the indemnity provisions described in "Types of Debts and How to Divide Them," above, the right to sue might provide little comfort as the person who didn't pay the taxes might never pay back the other spouse, either.

Nonetheless, it's worth including in your settlement agreement and judgment. If one spouse has a greater ability to earn income, it is fair to place the entire tax burden on that spouse, assuming you could trust that the spouse will indeed pay the taxes (and has the income to do it). One way to protect the other spouse is to estimate the tax liability and agree to put assets into a trust specifically earmarked for paying the taxes. If the tax liability never materializes, the spouse who had the responsibility to pay ends up keeping those assets.

If you can't come to an agreement about how to allocate liability for income tax debts, you'll have to ask a judge to decide that issue. The judge knows that an order for one spouse to pay future tax liability is not binding on the IRS. And if both parties benefited from the income that generated the tax obligation, as is usually the case, judges tend to order spouses to share the taxes owed, including interest and penalties. Even when one spouse is guilty of tax evasion and is the one who prepared the joint return, the liability might be assigned to both spouses. Courts view marriage as an economic partnership, and often believe that if wealth was acquired through unlawful means and both spouses benefit from it, both should share in the consequences.

However, the innocent spouse rules might protect a spouse who innocently signs returns prepared by a spouse who exercised control over the marital finances. An innocent spouse could be protected from tax liability provided:

- the spouses filed a joint return
- a substantial understatement of tax is attributable to grossly erroneous errors made by the spouse who prepared the return
- the innocent spouse establishes "lack of knowledge," and
- it is "inequitable" to impose the tax on the uninvolved spouse.

The IRS or a tax court, not the divorce court, decides whether the innocent spouse rules apply. To avail yourself of this rule, you need a tax specialist, but you could learn more about it in IRS Publication 971, *Innocent Spouse Relief,* available at www.irs.gov.

If the divorce decree says who is responsible for past taxes, it should also say which spouse is responsible for maintaining relevant records and for how long, which spouse chooses the CPA or tax attorney who helps with amended returns or audits, who pays for those services, and which spouse has authority to settle with the IRS. It should also address the possibility of a refund and say who receives it if there is one.

Taxes in the Year of Divorce

Divorcing couples often face questions about whether to file jointly or separately while their divorce is in process. You can file a joint federal income tax return only if you have been married for the entire tax year, so if your divorce isn't finalized on December 31 of a given year, you could file jointly for that year (and conversely, even if you get a final judgment on December 28, you could not file jointly that year). If you have reasons to want to file jointly, you could wait to finalize the divorce until after January 1.

Often, spouses are separated for the entire tax year before their divorce is finalized and decide to file separate returns for that year. Although they're filing separately, there's still a question about who should be responsible for taxes for that year. The biggest issue is how to allocate income for tax purposes, when spouses might not be sharing income as they did when living together. One option is for each spouse to pay taxes on that spouse's income only; another is for each to pay taxes on half of the combined income (if you live in some community property states, that's what you're required to do). You could ask a tax preparer to work out which way is more advantageous for both of you and then make your decisions.

You might also need to decide who will claim deductions for property tax and mortgage interest payments. Often, the person in the higher tax bracket could gain significant advantage from these deductions, and if you agree to even things up through a cash payment or moving something else around on the division spreadsheet, then you could join together against the common enemy, the IRS, in a win–win situation. You should also address, in your written settlement agreement, the topics described in "Past Tax Liability," above: who maintains records, selects tax return preparers, and handles refunds.

Being creative about who's responsible for taxes could help you create an equitable property settlement—but be sure your agreements are in line with IRS regulations. Again, rely on the guidance of your tax experts.

> ⚠️ **CAUTION**
>
> **Watch out for estimated tax payments as a way to hide assets.** It is possible for a sneaky self-employed spouse to hide money with the IRS by overpaying estimated taxes during the divorce year, with the expectation of receiving—and keeping—a big refund that the other spouse never knows about. Being vigilant in the discovery phase of your divorce (see Chapter 4) should uncover this stunt.

How Taxes Affect Value

Before looking at tax issues related to specific assets, it behooves you to have a brief encounter with two important tax concepts: Section 1041 transfers and tax basis.

Section 1041

Section 1041 of the Internal Revenue Code provides that transfers between spouses as part of a divorce are not taxable events. This means that even if an asset like your home has increased in value since it was purchased—the relevant question for tax liability—the transfer made between spouses as part of the divorce is exempt from income tax. Nor are capital gains taxes or gift taxes generated in the context of a divorce.

However, Section 1041 has an enormous exception: If a third party (someone other than the two spouses) is involved in the transaction, then Section 1041 does not apply. The most common example is when spouses sell the family home to a third party; income from such a sale would be taxable gain (subject to the residence exclusions discussed in "Taxes and the Family Home," below). Here are two other examples of taxable transactions at divorce.

EXAMPLE 1: Spouse A is involved in a closely held corporation. The value of the corporate stock is significant, and Spouse B is awarded the value of half the marital shares. The corporation has a buy-sell agreement that provides that only certain people could be owners of shares, and Spouse B is not one of those people, so Spouse B can't keep the shares. Bylaws also require that the corporation be the party who redeems (buys) those shares awarded to Spouse B, instead of Spouse A actually making the purchase. Even if there were no such bylaws, the company might step in to purchase the shares if Spouse A did not have the money. If the company pays Spouse B $100,000 for the shares of this corporation, that is a taxable event because it's not solely between the spouses, as required for a 1041 transfer. Spouse B will receive less than $100,000 due to the reduction for taxes because the corporation, not Spouse A, is the purchaser.

EXAMPLE 2: In order to equalize the property division, Spouse A agrees to pay Spouse B the sum of $100,000 over a 10-year period. Because Spouse B is smart, she demands 5% interest on the payout. She assumes the total payment is tax free because Section 1041 makes divorce property transfers a nontaxable event. Wrong assumption—principal is tax free under Section 1041, but the interest income is not.

Basis of an Asset

The concept of basis is an important one to understand, as it is the starting point for calculating tax on any type of sale. Basis is the original purchase price of an asset for purposes of calculating tax-related gains and losses. (This general definition will suffice for our purposes, though tax basis can be more complex when dealing with business assets, or assets acquired through inheritance.) To calculate gains, losses, and taxes on the sales proceeds of an item requires knowing the basis of the item and its value at sale. The difference between those two numbers is the equity or profit, and is taxable (or, if the difference is negative, may be deductible). The basis of property could make a really significant difference in its value to you, so be sure you know what it is before making decisions about what you'll keep.

> **EXAMPLE:** At different times during your marriage, you purchase 100 shares of ABC Company for $50 each and then 100 shares for $100 each. At divorce, you are dividing the stock, which is now worth $150 per share. If you sell both batches of stock at the same time for the same price of $150 per share, then for each share you bought at $50, $100 would be taxed, because that's the difference between the basis ($50) and the sale price ($150). For each share having a $100 basis, $50 would be taxed. Assume that you are in the 15% tax bracket: The $50 basis stock would net you $85 per share and the $100 basis stock would net $42 per share. All assets are not created equal!

To avoid the problem shown in this example, divide stock or brokerage accounts proportionately, with each spouse sharing in all stock. In other words, don't award the AT&T stock to one spouse and the Verizon stock to the other; divide the shares of each so that each spouse gets some AT&T and some Verizon. This spreads the tax risks and advantages when stocks have various tax bases.

Basis isn't the only thing that could affect the amount of taxes owed. The length of time you own an asset could dictate the tax rate that applies to its sale—the ordinary income tax rate or the more beneficial capital gains rate, which can be as low as 0%, 15%, or 20%, depending on your taxable income (tax bracket) and filing status. Be aware that the capital gains rate is back in the political arena, where its fate is subject to change.

Taxes and Retirement Accounts

What if a marital estate has $200,000 in cash and $200,000 in a 401(k) retirement account, and the spouses agree that Spouse A will receive the cash and Spouse B will receive the retirement account. Is this an equal division? No.

Here's why: The money in the retirement account has not been taxed yet—Spouse B's contributions were made from a paycheck on a pretax basis. When Spouse B takes out the money from the 401(k) at some point in the future, Spouse B will have to pay taxes on that distribution. The cash that has been awarded to Spouse A comprises dollars that have already been taxed, so Spouse A will get to keep it all.

To resolve this disparity, you could calculate the present value of the taxes that will be due in the future, and compensate Spouse B. But if Spouse B is many years from taking a distribution from a 401(k), this is a very speculative calculation, because it's difficult to know what Spouse B's income tax bracket will be or the amount of the distributions. A better solution might be for each spouse to take 50% of the cash and 50% of the 401(k). This approach has each spouse bearing an equal risk of the unknown, and each one has the benefit of receiving an asset that will earn income tax free until distribution.

Taxes and the Family Home

For many tax policy reasons (along with political considerations), personal residences are blessed with tax advantages. For example, property taxes and interest on mortgage loans are deductible (up to a certain amount), and the capital gains exemption when the residence is sold allows some of the profits on the sale to escape taxation altogether.

The capital gains exemption means that the first $250,000 of profits from the sale of a primary residence is free from taxation for each spouse (increasing to $500,000 if married and filing a joint return). The house must have been owned and used by the taxpayer(s) as a principal residence for two or more years during the five-year period ending on the date of sale, but short temporary absences (vacations, seasonal absences) are counted as periods of use.

If one spouse stays in the home after divorce, but the other spouse receives a share of the equity when the house is sold later, then the second spouse will also be able to shelter up to $250,000 of profit. The nonresident spouse is considered for tax purposes to be using property as a principal residence during any period of ownership while a former spouse lives in the property under a divorce or separation instrument (a settlement agreement or divorce judgment).

If you net more than the excluded amount, the difference will be taxed at the capital gains rate, which is more favorable than your personal rate.

Alimony and Separate Support

The 2017 Tax Cuts and Jobs Act *eliminated* the federal tax deduction for alimony paid pursuant to divorce or separation agreements and decrees executed after December 31, 2018.

The old law's deduction still remains in effect for payments made under pre-2019 agreements—payments made under these agreements continue to be deductible from the payer's taxable income and included in the recipient's gross income (though spouses could always agree that spousal support was neither deductible nor taxable).

The impact of this change in the law will be major—it affects not just the taxation issues, but each side's divorce strategy and how to meet a spouse's support needs. You'll find an expanded discussion regarding alimony in Chapter 10, "Your Financial Survival."

The Health Care Puzzle

or anyone getting divorced, health care is often a significant concern. The U.S. Census Bureau estimates that 30 million Americans are still uninsured. More than half of the personal bankruptcies filed in the United States result from the inability to pay medical bills, and 80% of those people had some form of medical insurance. These numbers increase daily, and no divorcing spouse wants to join those statistics. This chapter will address concerns about health care after divorce and provide you with some strategies for putting together the pieces of the health care puzzle, including the pieces added by the Affordable Health Care Act.

Health insurance is a much bigger issue now than it was for you in your twenties, thirties, and forties. A major concern for most people is keeping the insurance they have or finding a way to obtain affordable health care coverage once the divorce is final. Unless you have a very secure job and employer-provided group health coverage, or cost is not a concern, you're going to find that health care coverage is an issue you must grapple with during your divorce. The good news is that pre-existing medical conditions are no longer the wrenching factor they were before January 1, 2014. But the challenges to the constitutionality of the Affordable Care Act continue, including the provision that disallows insurance companies from considering preexisting conditions. For example, the individual mandate in the ACA, which placed a penalty on individuals not having insurance, has been abolished.

With the affordability of health care back on the political football playing field, once again my clients—especially those who have preexisting conditions and who felt relief when the ACA went into effect—are expressing heightened anxiety over budgeting for rising medical expenses. I have few words of comfort, only advice to stay focused during the tumult while examining their options currently available.

Early Warning

If you're insured through your spouse's employment, you have valuable legal rights in terms of keeping that coverage both during and after the divorce. For one thing, in most states, once a divorce is filed, neither spouse is allowed to make any changes in insurance coverage or benefi-ciaries without the other spouse's consent. What this means is that if your spouse hasn't already filed, you may want to make sure you don't delay in getting the divorce on file, so these restraining orders are in place and you aren't blindsided by some kind of change in your insurance status.

If you are concerned about your spouse either intentionally dropping your dependent insurance coverage or failing to pay premiums, tell your attorney immediately. Few things are more frightening than discovering, in the middle of a divorce, that health insurance coverage has lapsed. Even if your state doesn't have automatic restraining orders, your attorney may be able to obtain a court order requiring your spouse to make timely insurance premium payments and to keep you covered until the divorce is settled.

Divorce and Your Health—More Questions Than Answers

A 2005 study in the *Archives of General Psychiatry* concluded that hostile marriages may have negative physical and mental effects on both spouses and that couples who argue often take more time to heal from (physical) wounds than those in less hostile relationships. It was reported that con-stant marital conflict may cause changes in specific proteins that increase the risk of diseases such as cancer, arthritis, heart disease, Type 2 diabetes, and depression. *In other words, maybe divorce will improve your health.*

Another research study, funded by the Household Income and Labour Dynamics in Australia, considered a sample of 2,300 Australians over age 60. One finding was that older divorced, widowed, and single women reported significantly better general health than their married counterparts. On the other hand, a man's health appears to be unaffected by his marital status. *Maybe divorce will improve your health, if you are female.*

A 2009 research study at the University of Chicago and Johns Hopkins University showed that divorce and widowhood might have a detrimental impact on health. This study of 8,652 people between the ages of 51 and 61 found that divorced or widowed people have 20% more chronic health conditions than married people. The chronic conditions include diabetes, heart disease, and cancer. *Maybe divorce will not improve your health.*

Be sure to investigate your health insurance options as soon as possible. It takes time to learn the terminology and details of available plan benefits and to compare costs. And because premiums are one of your largest budget items, you should know what to expect before you negotiate final figures for property division and alimony. When your divorce ends, your settlement agreement or divorce decree should address both spouses' obligations regarding health insurance coverage.

Group and Individual Coverage

In general, you can obtain health insurance from the following six places:

1. **Private market.** You still have the option to purchase an individual policy directly, especially if price is no object.

2. **Employer-provided group insurance.** This might be the least expensive type of insurance. If you're covered through your own secure employment, then you won't spend too much time on this issue in your divorce (unless you also cover your spouse, in which case you will have to comply with COBRA rules should your spouse elect continuing coverage). If your coverage is through your spouse's employer, you should carefully read the sections on COBRA and ACA coverage below, so you can make a smart decision on whether to take advantage of COBRA.

3. **ACA Health Insurance Exchanges.** These portals might be the most affordable coverage for individuals and small businesses (with up to 50 employees).

4. **COBRA continuation coverage.** This is for spouses who have received health coverage as a dependent on the employee-spouse's insurance plan; after COBRA terminates, the coverage may be converted to an individual policy.

5. **Medicare.** Available for those aged 65 and above.

6. **Medicaid.** Technically not a form of health insurance, Medicaid is a public, state-run program that provides limited hospital and medical services for people who have certain medical conditions, low income, or limited resources.

Types of Plans

If you have not been in the market for insurance in the last few years, you'll be amazed at the variety of options among individual insurance policies. Lower-priced plans place constraints on hospital and physician access, and more expensive plans give you greater access.

Some plans have no deductibles, no copays, and no waiting periods, while others offer many health services under one umbrella, including dental, prescription, and vision, along with general medical insurance. Preferred provider plans (PPOs), health maintenance organization plans (HMOs), catastrophic plans, and many others offer variations on coverage. Additionally, the Affordable Care Act created plan levels, including Bronze, Silver, Gold, Platinum, and Catastrophic, which provide coverage at competitive rates, as discussed in "Health Insurance Under the Affordable Care Act," below.

You could purchase an individual insurance policy directly from an insurance company or, if you have access, through mass purchasing groups, such as credit unions and professional or trade associations. For example, the American Association for Retired Persons (AARP) offers plans for those 50 and older (go to www.aarp.org, look under "Health and Wellness," and follow the links for individual health insurance information). Be careful with group plans that are not employment related, though—especially plans through trade associations that often see enormous premium hikes over a very short period of time. Don't buy trade association group insurance unless the association has been around for a very long time and the coverage is with a reputable company. And try to talk with people who've been covered under the plan for at least five years, to find out how their experience has been with regard to cost, claims, service, and consistency.

You can begin your insurance investigation on your own using the Internet, or contact an insurance agent (agents represent one company) or broker (brokers represent multiple companies). Consumer-oriented insurance websites include: www.healthinsurance.org and www.affordable-health-insurance-plans.org. You will get quotes for insurance as well as information. Two additional helpful websites are www.healthcare.gov and www.obamacarefacts.com.

Your Health Information

If you have applied for health, life, or disability insurance coverage in the last seven years, and especially if you have been denied coverage, you'll need to request your Medical Information Bureau (MIB) report. MIB is a membership corporation whose members are insurance companies. Its information bank helps insurers detect fraud by maintaining centralized records about people who seek insurance—very much like a credit report does for financial matters. Under the Fair Credit Reporting Act, you are entitled to access the information in your consumer health files. Specifically, you are entitled to one free MIB report annually. Not only will you see what is reported about your health conditions, but you have the right to question that information and correct it if necessary. The website for MIB is www.mib.com. The toll-free phone number for requesting a report is 866-692-6901.

Even if you are Internet savvy, you might want to consider talking to an independent agent at an early stage in your investigation. The agent can alert you to the types of provisions that are particularly important for you and teach you a bit about insurance terminology, which will make you more sure-footed if you go back to Internet research. Consider checking with the National Association of Health Underwriters, which provides a listing of licensed health insurance agents at www.nahu.org. But remember that insurance agents and brokers are salespeople first and foremost—their interest is in selling you a policy. Sometimes, they are not even particularly well-versed about the terms of the policies they're selling.

If you find that some provisions are especially important to you, insist on reviewing the actual policy language before you buy the policy. And talk to more than one insurance agent or broker—each represents only one or a few companies, and you want to learn about what's being offered by as many insurers as you can. When you shop for health insurance coverage, be sure to compare policies of the same type and with the same benefits; otherwise the price differences are meaningless.

Insurance Terms

Here are some terms you will undoubtedly bump into as you look around at health insurance options.

Deductibles. The deductible is a specific amount you must pay before expense reimbursement begins. The higher the deductible, the lower the cost of the plan.

Coinsurance or Copay. This is the percentage split between the individual and the insurer of covered expenses (after deductibles). A common coinsurance level is 20% of the expenses paid by the individual and 80% of the expenses paid by the insurer. The trend, however, is a higher percentage (30% and 40%) for the consumer.

Covered Expense. A covered expense is an eligible expense that will be reimbursed in whole or in part. An example is a doctor's visit. If an expense is covered, that does not automatically mean that you have unlimited coverage of that expense—insurers place limits on what they will reimburse. They may cap allowable payments for a procedure or service (like surgeries), limit the number of visits or days for certain types of care (including home health care), or allow a "reasonable and customary charge," with the balance payable by the consumer.

CAUTION

Honesty is the best policy when applying for a health insurance policy. If you fib and obtain coverage, you could find yourself in major trouble when you file a claim for reimbursement. Fraudulent applications are the most common reason for nonpayment of claims (and can result in cancellation of your insurance, too).

Health Insurance Under the Affordable Care Act

Since January 1, 2014, the Affordable Care Act (ACA) has changed the national landscape of health insurance. One keystone of this legislation is to do away with the cost barrier of preexisting medical conditions. Now, health insurance companies cannot deny you or subject you to harsh premium increases due to preexisting conditions.

Under the ACA, every state must create or participate in a health insurance exchange, a type of insurance marketplace that informs consumers of their available options and helps them shop for coverage. The exchanges are supposed to make it easier and more affordable for individuals and small businesses (with up to 50 employees) to purchase health insurance by promoting choice and competition. States can elect to operate their own exchange or to participate in a multistate exchange. You can use the exchange to find a private insurance plan from a menu of options and to compare costs and types of benefits. If your state does not operate its own exchange, you can purchase a health plan from a multi-state or regional exchange run by a government agency (for example, the federal Department of Health and Human Services).

The following are the five ACA benefit categories, ranging from modest to generous, but each plan must include basic, preventive, and comprehensive medical coverage and prescription drug benefits:

- Bronze: Your health plan pays 60% on average; you pay about 40%.
- Silver: Your health plan pays 70% on average; you pay about 30%.
- Gold: Your health plan pays 80% on average; you pay about 20%.
- Platinum: Your health plan pays 90% on average; you pay about 10%.
- Catastrophic: These plans pay less than 60% of the total average cost of care and are available only to people under age 30 or those who have a hardship exemption.

If you can't afford to purchase a plan in an exchange, you might be eligible for a government subsidy—facilitated by the government-run marketplace—based on your income and family size. And if your individual annual income falls below 400% of the federal poverty level (which comes to $51,040 annual income), you might be eligible to receive a subsidy to help pay for your premiums and out-of-pocket expenses. Online calculators can help you determine if you're eligible for a subsidy or tax credit: www.healthcare.gov; www.obamacarefacts.com; http://kff.org/interactive/subsidy-calculator.

Consumers have certain time periods, known as "Open Enrollment Periods," when they can enroll in the ACA exchanges. The periods' length of time has been reduced from three months to six weeks. Special circumstances (such as loss of coverage due to a divorce) allow individuals to enroll in an exchange outside of the Open Enrollment Periods; these are called "Special Enrollment Periods."

The ACA made many more changes to the health insurance industry. I'll just mention a few. The law prohibits insurers from establishing annual spending caps, limits deductibles, and stops the practice of charging older people premiums ten times higher than what younger insureds are charged. The penalty on those without medical insurance and who did not meet an exemption to the penalty, known as the individual mandate, has been repealed by the Tax Cuts and Jobs Act of 2017; however, some states require that all their residents have insurance coverage (as of this edition, Massachusetts, New Jersey, California, Rhode Island, and District of Columbia have done so).

The ACA provides that all existing health insurance plans must cover approved preventive care and checkups, without charging copayments. The ACA also requires health plans that insure children on a parent's plan to continue the child's coverage to age 26.

The websites at www.healthcare.gov and www.obamacarefacts.com provide links for each state so you can learn about the health care options and exchanges in your geographical area.

Health Savings Accounts and Flexible Savings Accounts

If your income is high enough so that you could benefit from tax deductions, consider opening a health savings account (HSA) with a bank, credit union, insurance company, or other government-approved company. Contributions into an HSA can be made before taxes or deducted from taxable income and can be used to pay qualified medical expenses at any time.

You must have an individual health insurance policy with a high deductible to be eligible for an HSA (you're not eligible if you're on Medicare). This means at least a $1,400 deductible in 2021; the annual out-of-pocket amount (including deductibles and copays) cannot exceed $6,900.

In 2022, you can contribute up to $3,650 per year to your HSA if the account is only for your expenses (not your dependents'). If you are over 55, you are allowed to make an additional "catch-up" contribution of up to $1,000 each year. Check the U.S. Treasury Department's website for current amounts: www.ustreas.gov. Contributions could be made in a lump sum or in smaller amounts at any frequency. You withdraw money when you pay out of pocket for qualified medical expenses. IRS Publication 502, *Medical and Dental Expenses*, provides a partial list of what qualifies.

The contributions roll over year after year, so you will not lose your money if you do not spend it all in one year. If you don't use the money, it grows tax deferred as an IRA does. When you enroll in Medicare upon reaching age 65, you can no longer contribute pretax dollars to an HSA, but you can use your HSA funds for Medicare premiums, deductibles, copays, and coinsurance (but not Medigap supplemental insurance). If you are over 65, you can withdraw the money for nonmedical expenses; you will pay income tax on those withdrawals, but no penalty. If you are under 65, you could withdraw the money for nonmedical expenses, but you will pay income taxes and a 10% penalty.

An FSA (flexible spending arrangement), like an HSA, is a tax-advantaged account that lets you save for "qualified medical expenses." But unlike an HSA, it is part of an employer's offered benefits. Another major difference between these two accounts is an FSA requires you to "use or lose" your contributions; this means that at year's end if money remains in your FSA, you lose it unless your employer offers a rollover option that would allow you to roll over no more than $550 (an IRS-imposed limit for 2021).

> ## Health Savings Accounts and Flexible Savings Accounts (continued)
>
> Here are the mechanics of an FSA: Pretax dollars are deducted from your paycheck in regular amounts; however, you could begin immediately to draw on your account against your selected annual contribution, which you establish at the first of the year. When calculating this contribution, think about covering your deductible, usual medication expenses, and anticipated physician visits. The maximum annual FSA contribution, as of 2021, is $2,750. As with an HSA, you will often be provided a debit card and you, in turn, will submit receipts to the administrator of the plan.

Cancellation and Renewal

Even though the ACA prohibits insurers from discriminating against individuals based on preexisting medical conditions, your policy can be canceled for other reasons.

Failure to pay premiums. You have to pay your premiums on time even as they increase (and you can count on that happening).

Failure to disclose relevant medical information. If asked, you must disclose all of your health conditions when you apply for benefits. Failing to do so is asking for certain cancellation. And if the insurance company paid any medical expenses related to the undisclosed condition, you will be held accountable to repay them.

Elimination of benefits. A form of cancellation could occur when the insurance company eliminates or reduces benefits under your policy. This could happen at any time unless the insurance contract prohibits it. You are supposed to receive reasonable notice of changes in benefits.

Try to find noncancellable, guaranteed renewable coverage. And if that is not an option, look for a "conditionally renewable" policy; this gives the company the right to cancel all policies in a particular category but does not leave room for them to single you out for cancellation.

COBRA and Similar Military Coverage

For anyone covered by group health insurance through a spouse's employer, COBRA (a federal law) applies to you. COBRA provides dependents an option for continued insurance coverage upon certain events, one of which is divorce. When you elect COBRA coverage, you do not continue as a dependent on your spouse's group policy. Instead, you continue as a member of the same group plan at your own expense (you pay the premium plus an administrative fee that compensates the employer for managing your coverage). Because the coverage is continuation coverage, you remain covered without undergoing a medical review.

The term COBRA is an acronym for the Consolidated Omnibus Budget Reconciliation Act of 1986. It is actually a part of ERISA (the Employee Retirement Income Security Act)—that helpful federal law we learned about in Chapter 6. COBRA applies to employers with at least 20 employees, employee organizations (unions), and state and local governments. Federal employees aren't covered by COBRA, but most have similar benefits (ask the personnel department at the specific agency).

For former spouses of military personnel, two programs called Tricare and CHCBP (Continued Health Care Benefit Program) might provide 36 months of continued health care coverage after the divorce, just as COBRA does. To be eligible for Tricare, the former spouse must fall under the 20/20/20 or 20/20/15 eligibility rules (see Chapter 7). If a former spouse is not eligible for Tricare, CHCBP coverage might fill the gap. The CHCBP eligibility requirements for the 36-month coverage, and potentially unlimited coverage, are complex, so begin your research by downloading the CHCBP Fact Sheet and Brochure at www.humanamilitary.com/beneficiary/benefit-guidance/special programs/chcbp. (Information about Tricare is at www.tricare.mil.) Better yet, seriously consider consulting with a family law attorney who has experience in military retirement and benefits law, to be sure you do not lose these important benefits because of a technical misstep.

COBRA Terminology

The terms of a group health insurance plan are in a document called a summary plan description (SPD). The employee spouse is referred to as the participant. The spouse of a participant is referred to as the qualified beneficiary. The qualifying event is the divorce, death, termination, or Medicare qualification of the participant. Election is the term for your decision to retain coverage.

Steps to Ensure COBRA Coverage

It's very important to meet COBRA's timing requirements. Within 60 days of the divorce or legal separation's becoming final, a qualified beneficiary must notify the health care plan administrator of the divorce and the need for COBRA coverage. If you do not know who the plan administrator is, contact the employer's human resources department. This notification is the minimum that you must do to ensure you get the coverage, but, in fact, you should be in touch with the plan administrator much earlier in the divorce process, to find out approximately how much the premiums will be. You'll need this information to plug into your expense budget and be an informed negotiator.

Once the qualifying event occurs and you notify the plan administrator —when the divorce becomes final—the plan administrator will send you a notice with instructions and time limits for electing coverage. Make sure that the plan administrator has your current address at all times, and when you receive this COBRA notice, pay close attention to it: It will contain information crucial to protecting your coverage.

Coverage

When you are covered under COBRA, you receive the same benefits as all other participants in the plan—you are still a member of the plan just as you were before. You should also receive benefit statements, identification cards, and plan summaries just as the other covered members do.

Cost

The qualified beneficiary (the nonemployee spouse) is responsible for paying the premium for the insurance coverage. The premiums can't be more than 102% of the plan's cost of providing coverage to non-COBRA participants. This cost includes the premiums paid by the employer for that person's coverage (whether the employee contributed or not), plus 2% for administrative fees. Premiums may be increased if they're increased for everyone on the plan—people on COBRA can't be individually singled out.

If you elect COBRA coverage, you must pay the first premium within 45 days after the election. It is your responsibility to make this payment, *even if you do not receive a bill from the insurance company.*

COBRA coverage might be more expensive than policies found through the ACA marketplace. Even if your divorce occurs outside of a marketplace Open Enrollment Period, your divorce might qualify you for a Special Enrollment Period with the less expensive ACA exchange option. If you decide to go with the marketplace at the time of your divorce, you cannot later decide to go with COBRA coverage. If you decide to go with COBRA coverage at the time of your divorce, and later want to change to an ACA exchange policy, your divorce would not qualify you for a Special Enrollment Period with the ACA exchange; you would have to wait for the ACA's regular Open Enrollment Period. Remember to investigate the dates for enrollment periods if you want to terminate COBRA and sign up on an exchange.

Beginning and End of Coverage

COBRA coverage begins on the date that the old coverage is lost, assuming all deadlines are met. Usually, this is the date the divorce becomes final. COBRA coverage for a former spouse ends 36 months after the date of the qualifying event unless one of the following events occurs earlier:

- Premiums are not paid on time.
- The employer stops providing a group insurance plan.
- The former spouse/beneficiary obtains equivalent group coverage.

- The former spouse/beneficiary becomes eligible for Medicare *after* electing COBRA coverage.
- The former spouse/beneficiary obtains individual coverage through an ACA marketplace exchange.

Coverage could also end if the employer closes or goes bankrupt. If there is no employer health plan, there is no COBRA coverage.

Conversion Coverage

After your 36 months of COBRA continuation coverage ends, some group plans provide an option to convert to individual coverage, known as conversion coverage. Many states require group plans to offer it. You can convert to an individual plan with the same insurance carrier you've had under COBRA after the COBRA coverage period has ended, without having to go through underwriting (medical evaluation). Strict deadlines almost always apply to the conversion—currently, COBRA rules say that you must notify the carrier that you want conversion coverage six months prior to the end of the COBRA coverage. Check the summary plan description; this notice requirement might be hiding in the small print. Premiums for conversion coverage will definitely be higher.

 RESOURCE

Several federal agencies administer the COBRA program.
The U.S. Department of Labor, Treasury Department, and Department of Health and Human Services are all involved. The toll-free number for COBRA information is 866-444-3272. The Department of Labor also provides information at www.dol.gov. Enter "COBRA coverage" in the search box.

State Insurance Risk Pools

State health insurance risk pools came on the scene in the mid-1970s to address inadequacies in the health care system. They have had a narrow focus, providing a safety net for those who could afford private health insurance, but were denied coverage because of preexisting medical conditions. These risk pools have been subsidized by the states. Their premiums often ran twice what a healthy person would pay.

The eligibility requirements for state pools vary, but almost all states having such pools require at least the following of all applicants:

- The applicant must meet state residency requirements.
- The applicant must not be eligible for Medicare Parts A and B.
- The applicant must not be eligible for COBRA coverage.
- The applicant must be unable to secure major medical insurance on the private market.

Because of the affordability of policies in the ACA marketplaces, coupled with no preexisting condition limitations, such risk pools were becoming a thing of the past until the U.S. House of Representatives passed the 2017 American Health Care Act in an attempt to repeal the Affordable Care Act (the bill did not pass the Senate). This bill would have resurrected the state risk pools. Stay tuned to this ever-changing health care debate. In the meantime, you will find the remaining risk pools on www.healthcare.gov, the HHS.gov website portal for the Affordable Care Act, which also identifies other options for health insurance coverage.

Medicare

Medicare is the federal government's health insurance program for people 65 and older. It also covers people under 65 who have specific disabilities, and people of any age with end stage renal disease or Lou Gehrig's disease (ALS). Medicare is financed by payroll taxes paid by both employers and employees and monthly premiums deducted from Social Security checks. Your income and resources play no role in qualifying for Medicare—it's an entitlement program and anyone who applies can receive it when they reach a qualifying age.

Medicare does not cover all medical care and long-term care costs. That is why so many people have private supplemental insurance for expenses that Medicare does not pay. Keep in mind that the ACA exchanges do not apply to Medicare recipients.

The Four Parts and Eligibility

Remember the alphabet soup of retirement plans from Chapter 6? We are about to jump into another one. This soup has fewer ingredients, though—just the A, B, C, and D of Medicare. There might be only four, but figuring out Medicare coverage can be a mind-bender. This section gives a broad overview, with links to resources that will illuminate the details.

These are the four parts to Medicare coverage and their eligibility requirements:

> **PART A: Hospital insurance for inpatient care in a hospital or skilled nursing facility, hospice, and other home health care.** You are eligible if:
> * you are 65 and
> * you receive (or are eligible to receive) Social Security benefits, or
> * you receive railroad retirement benefits, or
> * you (or your current or former spouse) worked for a specified minimum of years in a government job where Medicare taxes were paid, or
> * you are the dependent parent of someone who worked for a specified minimum of years in a government job where Medicare taxes were paid.
>
> Even if you are not eligible under the above criteria, you might be able to obtain Medicare coverage by paying a monthly premium. If you are younger than 65, you might be eligible for Medicare hospital insurance if you meet one of several disability requirements.
>
> **PART B: Medical insurance for doctors' services and other medical services (not covered by Part A) and supplies.** If you are eligible for Part A, you can enroll in Part B and pay a monthly premium, determined by your income, to obtain outpatient medical coverage. This part allows you to get an annual physical exam and many preventive services for free. Go to www.socialsecurity.gov/benefits/medicare for information on these rules.

PART C: Medicare Advantage. If you have Parts A and B, you can pay an additional monthly premium for a Medicare Advantage plan to help cover costs not paid by Parts A and B. Plans might be managed care plans, preferred provider organizations (PPO), private fee-for-service plans, or specialty plans for drugs, vision, or dental coverage. This type of plan is in lieu of a Medigap supplemental policy, and Medicare Advantage plans have special enrollment periods. Starting in 2014, the Affordable Care Act required these plans to spend at least 85% of the premiums they collect on medical care, and prohibits them from charging higher copayments than traditional Medicare for some services.

PART D: Prescription drug coverage. If you have Part A, Part B, or a Part C Medicare Advantage plan, you are eligible for Part D drug coverage. Part D is voluntary and involves yet another monthly premium—and it's important to sign up at the right time. If you delay your enrollment in Part D because you have other prescription drug coverage, you might end up paying a costly penalty.

If you opt for Part D coverage, you must enroll in a private insurance plan for your prescription coverage. It's especially important to compare coverage on different plans for the medications you take. Do an Internet search at AARP, U.S. News & World Report, and Consumer Reports to compare private insurance plans that offer Part D drug coverage options.

You have probably heard of the Part D "donut hole," or drug coverage gap. This gap is now closed, and everyone with Part D coverage will be responsible for 25% of the cost of their drugs.

Where Do You Start?

If you are receiving Social Security retirement or disability payments, you will be notified a few months before you are eligible (age 65) for Medicare coverage. Enrollment in Parts A and B are automatic, but you have the option to turn down Part B because it involves paying a premium. However, if you do not initially enroll in Part B, you could end up paying more for coverage if you decide you want it later—so err on the side of caution. If you are not receiving Social Security retirement or disability payments, then you should contact the Social Security Administration at least three months before you turn 65 so you could sign up for Medicare.

After you are enrolled, you will receive a Medicare card showing which parts you are enrolled in; like your Social Security card, keep your Medicare card in a safe place.

If you need help paying your Medicare premiums, you might qualify for state aid, called the Medicare Savings Program, which might also pay your Medicare deductibles and coinsurance. These programs have income and resource requirements, determined by each state. For more information, go to www.medicare.gov and search "medicare savings programs."

If you have private insurance or group coverage or you are a dependent on your spouse's employment-based insurance, and you are approaching Medicare eligibility, talk with your insurance agent (or the employer's group plan administrator) to be sure coverage is coordinated. Whatever you do, do not cancel any health insurance until your Medicare coverage is secure and has begun. And remember that Medicare eligibility terminates COBRA coverage and any policies purchased on the ACA exchanges.

Supplemental (Medigap) Coverage

If you wonder why supplemental insurance coverage is important when you're on Medicare, take a look at the following list of health care services that Medicare does not cover:

- dental care (routine check-ups, fillings, dentures)
- vision care (eye refractions, contact lenses, glasses, except after cataract surgery)

- most nonemergency transportation
- alternative medicine, including experimental procedures and treatments
- cosmetic surgery
- hearing aids and fitting exams
- long-term care (custodial care)
- nonmedical services (for example, copies of x-rays, hospital television and phone, and private hospital rooms), and
- some preventive care.

For more services not covered by Medicare, search www.cms.gov.

Even for the services it does pay for, Medicare does not pay 100% of the cost, and you must pay out of pocket for premiums, deductibles, and coinsurance. In all, Medicare might pay less than 50% of senior health care costs—a sobering reality if you were thinking everything would be fine if you could make it to 65 with a relatively clean bill of health.

What this should tell you is that supplemental Medigap coverage is extremely important. To obtain this insurance, you'll return to the world of individual health insurance described in "Group and Individual Coverage," above. Supplemental coverage will be cheaper than a full private policy, but you must do your price and benefit comparison shopping just the same. Note that the most comprehensive Medicare supplement insurance plan is Plan F, which covers all available benefits. Because supplemental Medicare coverage is not offered on the ACA exchanges, they won't do policy comparisons for you.

RESOURCE

Medicare's website is www.medicare.gov. It has many tools to help you through the labyrinth of information. You can also call 800-633-4227. Another resource is the Medicare Rights Center, a national nonprofit consumer service organization that works to ensure access to affordable health care for older adults, at www.medicarerights.org and www.medicareinteractive.org. For free personalized assistance regarding Medicare, contact your State Health Insurance Assistance Program: www.shiptacenter.org.

Medicaid

Medicaid is not a form of health insurance like Medicare. It is a public, state-run program that provides limited hospital and medical services for people with low income and limited resources. States manage Medicaid programs with combined federal and state funds. The federal government monitors Medicaid programs and issues guidelines for state use of Medicaid funds through the Centers for Medicare and Medicaid Services (CMS). CMS makes the general rules for delivery of services, funding, quality, and eligibility standards.

State participation in Medicaid is voluntary, but all states participate. Each one layers its own rules on top of the CMS rules, and the rules differ considerably from state to state. For example, some states are introducing work requirements and drug screening for Medicaid eligibility; some are ending Medicaid retroactive coverage. Even the names of Medicaid programs vary: Medi-Cal in California, MassHealth in Massachusetts, and so on. To add to the confusion, a state's Medicaid program might be administered together with other non-Medicaid state-funded programs.

Medicaid pays directly to health care providers or private health insurance companies acting as subcontractors. There are restrictions on who could provide the services, and service costs might only be partially paid by Medicaid. Many physicians, for example, are reimbursed for only a part of their service costs—but the medical providers know the patients can't pay them, either. This has led to some physicians limiting the number of Medicaid patients they will see in their practices.

As a result of the economic downturns and congressional attempts to reduce "entitlements" in the federal budget, states began charging higher premiums and copayments to Medicaid participants. The purpose of this, of course, is to generate revenue for the programs. This is but one indicator that the burden of the financial responsibility is beginning to shift to Medicaid recipients. While the Affordable Care Act did provide major expansion and funding for Medicaid programs, unfortunately, 39 states, for a variety of political reasons, have opted out of implementing these provisions and receiving substantial federal monies to fund them.

For more information on the status of your state's Medicaid program, go to www.medicaid.gov/about-us/contact-us/contact-your-state-questions/index.html.

Eligibility and Coverage

It is possible to be eligible for both Medicare and Medicaid. But to be eligible for Medicaid, you have to meet both income and eligibility group requirements. Income thresholds are established by each state, but income alone does not qualify you for Medicaid. There are asset limits as well, $2,000 (with $603,000 to $906,000 home equity excluded as of 2021), and each state will have specific regulations for measuring asset values. You also must fall into one of the eligibility groups that Medicaid targets: low-income parents and children, and people with disabilities, including blindness, pregnancy, and HIV, as well as simply being elderly. Nursing home coverage for the aged is the fastest growing eligibility group of Medicaid. Within each eligibility group additional requirements apply—for example, you must have no health insurance coverage or very limited coverage.

Eligibility requirements could be revised at both the federal and state level as funding ebbs and flows. The Affordable Care Act expands Medicaid eligibility to everyone under age 65 earning up to 138% of the federal poverty limit, which is less than $12,880 for an individual. To accomplish this, the federal government substantially increased its share of Medicaid's costs from the current 57% to 90% after 2020; however, many states have opted out of the expansion and the federal dollars that went with the expansion.

Each state has its own list of covered services, but typical services include inpatient and outpatient hospital services, lab and x-ray services, skilled nursing home care, services by physicians, physical therapy, hospice, and rehabilitative services. Services might be provided by hospitals, community clinics, or private physicians.

Programs

As noted, Medicaid coverage can be provided through different types of insurance programs. In managed care programs, Medicaid recipients enroll in private health plans that contract with the state, which pays a fixed monthly premium on behalf of all members as a group. Most states have managed care plans; in fact, about 60% of Medicaid enrollees—mostly the parent and children eligibility groups—are covered by managed care. The aged and disability groups remain in "fee for service" programs.

The Health Insurance Premium Payment (HIPP) program allows a Medicaid-eligible person to obtain private insurance with Medicaid paying the premiums. This is also known as a premium assistance program. Few states have opted into this type of benefit program.

Medicaid and the Friendly Divorce

You may have heard of "friendly" divorces as a way for people to qualify for Medicaid benefits. Some elder care planners advise people seeking Medicaid services to adopt financial strategies that will protect their assets if nursing home admission is likely. One way to do this is for seniors to transfer assets to other family members in order to qualify. Another method that some couples use to create Medicaid qualification, especially nursing home benefits, is divorce. It is a way to reduce countable assets to the near-subsistence level of income and resources needed to qualify. Note that a prenuptial or postnuptial agreement does not protect you when it comes to qualifying. Medicaid ignores marital agreements and all assets of both spouses are considered available for the care of either spouse.

This unfortunate strategy is most often employed when insurance is not available, when the couple cannot afford to pay for nursing home care from personal assets, and when there appears to be no other option. The divorce process results in one spouse becoming impoverished while the other one ends up with all the assets, by agreement. The spouse left with little or nothing then qualifies for Medicaid. This strategy is legal, believe it or not, and some couples employ it while continuing to live as husband and wife in all but legal status.

Obvious emotional and financial downsides accompany a "friendly divorce." The upside, which leads couples to take this extreme step, is that the spouse who ends up with nothing benefits by qualifying for nursing home care that would have otherwise been unaffordable. Please consult with both an elder care attorney and a family law attorney before resorting to divorce under these circumstances.

RESOURCE

There are many websites to help you through the Medicaid maze. One is the Kaiser Family Foundation's site for information and links to state Medicaid programs and other low-income health programs: www.kff.org/medicaid. And the federal government offers Medicaid program resources: www.cms.gov.

Long-Term Care

Long-term care is highly relevant to spouses divorcing later in life. In happy times, most people assume they have a built-in caretaker as age and health issues take their toll. This expectation is shattered in a late-life divorce. Who will step into this role? An adult child, another relative, a friend, or a private or publicly funded provider? Who has the skills and the time to provide social services or health aid? If you have ever been in a caretaking role, you know how taxing, demanding, and costly it can be. And, consider the scenario of a divorcing spouse who takes care of an elderly parent living in the spouse's home or helps that parent remain independent at home. If the spouse needs to return to the workforce after the divorce and will no longer have the time to provide help to that parent, much less pay someone else to provide those services, the effects of the divorce continue to ripple into the life of that needy parent.

This might be the time for you to explore the affordability of long-term care insurance. You might even try to quantify the value of your spouse's future caretaking and make the argument to a judge or in negotiations that you should be compensated for those "services" that your spouse will no longer provide as a consequence of a divorce.

If you and your spouse purchased long-term care insurance as a married couple and received a discounted rate, your carrier might require notification of the divorce and might increase premiums as a result.

Carriers operate under an underlying assumption that the married couple will provide caretaking to each other and thus delay a move into a more expensive long-term care facility. A joint policy might need to be split into individual policies with a likely increase in premiums.

A very helpful website developed by the U.S. Department of Health and Human Services is a good starting point to navigate through these increasingly relevant and complex issues: www.acl.gov/ltc.

Bridging the Gap

Many older divorcees might experience a gap in health coverage, between the time the divorce is final and the time Medicare eligibility kicks in at age 65. For those under age 50, serious health problems might not have surfaced. Those 65 and older have the Medicare cushion. While neither side of Medicare eligibility is safe or fully protected, the 50–65 age bracket creates a dangerous insurance gap for many people. This is a serious concern and is one that manifests often in late-life divorces.

It's important that you begin early to investigate options for health insurance coverage available to you in light of your health and financial situation. It takes time to research and identify the best policies and configuration of benefits; it takes time to fill out lengthy application forms; it takes time to gather medical records; and it takes time to await acceptance or rejection of your applications and to appeal rejections, if you so choose. And you are doing all of this while you are engaged in all the other aspects of your divorce.

Once you have cost estimates, you are ready to negotiate how the costs will be paid—whether through alimony, the allocation of income-producing assets, or your own income generated by employment. You might even consider using alternatives to divorce, such as postmarital agreements, to bridge gaps in insurance coverage. Most likely you will not be able to rely upon a single approach to health care coverage—you might end up using a variety of materials to construct your bridge.

The rising cost of health care touches all of us, as the ongoing debate over reform shows. While the Affordable Care Act offered some relief from the anxiety of having preexisting medical conditions—a core issue in late-life post-divorce finances—the relief is transitory. The politics of health care are unpredictable. But one thing is not: The cost of health insurance and medical expenses will likely continue to make a large hole in your post-divorce budget. ●

Your Financial Survival

The financial aspect of divorce both exposes nerves and unleashes creativity. During your separation, you and your spouse are still legally bound, and you will have to stretch possibly limited resources between two households. Once your divorce is final, you'll be on your own—a separate financial entity. To prepare for this eventuality, your next task is to get closely acquainted with your living expenses—current and future. In this chapter, I offer a little bit of tough love, encouraging you to bite the budget bullet and calculate your current living expenses and your projections for the future. Doing so will help you understand where you are now and reassure you that you will get through the divorce and survive alone after all is said and done.

Once the budgeting is out of the way, you'll take stock of your resources for generating income, including an exploration of potential income streams you might not have considered. For over 44 years, my clients never ceased to amaze me with their ingenuity in using their inner resources to find outer resources. You will, too.

Budgeting—The Four You've Gotta's

If I could excise the word "budget" from this chapter, I would, because I know you don't like it. Most people resist budgeting, and it's true that it's a challenging task. But you absolutely have to do it. First, the budget you prepare at the outset of your case will reflect your living expenses at that time and will establish the baseline for negotiations and court orders for temporary support. Next, your budget will reflect what you anticipate you'll need postdivorce, which is relevant both to setting alimony and dividing property and debts.

In my practice, before I asked my clients to begin working on budget preparation, we'd have a frank conversation about what I call The Four You've Gotta's:

- You've gotta keep denial and resentment at bay.
- You've gotta be honest with yourself.
- You've gotta know where your money goes.
- You've gotta isolate the necessaries.

#1: You've Gotta Keep Denial and Resentment at Bay

Money and emotion collide during a divorce (just as they often do during a marriage). The thought of being deprived leaves you angry, frustrated, and probably scared. You resent having to spend time combing financial records. You will procrastinate and try everything to avoid looking at exactly where your money goes.

Our relationships with money are established early in life—sometimes modeled after our parents, sometimes shaped by life experiences. We use money to act out, to punish, and to reward. We feel empowered by it. We play games with it. Every emotion we have could become the catalyst for some action we take with our money, whether it's spending, saving, or giving it away. Denial, fear, and anger all affect your experience of finances during divorce.

Denial. Some of us wear blinders. We know that our income vanishes as quickly as it comes in, yet we take for granted there will always be enough. We avoid facing bad spending habits or confused budgeting. Your divorce might be the first time you pull your head out of the sand of denial. If so, don't worry about being judged. From my years of being privy to people's spending habits, I can tell you that no matter how high the income and whatever the bottom line value of a marital estate might be, the vast majority of people somehow manage to spend all of what they take in—or more. And many people have disordered record-keeping habits and only vague knowledge of their own situations. If that describes you, you are not alone.

Fear. By far the most common fear that surfaces during a late-life divorce is of not having enough income to make ends meet. This fear goes to the core of survival, and it can be paralyzing. There's no doubt it's based in reality, either; many people, primarily women, are significantly worse off financially after a divorce. Still, you need to conquer your fear—or at least overcome it well enough that you're able to evaluate your situation and advocate for yourself financially.

Anger and resentment. One spouse's anger about the other's spending patterns might be the straw that breaks the back of the marriage. And the consequences of divorce could create even more resentments:

- You have a job, but you have been counting on a future when you would not have to work. Retirement was on the horizon. *Not now.*
- You dreamed of traveling or spending more time with children and grandchildren. *Not now.*
- You have retired and already embarked on a more leisurely lifestyle in your prime-time years. You were ready to coast. *Not now.*
- For the first time in decades, after working at raising your family, you might have to find a job outside the home. *Yes, now.*

Whatever your situation, it is natural to resent the deprivations that divorce could lead to—the loss of financial security as well as being deprived of plans, dreams, and the sense of control over your own destiny.

You'll be best off if you acknowledge these emotions and deal with them, possibly with the help of an appropriate counselor. In the meantime, try to put aside your resentment. It will serve you better to pay attention to the details upon which you will rebuild your future.

#2: You've Gotta Be Honest with Yourself

Don't fudge the figures as you dive into the logistics of budgeting. Be honest with yourself. The more accurately your calculations reflect your current outflow of funds, the better positioned you are to make wise decisions regarding cutting back and generating income. Your choices later will be smarter because you are dealing with facts, not wishful thinking or imagination.

#3: You've Gotta Know Where Your Money Goes

The first step in your financial survival plan is to look at your spending patterns and living expenses. Appendix B contains a list of expense categories, designed for the purpose of jogging your memory. There are no blanks to fill in, for two reasons. First, your attorney will most likely provide you with a financial questionnaire that is either specific to your local court or that the lawyer has prepared and likes to use. Second, I know you'll be frustrated if you break down expenses one way, and my budget format does it another way. To avoid this becoming a distraction and an excuse to stall, use Appendix B simply as a memory aid.

> **TIP**
> **Don't stay in the dark about your expenses.** If you do not have access to your household expense records, your attorney will help you get them, using the discovery methods explained in Chapter 4, "Your Divorce Options." You are entitled to see them.

Here are some tips as you start your examination:

- Tackle this task over a span of days. Identifying your living expenses accurately takes time, is tedious, and requires focused attention. It is too much to accomplish in one sitting.
- Work on your budget during a time of day when you are freshest and free from interruptions or distractions.
- If you prefer paper and pencil, use a loose-leaf notebook or notepad. Assign at least one page for each category in Appendix B. This will give you plenty of room to make notes, list items, and make calculations. Or, make a folder for each expense, where you can also keep related paperwork. (Just make sure it doesn't become your "bills to pay" file.)
- If you want to use your computer or tablet, use a program like Microsoft *Excel* or Apple's free *Numbers* app. Open a new tab for each category.
- Calculate either annually or monthly—just be consistent. It is a good idea to break down the last 12 months of expenditures so you could spot seasonal fluctuations and annual payments.
- Be thorough. That is why Appendix B is so lengthy. If you think of additional categories, include them.
- Start with the predictable expenses, then think about the surprises—the major car repair or unexpected root canal.

- Put your monthly and annual figures on separate tally sheets. If you don't use a computer program that will list and calculate numbers for you, use a desk or hand calculator with a tape. This will save you time and headaches when you double-check figures or try to find an error.

#4: You've Gotta Isolate the Necessaries

Once you have completed your tally sheets, use a highlighter to mark all expenditures that are absolutely necessary—basic for your survival. It is important to differentiate these unyielding expenses from others that are discretionary.

What Is Necessary?

You've reached the time for some soul-searching about the sometimes vague line between necessary and discretionary expenses. Here are some questions to spark your thinking: Do I really need a housekeeper once a week or could I get by with twice a month—or not at all? Do I really need a monthly manicure? Can I reduce my cell phone minutes or my wine or beer budget? Is fast food really that economical? Do I really watch all those streaming channels? Can my neighbor's son mow my lawn more cheaply than the landscape company, or wash my car? What if I reduce the number of times I run my sprinkler system each week? Could I raise or lower the thermostat by a couple of degrees? What if I get my hair cut every six weeks instead of every month? Could I be more creative at holiday time and shop sales in advance? Do I really read all of the periodicals I subscribe to? Just taking some simple steps could make a difference in your bottom line.

Finally, prepare a summary page of the monthly average and annual total of your absolutely necessary expenses; then do the same for the remaining discretionary expenses. Your totals might change during the divorce, as you continue to rethink your relationship with money and find more ways to economize.

Once you're finished, reward yourself—frugally, of course—because your budgeting efforts will pay off in more ways than you can imagine.

RESOURCE

As you discriminate between what is necessary and discretionary, consider things and services you could share more economically with others. You'll be surprised how much sharing could lighten your budget load. Consider checking out www.mint.com and www.budgetpulse.com, free online budget and money management systems, as well as the app for IExpense online.

Getting Help

Sometimes the perspective of an outside person can jar your thinking productively. A certified financial planner, a trusted friend, an accountant, or your attorney (or staff) could look at your expenditures. This could be incredibly helpful to understanding where your money goes. There are also some fantastic books on the market full of sound advice and guidance for budgeting: *The Budget Kit: The Common Cents Money Management Workbook,* by Judy Lawrence; *The New Savage Number: How Much Money Do You Really Need to Retire?,* by Terry Savage; *The Single Woman's Guide to Retirement,* by Jan Cullinane; and *Suze Orman's Financial Guidebook* and others in her series. It is beyond the scope of this book to cure you of harmful spending habits. But if you have problems managing money, now is the time to get help. If debt is overwhelming you, talk to a credit counselor. If you think you need to consider bankruptcy, talk to a bankruptcy attorney. (There's more about bankruptcy in Chapter 8, "The Bad News: Debts and Taxes.")

Exploring Potential Income Streams

A clear picture of your living expenses is only Step One in figuring out your future needs so that you could engage in meaningful negotiations about alimony and property division. The next step is reviewing all the potential ways that you could meet those needs.

If you are employed, your wages (and any bonuses and commissions) are your first and most obvious source of money. But whether you're supplementing your work income or establishing your means of support, you might have other potential income streams you could tap into.

Passive Income

Passive income might best be defined by what it is not: It's not earnings from wages you work for, or profit from a business that requires your active participation. It's also not capital growth (that's when an asset increases in value, not from your efforts, but from market conditions). Examples of passive income include interest, dividends, rental income, royalties or licensing fees from intellectual property, and royalties from oil, gas, and mineral rights. Income from a business that does not require your direct involvement is also passive income.

Social Security, alimony, and income streams from retirement resources are also technically passive income. They're addressed separately later in the chapter.

When you prepare your budget and calculate income, do not forget to include passive income; you might need to rely upon it to make ends meet. And it's important that you evaluate the potential of each of your marital assets for generating passive income. This potential might be a deciding factor in whether you choose to negotiate for those assets.

Often, passive income is automatically reinvested, but you could change that default if you need the income to meet your living expenses now or intend to use it for support in the future.

Whatever you're going to do with it, you need to know the earning history and the earning potential of each passive income vehicle. For savings and investment accounts, as well as royalties and lease income, historical information should be on your personal tax returns and on statements from financial institutions. For rental income properties, tax returns provide income and expense history. Income-producing real estate requires further investigation. For example, find out when leases expire, what the occupancy history of the property is, whether tenants are responsible and timely in their rent payments. You might need to request this information from the property's management company or your spouse, if you are not directly involved in the property management.

How valuable an income-producing asset is to you depends in part on how predictable the income will be. Markets and unpredictable tenants add uncertainty to the soundest of investments, so make sure you consider future possibilities when taking on an asset like that.

Review Assets Thoroughly

If you have an investment portfolio, you should review it with a financial adviser or a divorce financial analyst. If you don't already have a financial adviser, ask your attorney to recommend one who could give you future income projections concerning your stocks, bonds, and mutual funds. A financial planner might also have recommendations about selling and reinvesting in light of your future plans—and about what you might want to keep in the divorce. People going through divorce often fail to examine their assets carefully for income-producing potential. Passive income is good, but passive negotiating isn't—don't fall into that trap.

Bargaining for Alimony

Alimony, also called spousal support or spousal maintenance, means financial support that moves from one former spouse to another after a divorce. Whether you are the spouse paying alimony or the one receiving it, there's a lot to know.

RESOURCE

Because most people over 50 don't have minor children living at home, we don't deal with child support here. You can learn more about child support in *Nolo's Essential Guide to Child Custody & Support*, by Emily Doskow (Nolo).

Large alimony awards make the news and provide material for late-night comedians. Most of these cases are outliers and have no bearing on 99.9% of divorces. Likewise, if friends who live in other states have shared their alimony stories with you, put those out of your mind. Alimony laws and practices differ enormously from state to state; they could even vary from county to county and among judges in the same county. That's why your best advice on this subject will come from an attorney who practices in the area where you live. If you don't have a lawyer representing you in the divorce, and you want to claim alimony, this is a good time to get some advice before going forward.

You and your spouse could agree to alimony as part of your settlement or argue the issue in court and let the judge decide, in which event, the judge has discretion, meaning a lot of room, in making a decision. While there are certain factors that most judges consider (see "Amount, Duration, and Payment of Alimony," below), alimony is very different from child support, which is determined by state guidelines. Instead, alimony depends on a judge to weigh the facts and circumstances of each case.

Types and Purposes of Alimony

These are the five types of alimony that you might be eligible for—but all states do not have all types. Ask your lawyer which ones are applicable to you:

- **Temporary alimony** (also called interim support) is paid while a divorce is pending, or for a defined and relatively brief period after the divorce is final. For example, temporary alimony might end when the receiving spouse is eligible for Social Security.
- **Permanent alimony** usually is paid after long-term marriages end or when one spouse is mostly or completely dependent on support from the other spouse. The word permanent does not

mean that the alimony never ends; the final court order (or state law) will provide the terminating circumstances. The most common are the death of either spouse or the remarriage or cohabitation of the recipient spouse, but other conditions could apply, such as the sale of the family home or retirement of the paying spouse. Here, the goal is to allow the receiving spouse to continue living in the manner to which they have become accustomed because of the length of the marriage and the history of dependency. Historically, wives have received alimony after a traditional marriage in which the husband worked and the wife stayed at home, but today, permanent alimony is growing less and less popular as more women join the workforce. More women are paying alimony to ex-husbands, too.

- **Rehabilitative alimony** has the goal of helping the receiving spouse achieve financial independence. The spouse who seeks rehabilitative alimony might be required to prepare a plan detailing the education and training that will lead to becoming self supporting. The plan will include a time frame for attaining the goals, and some states have a predetermined maximum time period for rehabilitative alimony. Remarriage often does not terminate this type of alimony, as long as the receiving spouse is still pursuing education and training.

- **Reimbursement alimony** is available when one spouse provided support for the other's education during the marriage, expecting to participate in the fruits of that education—made possible by the educated spouse's increased earning capacity—and the divorce interfered with that expectation. The amount of alimony might be based on the amount expended by the supporting spouse or upon the enhanced earning capacity of the supporting spouse. Remarriage is often not a terminating event for reimbursement alimony.

- **Lump sum alimony** is a single payment made when the divorce is final or scheduled for a later date. This type of payment might represent a property buyout or not.

Eligibility for any type of alimony might depend on other factors, the most common qualifiers being length of marriage and financial need.

TIP

Consider creative ways of planning alimony payments. If you are the paying spouse and your income fluctuates, you might want to describe alimony not in a fixed amount but as a percentage or a fixed portion of income. For example, if your income is mainly from rental property and varies depending on how many units are rented at any given time, you could argue for alimony to be a percentage of monthly income.

Section 529 Plans

You might have used a 529 college savings account for your children, but did you know these accounts are not limited to children, but could be used for anyone's education—including that of a spouse after divorce? If you know that you want to return to college and could save toward that goal, even after retirement, you (or your spouse before a divorce) could save in a 529 plan for that purpose. The benefit to 529 plans is that income earned in the account is not taxed if used for qualified education costs. Additionally, you might be able to transfer the account to a child or grandchild if you end up not using it for yourself. A 529 plan might be a negotiating tool at time of divorce—for example, imagine that you want a greater share of the marital estate so that you could return to college and increase your future earning power, but your spouse is resistant. Earmarking funds for a 529 plan before the divorce is final could offer tax benefits, and more important, it assures your spouse that if you don't carry through on your plan, your children stand to benefit. Explore college savings plans at www. collegesavings.org and www.savingforcollege.com.

Alimony could be a way to make a divorce settlement more equitable. For example, if it's difficult to reach an equal (or equitable) division of the marital estate with the assets on the table at the time of divorce, then the promise of future income in the form of alimony might create a more equitable resolution. In some states, however, alimony is treated as separate and apart from the division of the marital estate, and can't be used to make up for a deficit in the property division.

Amount, Duration, and Payment of Alimony

Every state does not use the same factors to make alimony decisions, but all judges consider some fairly common elements. All of these factors could be meaningful to whether alimony is awarded, how much is awarded, and how long the alimony lasts.

Length of the marriage. Marriages of 10 years or more are often considered to be long-term marriages and some states consider 10 years a threshold for alimony. The length of a marriage has a bearing on both the amount of alimony and its duration.

Needs of the requesting party. Some states take a narrow view of needs. They interpret the word to mean basic necessities or minimum reasonable living expenses. Other states take a broader view and consider the marital standard of living. Because the court cannot engage in speculation about needs, the requesting side will need evidence to prove it. This is where your careful budget preparation will serve you well.

Ability to pay. A spouse's ability to pay is measured at the time of the divorce. Earning capacity, income from assets awarded in the divorce, and standard of living are all components of this factor. Courts can even impute income if a spouse isn't earning a reasonable income. For example, if your spouse is a doctor who quit practicing medicine to pursue a career as a painter, the judge might order alimony in an amount that's more consistent with a doctor's salary than a painter's.

Contributions to a spouse's income-earning capabilities. One spouse might have contributed to or enhanced the other's training, education, professional licensure, or career success. A spouse might have foregone or delayed education, employment, or career opportunities (for example, to raise children). Even where the alimony requested isn't reimbursement alimony, this factor could be relevant.

Allocation of assets and debts. How property is divided could affect alimony awards. The size of each spouse's sole or separate estate is also a consideration.

Employability. A judge will consider whether the receiving spouse has employable skills or needs time to develop some. If the couple has children whose custody interferes with a parent's ability to be employed, alimony is more likely. The ability of the spouse who seeks alimony to become self-supporting, and the time and training needed, could affect both the amount and duration of support. Be prepared to offer detailed evidence about all efforts to find employment, plus efforts and future plans to reeducate or train to acquire the necessary employment skills.

Health and age. Either spouse's age or medical condition might matter in a decision about support.

History of domestic abuse. Alimony is technically not supposed to be punitive, but some judges will take a hard line against perpetrators. This response is not without merit: Domestic abuse could impact the victim's emotional and physical ability to function effectively and at full potential in the workplace; extreme cases involve abusers who prohibit their victims from working outside the home at all. Even those suffering verbal abuse that undermines self-esteem and self-confidence could find their employment skills diminished. The need for counseling or job training might be factors in these circumstances.

Fault factors. In some states, fault is considered a factor in setting support. If one spouse dissipated (wasted) marital property, support might be used to make up for the other spouse's losses. If a spouse's behavior caused the breakup of the marriage, that fact might be another reason to award alimony. Again, alimony is not supposed to be punitive, but judges might be more likely to order it under fault circumstances.

Presence of children and others in the household. If either minor or adult children, or even elderly parents are living in the home, the spouse living there with them might have more need for support.

Other equitable factors. The term equitable is a catch-all for anything else that the judge thinks is fair and relevant to the award, duration, and amount of support.

Alimony orders are based on the facts existing at the time of the divorce. The terms of alimony, whether set by agreement or by a judge's decision, are included in the final judgment issued by the court. Usually the paying spouse sends a check to the receiving spouse each month or pays by automatic bank withdrawal. But alimony payments could also be paid to a third party on behalf of the receiving spouse—for example, paying health insurance premiums directly to the carrier.

Terminating and Modifying Alimony

Even though some people complain loudly about how long it lasts, most alimony doesn't go on indefinitely. Most settlement agreements or divorce decrees set an ending time. Sometimes it's a specific date; sometimes it's the occurrence of a particular event. And sometimes, circumstances change, leading to a modification of the amount or duration of alimony or even a termination of the alimony order.

Alimony ending on a specific date. Some orders state that the alimony ends on a particular date, regardless of the circumstances existing when that date arrives. Changes of circumstance aren't really relevant to these types of orders.

Alimony ending upon occurrence of certain circumstances. It's not uncommon for alimony to end upon the remarriage (or cohabitation) of the receiving spouse, upon that spouse's completing an educational program or other career training, or even upon the occurrence of something like the death of the receiving spouse's parent, because of an expected inheritance. The key is to be specific in describing or defining the terminating event; for example, define "cohabitation" to be sure everyone is on the same page about its meaning.

Changed circumstances. Some states will allow either former spouse to petition for a modification (adjustment) of alimony if a change in circumstances is relevant to the alimony payments, unless the final divorce decree states otherwise. In other states, the only things that end alimony are the death of either spouse or the circumstances specified in the final divorce judgment. In those states that do allow modification, the spouse who wants to make the change has the burden of proving that the circumstances have changed and justify a modification. Relevant changes could include:

- Either spouse opts for early retirement or makes voluntary changes in employment.
- The supported spouse is no longer in need.
- The supported spouse did not make good-faith efforts toward self sufficiency within a reasonable period of time.
- The supported spouse remarries or cohabits.
- Either spouse loses a home or becomes ill or disabled.
- Either spouse experiences a substantial increase in the cost of living.
- Either spouse's income decreases, including decreases due to illness or disability.
- It is just and equitable to terminate or modify support.

Security for Alimony

Especially when alimony is expected to last for an extended period, the recipient spouse should consider seeking a guarantee that payments will continue even if something happens to the paying spouse. Most often that means purchasing life or disability insurance in an amount that would replace the value of the alimony payments. The amount of insurance might decrease along with the remaining balance of alimony. It's also possible to create an interest in real property—in other words, a lien—to protect the receiving spouse's interest. If the paying spouse expects to retire before alimony terminates and will receive pension benefits, then the qualified domestic relations orders, discussed in Chapter 6, "The Big-Ticket Items: Your Home, Your Retirement, and Your Family Business," should secure the payment stream. Learn more about calculating present and future values of alimony awards in in Chapter 5, "Marital Property: Steps to a Fair Division."

Significant Alimony Tax Change

As mentioned in Chapter 8, Congress eliminated the federal tax deduction for alimony (removing the paying spouse's ability to deduct it), beginning with separation and divorce agreements and decrees executed after December 31, 2018.

Those finalized before that date will not be affected, with the exception of the rare modification of an older alimony agreement. The impact of this action, made with little forewarning to or input from the matrimonial bar associations, is still unknown in the divorce trenches.

Alimony has long served as a settlement tool when trying to negotiate movement of assets or cope with income disparity between spouses. There's something about the words, "But your payments will be tax deductible" that softens the payer's grip on the purse-strings.

Some matrimonial law commentators have proclaimed "The sky is falling," predicting that more divorces will be litigated as a result of this tax law change. Others believe that alimony agreements and awards will drop, arguing that the parties (or judges) will anticipate the taxation sting to the paying spouse. If that happens, women—who continue to receive alimony in greater numbers than men—will suffer even more from their already lagging post-divorce income as compared to men.

My opinion is that family law attorneys are going to have to be more creative when they negotiate the pros and cons of alimony, no longer based on the familiar numbers game of deductibility, but based on the fact picture each individual case presents.

Timing Withdrawals From Retirement Assets

You might negotiate to receive retirement assets as a way to provide security for your future. However, in extreme circumstances, these assets could provide a source of cash during and after your divorce. This certainly should not be your first line of defense, as you might incur penalties and other consequences—and of course, if you take withdrawals or loans but don't repay them, the money won't be there when you planned on being able to count on it. If you do find yourself in a situation where you need to access your retirement funds, you could tap into them through loans, hardship distributions, and withdrawals.

Loans

Loans are an option with some 401(k) plans, and an increasing number of people are taking out such loans. Borrowing from your own 401(k) is tempting, because you think you are paying interest to yourself, and borrowing from yourself instead of from other sources. So it might appear, at first glance, to be a good way to cover expenses. But let's look at how a 401(k) loan works.

It starts logically enough: You borrow money from your 401(k) account and promise to repay it, along with interest, at a later time. You proceed to earn more money, which you use to repay the loan and pay the interest. Sounds like you are paying yourself back and earning interest, right? But when you repay the 401(k) loan principal, you are doing it with money you already have—in other words, taking it from one of your own pockets and putting it in another. More importantly, you're probably paying the loan back with money you've earned at work, which means money that has already been taxed, unlike the original money you put into the account, which was withdrawn from your paycheck pretax. That money will be taxed again when you withdraw it from the account later.

Likewise, when you repay a 401(k) loan's interest, you again are using already-taxed money, just like your principal payments. (This differs from the interest you earn on your 401(k) investments in general, which comes from the market, not from you.) In the future, when you withdraw those interest dollars, you will pay taxes on them again.

If you lose your job with a loan outstanding, it must be repaid immediately. If you cannot repay it, the loan balance is deemed to be a distribution on which you will owe income taxes and perhaps a 10% penalty (depending on your age).

In sum, borrowing from your 401(k) account might not be the attractive option you think it is. If you must do it, look before you leap, and keep the loan to a minimum.

Hardship Distributions

Retirement plans may, but are not required to, provide for hardship distributions to participants. If they do, what constitutes a hardship must be spelled out clearly in the plan, and the Internal Revenue Code limits eligible expenses to certain categories.

TIP

The concept of hardship distribution doesn't really apply to IRAs because you could take IRA distributions at will. But early distributions are likely to be taxed and penalized unless they are used to pay expenses similar to those that might be eligible for a hardship distribution under a 401(k) plan (listed below).

401(k), 403(b), and 457(b) plans all might permit hardship distributions. These distributions, unlike loans, are not paid back to the retirement account; once you take it out, the transaction is complete. The distribution could not be more than the employee's elective contributions into the 401(k)—in other words, you can only take out what you contributed, and you must leave your employer's matching contribution and your account earnings. Although you escape penalties on your hardship distribution if you are 59½ or older, you do still have to pay income tax on the money.

The standard for hardship distributions is that the distribution must be on account of an immediate and heavy financial need of the employee (or a spouse or dependent), and the amount of the distribution must be necessary to satisfy that financial need. In addition, all of the following must be true:

- The employee must not have other resources available to meet the need (including a spouse's resources).
- The amount of the distribution must not exceed the need (but could take into consideration the amount needed to pay taxes or penalties resulting from the distribution itself).
- The employee must have obtained all available loans and other distributions under the employer's various plans before taking the hardship distribution.

- The employee could not make any elective contributions to the plan or to any other employer plans for six months after receiving the hardship distribution.

If all of these requirements are met, you might obtain a hardship distribution that falls into one of the four categories of expenses that the IRS has determined meet the hardship standard:

- a down payment on a first home (but not mortgage payments)
- medical expenses
- educational expenses, and
- expenses necessary to prevent eviction or foreclosure on a principal residence.

Your plan might stick with these IRS categories, or list other expenses that qualify, such as burial or funeral expenses and expenses for repairing damage to your house. A plan might elect to allow only one or two types of hardship distributions or allow no hardship option at all.

As you can see, it isn't easy to tap funds for a hardship distribution —and this is for good reason, as this option is even more detrimental to your retirement planning than taking a loan, because you are not required to pay the money back.

Withdrawals

A third way to get money from your retirement funds is to withdraw it. However, it's not as simple as that sounds. Some plans don't allow withdrawals at all. If your plan does, you're still subject to taxes and penalties.

If you are under 59½, a withdrawal could incur a 10% penalty and put you in a higher income tax bracket, but you might be able to avoid penalties and taxes if you take substantially equal periodic payments each year for at least five years or until you reach 59½, whichever period is longer. This is called a 72(t) premature withdrawal. After the five years (or when you're 59½), you could stop receiving the payments or change the amounts. The payment amounts are calculated by one of three methods allowed by the IRS. Your tax adviser can calculate which one produces the best tax consequences for you.

CAUTION

If you're over 72, you must withdraw funds. If you're older, you face the opposite problem—you have to withdraw a minimum amount of money each year. The amount is calculated by dividing your account balance by the number of years you are predicted to live under standard actuarial guidelines. If you withdraw less than the IRS allows, you will owe a 50% penalty on the amounts that were not withdrawn in time.

Withdrawal Guidelines

Financial professionals follow industry guidelines that establish the order in which withdrawals should be taken from retirement savings accounts. The withdrawal hierarchy, set out below, might be of value to you if you're considering using retirement assets to supplement income after your divorce. As with any general rule, the rules below have many exceptions. Your financial adviser will tell you whether you are the rule or an exception, and can help you calculate the tax and other consequences of your withdrawal scenarios. Accepted guidelines suggest the following:

- In taxable accounts (those in which you invest already-taxed dollars), consider liquidating investments first that are worth less than their tax basis (usually the cost of the asset). This will produce losses, which can be used to offset ordinary income (salary, interest, and wages) up to $3,000 per year. Unused losses could be carried forward for use in future years.

- Consider selling next those assets in taxable accounts that will generate neither capital gains nor capital losses. This might be money market funds or other cash or cash-equivalent investments. Don't forget to leave funds for short-term financial emergencies.

- Tap into the assets that will generate the smallest gain or largest loss. If you liquidate assets in a taxable account, sell those with long-term capital gains first; the taxes might be at lower rates than short-term gains. If you have made contributions that are not tax deductible to a tax-deferred savings vehicle (traditional

IRAs or variable annuities), and if you want to withdraw from that account, you will need expert guidance in apportioning withdrawals between taxed and nontaxed dollars.

- Consider withdrawing money from tax-deferred accounts funded with pretax contributions, such as 401(k) accounts, traditional IRAs, or tax-exempt accounts, such as Roth IRAs.

Withdrawals from retirement assets are subject to quick changes in the law, which might affect your options. This is yet another reason to consult with knowledgeable tax and financial advisers. Retirement investments are the lifeblood of your later years. Investing in tax and financial advice will help you stretch the life of your savings and, if you are forced to use them for living expenses after your divorce, help you minimize the impact of that decision.

Counting on Social Security

The sole source of income for over 32 million Americans in their later years is a Social Security check. Whether you expect to be—or are—one of those 32 million, or whether you have other income and use Social Security as a supplement, it's an important income stream. This section discusses Social Security retirement benefits and survivor benefits. We don't address disability benefits, which are not automatic but are needs based.

The Basics

All Americans who have an earnings record are automatically entitled to full Social Security retirement benefits upon reaching full retirement age. The amount of the benefit is determined by the worker's age and lifetime earnings record. You are eligible to begin drawing 80% of your benefits at age 62. But if you wait to start receiving your benefits until you reach your full retirement age—between 66 and 67, determined by your year of birth—you will receive full benefits. A chart on the Social Security Administration (SSA) website tells you your full retirement benefit age and calculates your benefits if you retire early: www. socialsecurity.gov/retire2/agereduction.htm.

Social Security benefits are technically not property, and a judge cannot award you all or part of your spouse's Social Security retirement check. But in some equitable distribution states, who is receiving what benefits could influence judges on subjects like alimony and how to divide assets; for example, a judge might consider the disparity between spouses' estimated or actual Social Security benefits. A minority of jurisdictions (Alaska, California, Illinois, Nevada, New Mexico, North Dakota, Oregon, and Tennessee) don't allow courts to consider Social Security in divorce property divisions in any way.

Social Security benefits can be garnished for child support and alimony, depending on the type of benefit being received. Old-age retirement and disability benefits can also be garnished; however, Title 16 Supplemental Security Income (SSI) cannot. This is because Social Security benefits are funded by employment taxes paid into the Social Security Trust Fund and are considered a substitute for income, while SSI is a need-based supplement for clothing, housing, and food expenses, and those benefits are funded by general tax revenues.

In the course of gathering your financial information, you will find out your own and your spouse's Social Security benefits earned to date. You can request a copy of earnings records at www.socialsecurity.gov. You can also access your earnings history and estimate your retirement benefits based on different retirement scenarios at www.socialsecurity. gov/estimator.

Retirement Benefits

If your marriage lasted 10 years or more, you can collect retirement benefits on your former spouse's Social Security record even after your divorce—especially welcome news if you've been out of the workforce during your marriage. Even if you have accumulated some work credits, it is worth comparing your earned benefits to the portion of your spouse's benefits to which you might be entitled, so that you can choose the benefit that's higher.

Two threshold requirements must be met before you can draw Social Security benefits based on your former spouse's earnings credits:

- Your marriage was or is valid under your state's law, and this includes a common law marriage if your state recognizes it.
- Your marriage lasted for at least 10 years before the final divorce order was entered.

If you meet both requirements, and as long as you aren't entitled to an equal or higher benefit from your own earnings, then you might be entitled to a spousal benefit in an amount equal to one-half the benefit that is paid to your former spouse during that their lifetime. You're entitled to whatever the benefit is at the time—you get half of the amount your spouse is entitled to whether it's full or partial benefits. You might also be entitled to survivor's benefits if your former spouse dies before you do—more about that in "Survivor Benefits," below.

> **TIP**
> **If you are the wage earner, don't worry.** The amount your former spouse receives does not reduce your own benefit at all.

You must file an application for spousal benefits with the Social Security Administration. You can't do this until you're 62 or older, but your right to do it never expires—in other words, it doesn't have to be right after your divorce. However, if you remarry, you might not be able to collect these benefits unless your later marriage ends.

Here are a couple of financial strategies developed under current law, but note the sidebar below, "Caveat: Significant Changes to Social Security Laws." First, you could begin receiving retirement benefits either on your own or your spouse's record at age 62, then switch to the other benefit when you reach full retirement age if the other one is higher.

Second, once you've been divorced for at least two years, you'll be entitled to benefits through your former spouse even though your former spouse is eligible but not yet receiving benefits. In other words, you could start earlier than your former spouse in receiving benefits from the account. (Your spouse might be delaying for tax reasons or to reap higher benefits.)

Benefits derived through a former spouse end when the first of the following events occurs:

- when you die
- when your former spouse dies (but see "Survivor Benefits," below)
- when (or if) you become entitled to retirement benefits based on your own work credits in an amount equal to or greater than that of your former spouse (but see the paragraph below), or
- when you marry, before age 60, someone other than your former spouse.

When you become eligible for retirement benefits on your own work history record—in addition to your former spouse's benefits—the SSA will pay your retirement benefit first. If the benefit on your former spouse's record is higher, you will receive an additional amount on your ex's record so that the combination of benefits equals that higher amount.

Survivor Benefits

If your former spouse dies, you might be eligible to receive survivor benefits of 100% of your former spouse's benefit. You must apply for the benefits and meet the following requirements:

- You and your former spouse were validly married for at least 10 years before the divorce was final.
- You are at least 60 years old (or at least 50 years old if you are disabled).
- You are not entitled to retirement benefits in an amount that is equal to or greater than that of your former spouse's benefit.
- You have not remarried, unless you married again after you turned 60 or you are currently 60 or older and you remarried between the ages of 50 and 60 (or, you are at least 50 years of age, remarried after turning 50, and are disabled).

Caveat: Significant Changes to Social Security Laws

In November, 2015, Congress passed the Bipartisan Budget Act of 2015, which includes provisions changing Social Security law to address perceived "loopholes." Here are two important changes to consider.

First, the law creates some limitations on the "file and suspend" strategy for maximizing Social Security benefits. Before this Act passed, a primary worker who had reached full retirement age could file for retirement benefits and then suspend them in order to continue to earn delayed retirement credits through further employment. Prior law provided that a suspension of benefits did not suspend the benefits of others (spouse, former spouse, or other dependents) whose benefits were based on the primary worker's earnings record. The 2015 Act suspends benefits received by spouses, former spouses, and other dependents, as well as former spouses' benefits, *until the primary worker reactivates retirement benefits.*

Second, divorcees will continue to be able to claim either 50% of a former spouse's Social Security retirement benefit or their own retirement benefit (whichever is larger), *but divorcees born in 1954 or later will not be able to switch from one to the other at a later time.*

Social Security laws are complicated and getting more so. For many people, these benefits form a large part of their retirement income, so it's imperative to consult with legal and financial professionals who are knowledgeable about these changes, their effective dates, and additional amendments that may be coming down the pike.

By the way, if other survivors are entitled to benefits (such as a subsequent spouse or children), your benefits will not affect the amount of any benefits to which they might be entitled. Yes, multiple 10-year marriages could produce multiple former spouses, each of whom receives an amount equal to more than 100% of the deceased's benefits!

If you are collecting divorce-derived benefits based on your former spouse's Social Security retirement, you could switch to receive the higher amount of survivor benefits upon your former spouse's death. If you are collecting survivor benefits, you could switch to your own retirement benefits as early as age 62 if your retirement benefit is higher than the survivor benefit.

Additional Issues to Consider

Here are a few more important points to think about in Social Security planning.

Consider your timing. If your divorce is occurring near the ten-year mark in your marriage, talk with your attorney about the possibility of slowing down the divorce process so that the divorce isn't finalized until after your tenth anniversary. A delay does not harm the higher-earning spouse, whose benefit is not reduced at all by the lower earner qualifying to receive benefits—and it might even help avoid or reduce postdivorce support.

Check the impact of other retirement benefits. If you receive a pension based on work that is not covered by Social Security (for example, certain government or foreign employment that doesn't qualify as Social Security earnings), your ability to piggyback on your former spouse's benefit might be affected. Check with the Social Security Administration if you think this might affect you.

Knowing about your Social Security rights is crucial. The benefits are a part of your present or future income and are an important number to include in your postdivorce budgeting.

When Should You Start Receiving Benefits?

You have a choice between taking partial benefits after age 62 or waiting until you're entitled to full benefits. What should you do? The advantages to taking benefits as early as possible are cash in hand and the possibility that you might collect benefits for a longer period of time. The disadvantage is that your benefit is permanently reduced, and if you wait you might earn additional work credits in the meantime that would increase your monthly benefit. One little known option with Social Security is the one-year pay- back option. If you decide to start taking lower benefits before your full retirement age, and if you then decide you want to undo that and start retirement at age 66 or 67 (your full retirement age), you may be allowed to pay back the benefits you have received for up to one year (free of interest or penalties) and then draw higher benefits later. This option might be worth your serious consideration if you are not dependent on your Social Security income, if you're willing to bank your benefits, if the benefits do not increase your taxes substantially, and if you want the interim security of the accumulated funds should you need them for an emergency. This option has some tight timelines, so check with the SSA to learn about those if you consider this "pay back" option.

Being Inventive in Your Financial Life

As a result of your late-life divorce, you might be looking at working longer than you expected—or returning to a workforce from which you have been absent a long time. Maybe you will work part time. Maybe you will take this opportunity to change careers. All of this might feel scary to you, or it might fill you with a sense of possibility.

Many people going through late-life divorce freeze with anxiety when they think about their financial circumstances, particularly the likelihood of a reduced income, after their divorce. Even those who will come out of the divorce financially secure sometimes can't escape that anxiety.

In my experience, the sooner my clients unlocked their fear and moved through it, the sooner they were able to gain some confidence, start focusing on their inner resources, and get creative about generating income.

RESOURCE

There are many books on the market about later-in-life career options. I encourage you to stroll through your local bookstore to find them. You could start with the classic job-hunting reference series by Richard N. Bolles, *What Color Is Your Parachute?* Another book that crossed my path is *The Third Chapter: Passion, Risk, and Adventure in the 25 Years After 50,* by Sara Lawrence-Lightfoot, which reports on the author's work with 40 people in this age group and describes how her subjects embraced late-life crises and redefined themselves. She challenges stereotypes of aging and underscores the incredible creativity that could be tapped and unleashed at this stage of life. The subjects of Boomer employment in lieu of full retirement and changing paths later in life are popular topics these days. From career counseling seminars and workshops to websites and social networking, you will find guidance and learn about other people who share the boat you're in.

Remember the three lists I mentioned in Chapter 2—100 Things I Want to Be, 100 Things I Want to Do, 100 Things I Want to Have? Completing that simple exercise is another way clients began to garner a sense of direction. I'm not sure how or why this worked. But my clients taught me this: We all carry vast resources for creative problem solving, and the trick is finding a calm and reflective way to tap the resources within. Never underestimate how resourceful you will be on the other side of a late-life divorce.

An Encouraging Survey About Women, Work, and Age

If you are a woman contemplating a return to the workforce, you might find encouragement in research conducted by the National Center on Women and Aging at Brandeis, which surveyed 1,001 women age 50 and older about work attitudes. A few of the survey's results:

- 85% of women 50 and over who work said they were in good physical health versus 68% of those who do not work.
- 57% of women 50 and over who work say aging is better than they thought it would be, while only 50% of those who do not work feel the same way.
- 44% said their financial situation will be better in five to 10 years, compared with only 22% of those who do not work.
- A majority of women 70 and older who still work say they will never retire; and about 25% of working women between 50 and 69 say they will never retire.

Researchers concluded that women age 50 and older who work are healthier and have a more positive attitude than women who do not work.

Yes, this is a small sample. But it echoes my own impressions drawn from my female divorce clients, many of whom had no choice but to return to the work world after their divorce—some dreaded it, many were fearful and lacking in self confidence, but the vast majority met the challenge and pleasantly surprised themselves in the process. They were satisfied and happy with their work lives when I met up with them later.

Estate Planning and Divorce

When you're dealing with a divorce, related legal issues often come into play, and the most significant of these is the need to be on top of your estate planning. The term estate planning refers to the process of structuring your finances in preparation for your eventual death. It also encompasses things you do to prepare for the possibility that you could become incapacitated and unable to care for or make decisions for yourself.

Estate planning plays a major role in late-life divorce. Most people don't like dealing with these difficult issues even in the best of times, and it can feel like adding insult to injury when you must turn your attention to estate planning while you're coping with the challenges of your divorce. But during and after your divorce, it's more important than ever for you to create and maintain current documents, including a will or trust, medical directive, and financial power of attorney. These documents say what happens to your property after you die (and sometimes, during your lifetime), and allow others to manage your property and your health care if you become incapacitated.

The legal work of estate planning is similar to that of family law, because both deal in the transfer of property ownership—one when your marriage dissolves and the other at the time of death. Just as you must do in connection with your divorce, when you engage in estate planning you must identify and characterize your property. And choices made in one area could influence those in the other areas.

In this chapter, we'll consider the before, during, and after of estate planning in relation to your divorce. I'll explain the basic components of estate plans, so that you can understand and review your existing documents, look at how to deal with estate planning preferences while the divorce is pending, and conclude with a reminder of how important it is to put an updated estate plan in place after the divorce is final.

You and your spouse might have done estate planning during your marriage; if you're over 50, I certainly hope you already have an estate plan in place. At divorce, how you have planned your estate could affect how you divide your assets. As you work toward a divorce settlement, your future estate planning should never be far from your mind.

Before the Divorce: Beware the Traps

Your first step is to assess what is already in place in your estate plan. If you're exploring options and gathering information before you file for divorce, evaluating your estate plan should be part of that process. If you do have an estate plan, you need to know its components—do you have only a will, or have you created trusts, powers of attorney, and medical directives? Are your assets titled consistent with your estate plan? Do your children know of your plans? An estate plan has many moving parts, and you need to be on top of all of them.

Basics of Probate and Assets

The word probate refers to a court process that deals with property at death. A probate court is involved in the distribution of the deceased person's property and the appointment of the estate's personal representative. Probate can be cumbersome and expensive (and it's a public proceeding in most jurisdictions), and many people structure their estate planning with the primary goal of avoiding it. Even if you're not able to avoid it entirely, some assets don't have to go through probate; most estates contain some nonprobate and some probate assets.

Nonprobate Assets

Transferring nonprobate assets occurs outside of the will or probate court—it's usually done by the entity that holds the asset. The owner has given the holder instructions on what to do when the owner dies; and when that happens, the asset passes automatically or by a simple process of verifying the person's death. The beneficiary receives the property directly from the institution or organization that's been holding it, and the court is not involved. Nonprobate transfers are usually based on some kind of document that is separate from a will. Here are some examples of nonprobate assets.

Life insurance proceeds. The fact that life insurance circumvents the probate court is one of its most attractive features. In most cases, the insurance company pays benefits directly to a beneficiary (or to a guardian, if the beneficiary is a minor), usually much faster than if it were done through probate. However, it is possible for life insurance proceeds to end up in probate if the policy owner names the estate as the beneficiary, fails to name a beneficiary, or if the named beneficiaries do not outlive the decedent.

Retirement accounts. These are also paid directly to a named beneficiary. Examples are IRAs, 401(k) accounts, and pension benefits.

Trust assets. Trusts are a way to transfer assets outside of probate. (See "Trusts," below.)

Payable-on-Death (POD) accounts. You can place a POD designation on bank accounts, CDs, and other investment accounts, allowing the POD beneficiary to become the automatic owner of the account when the primary owner dies.

Joint Tenancy With Right of Survivorship (JTWROS). You can also avoid probate by holding title to a bank or brokerage account in the form of JTWROS. Some states also allow homesteads and other real estate to be held in this way. JTWROS means that two individuals (usually spouses) share ownership in property with an explicit requirement that upon the death of one, the other automatically inherits the property directly, without the necessity of approval from the probate court. Holding title in JTWROS controls the disposition of the property, even if a will says the property goes to someone else.

The deed or account agreement, usually the signature card, must include the magic words "with right of survivorship," for the ownership to pass at death. When joint accounts do not have a right of survivorship, the balance does not automatically go to the surviving joint tenant. For these accounts, the joint tenant owns only that person's contributions to the account (or asset), and the contributions of the deceased joint tenant are part of the deceased's estate.

Transfer-on-Death deeds (TOD). About half of the states acknowledge TODs, which transfer real estate to a grantee on the date of the grantor's death; it has no force or effect before that event and usually does not affect the grantor's rights to use the property or limit the grantor's creditors' rights to the property. However, to be effective the deed must be recorded before the grantor's death in the deed records office of the county where the property is located. The grantor can file a cancellation or revocation of the TOD any time before the grantor's death.

Complications could arise if you are a joint owner of the property, including owning property with a spouse, so be sure to consult with a probate attorney who practices in the state where the property is located.

Probate Assets

Probate assets are all other assets that pass from the deceased person's estate to a named beneficiary by way of a written will. When the decedent did not leave a will (or a valid will), these assets pass in a particular order according to state laws called laws of intestacy or inheritance. Spouses and children are always first in line, but the order and the amount given to each could differ from state to state (and also depend on whether the asset is separate or marital property).

Examples of probate assets are your house, your bank and investment accounts that aren't designated as payable on death or joint tenancy with right of survivorship, and your personal property, which includes everything from your costume jewelry to your expensive art collection.

You might have guessed already that the probate court deals with probate assets. But just how involved the court will get depends on your state laws, the particular court's procedures, how well your will is written, and the facts of the case. On one end of the spectrum, a probate court might do very little: If a valid will appoints an executor (representative of the estate), the probate judge might simply issue orders that confirm the executor's authority to carry out the wishes of the deceased person with relatively little supervision.

On the other end, a probate judge might be very involved with the administration of the estate. If the deceased left property and debt and didn't write a will, you can count on it: The judge must appoint a representative of the estate and oversee the payment of debts and the inventory and distribution of property. Even when the deceased did have a will, there might be an argument over the validity or interpretation of the will that a judge must rule on. The more involved the probate court, the more costly the process.

Wills

A will might be the only document in an estate plan; it is certainly the most important. Your will dictates who will receive your property and designates someone, called an executor, to manage your estate upon your death. You could name an individual as executor or choose an entity, like a trust company. An executor occupies a fiduciary role that is held to a high standard of trust and good faith; the tasks of the executor include paying the decedent's bills, filing tax returns for the decedent and the estate, and distributing assets according to the will.

Because wills are so important, the law imposes certain formalities when you sign a will. You must sign in front of witnesses or a notary—each state has its own rules. You can change your will with a codicil (an amendment), which usually requires the same signing formalities.

CAUTION

Do not ever make written changes directly on a will. Your handwritten changes will be ignored by the court or might invalidate the entire will. (I don't recommend handwritten wills or codicils, even if they're legal in your state—they're simply too easy to challenge.)

If you think your will is out of date, don't just tear it up. For one thing, in the absence of a will, inheritance laws dictate who receives your property—which might not conform with your wishes. If you want to change your will before your divorce is filed, check first with your divorce or estate planning attorney. If there is no problem with your doing so, create an entirely new one.

After your divorce is final, you'll need to prepare a new will, even if you have changed your will in the interim. You are free to leave money or property to your ex-spouse after the divorce is final, if you want to, but you need to do it in a will that's signed after your divorce. (See "After: Taking Care of Business," below.)

Trusts

A trust is a way of holding title to property. Instead of a person owning assets, the assets are transferred to a trustee who holds, manages, and distributes the assets on behalf of the trust.

Don't worry that trusts are too complex to understand; I'm going to make this simple. We'll start by explaining the three roles that exist in every trust:

- **Grantor/Trustor/Settlor.** This is the person who originally owns the property and who creates the trust. The grantor determines what assets are transferred into the trust, who will receive the assets and when, and what conditions and terms apply to the use and distribution of the assets.
- **Trustee.** This is the person (or entity, in the case of a trust company) who manages and administers the trust. The trustee follows the instructions in the trust document and distributes assets and income accordingly. Trustees, like executors, are held to high fiduciary standards.
- **Beneficiary.** This is the person or entity who receives part or all of the assets and income placed in the trust. There might be one or more beneficiaries.

The principal assets transferred into a trust are called the trust corpus (Latin for "body"). The corpus might earn interest or dividends or generate other types of income, depending on the nature of the property. The law recognizes three general categories of trusts: revocable, irrevocable, and testamentary.

Revocable Trusts

The term revocable means what it sounds like—the grantor can revoke or modify the trust at any time. Most revocable trusts are created for the purposes of avoiding probate, allowing others to manage property, maintaining privacy, and segregating separate property. A revocable trust might also be called a simple trust, a management trust, or a living trust.

In a revocable trust, the same person could fill all three roles of grantor, trustee, and beneficiary. With a revocable trust, you transfer assets to yourself as trustee of your trust, and you are also the beneficiary of the trust during your lifetime. This means you can still manage all of the property in the trust. You name a successor trustee so that if you become ill and can no longer serve as trustee, there's someone to take over your role as trustee. The successor trustee continues to manage the trust property and pay your expenses—a process that is far more flexible and inexpensive than a guardianship or conservatorship. (See more discussion in "Revocable Management Trusts" in Chapter 3.)

Following your death, the trustee distributes the trust assets to the people you have named in your trust agreement, so it works pretty much the same as a will does, but without probate.

> (!) **CAUTION**
>
> **Some people make the mistake of writing the trust agreement but failing to transfer the title of bank accounts, brokerage accounts, and real property to the trustee of the revocable trust.** If the trustee does not have title to the assets, then the trust does not work: The trustee will have no assets to manage if you become incapacitated and no assets to distribute following your death. Consider asking an attorney to help you prepare a revocable trust and transfer the title of your assets to the trust.

Let's go through some of the reasons for creating a revocable trust in addition to the primary goal of keeping property out of probate.

Asset protection. Revocable trusts are sometimes touted as a way to protect assets from creditors. In theory, if someone who created a trust is sued, the assets in the trust are out of reach, because they are owned by the trust, not the individual. If you think this seems too good to be true, you are right for two reasons. First, it's illegal to defraud creditors. If it's clear that the trust was designed solely to protect assets against creditors, the creditor might be allowed to invade the trust. Second, what protects against creditors in one state might not afford the same protection in another state, where the laws are different. On the other hand, if your trust has existed for a long time, you might escape with your assets intact.

CAUTION

Portability across state lines is a potential problem with wills and revocable trusts. Because probate and divorce laws vary from state to state, what works in one state might not in another state.

Property management. Revocable trusts are popular among older people who decide that they do not want to manage property any longer. They want someone else, a trustee, to deal with renters or make investment decisions about stocks and bonds.

Privacy. Probate records are public and require that your will be part of the public records. If you don't want your financial business to be accessible to others after your death, a revocable trust is one way to avoid public attention.

Segregating property. Revocable trusts can be used to segregate certain property. For example, someone who brings assets into a marriage and wants to keep them separate might put them into a revocable trust to avoid commingling with marital property and to maintain clarity about the separate property character of the assets. Whether segregating such property in a trust will resolve all potential characterization questions depends on state law and whether the assets produce income.

Revocable trusts are the most common type of trust. If you have a revocable trust, the assets being held in it are subject to division at divorce just like all the rest of your assets. There's nothing about the trust that should get in the way of your divorce, but it is not unusual to revise or dissolve these trusts during a divorce.

RESOURCE

Nolo has a number of useful products you can use to create your own living trust. *Quicken Willmaker Plus* is interactive software that will help you to prepare a living trust, as well as a will and medical directives. *Make Your Own Living Trust*, by Denis Clifford, includes trust forms for you to fill out and instructions for transferring assets. And you can create a living trust online at www.nolo.com. But if you think it's possible you might not follow through on transferring assets, get a lawyer to help you create your trust.

Irrevocable Trusts

An irrevocable trust is a very different animal, used primarily to reduce exposure to estate and gift taxes for large estates, for asset protection against creditors, or to make gifts to children. Usually the creator cannot also be a beneficiary, because the creator gives up any use of, or benefit from, the property during life. These trust transfers are truly irrevocable gifts. One example of an irrevocable trust is when a parent wants to make a gift to a child who is a minor or still young enough to need help managing money. The parent names a trustee to manage and distribute property until the child is mature enough to manage it.

Irrevocable trusts can create some interesting issues in divorce. In general, marital assets transferred into an irrevocable trust are no longer in the marital estate and thus aren't subject to division in a divorce; they simply stay in the trust and transfer to the beneficiary at the trustee's death, just as they would have in the absence of a divorce. But if one spouse didn't consent to making the trust, that spouse might raise an argument at divorce that property transferred to the trust should be returned to the marital estate. A divorce court can't undo the trust unless fraud was involved in its creation, but the spouse who made the trust might be required to reimburse the other spouse for that second spouse's share of the marital assets that were put into the trust.

Testamentary Trusts

A testamentary trust is a trust created by a will that provides for the transfer of property into the testamentary trust at the time of the grantor's death. Parents with minor children often make testamentary trusts; in the event that both parents die, the parents' assets go into trust for the children until they reach adulthood. Testamentary trusts could also provide a way for the creator to control the management of property left to a spouse or an adult child who the creator thinks is not qualified to manage the assets without the help of a trustee.

Trusts that fall into this category go by several names: bypass trusts, marital trusts, and generation-skipping trusts. They are often used to reduce exposure to federal and state gift, estate, and inheritance taxes. Details about these trusts, which can be complex, are beyond our scope, but you can learn more about all types of trusts and other estate planning issues at www.nolo.com or in *Plan Your Estate*, by Denis Clifford, *Estate Planning Basics*, by Denis Clifford, *8 Ways to Avoid Probate*, by Mary Randolph, and *Make Your Own Living Trust*, by Denis Clifford, all published by Nolo.

Family Limited Partnerships

A family limited partnership (FLP) is another way to avoid or reduce estate taxes and protect against exposure from lawsuits. An FLP operates like a limited partnership; it must have at least one general partner who manages the FLP, and limited partners whose liability for partnership debts is limited to the value of their capital contribution to the entity— in plain English, the amount they put in to create the entity. The general partner, however, is personally liable for the entirety of any debt or obligation, regardless of the size of this partner's contribution.

When an asset is transferred to an FLP, the original owner acquires a percentage interest in the FLP entity along with other partners, rather than owning the asset itself. A limited partner doesn't have control over the asset's management, and as a result, the interest in the FLP has a lower value than full ownership of the same asset outside of the FLP. Lower value equals lower taxes—so as you can guess, the IRS is not enamored with FLPs and scrutinizes them carefully.

Because assets transferred into an FLP no longer belong to the original owners, but to the members of the FLP, what's divided at divorce is the limited partnership interest, not the asset itself. It's important not to be fooled into thinking an asset in an FLP is worth more than it actually is.

EXAMPLE. Both spouses own a piece of real estate worth $100,000. During their marriage, as part of their estate plan, they transfer the property into an FLP to lower their eventual estate taxes. Each spouse, as a limited partner, now owns an interest in the FLP. When they divorce, Spouse A agrees that Spouse B can retain the entire interest in the FLP. Spouse A thinks it will go on Spouse B's side of the ledger with a value of $100,000, and that Spouse A will get other property valued at $100,000. But the asset is the FLP interest, and it's subject to the minority interest discount, making it worth significantly less than $100,000.

Powers of Attorney and Guardian Designations

Powers of attorney are discussed in detail in "Delegating Authority Using Powers of Attorney and Medical Directives," in Chapter 3. These documents grant specific authority to act on behalf of another person with regard to finances or medical treatment. Some powers of attorney are effective immediately; others spring into effect when one or more physicians certify that the maker of the power of attorney is incapacitated. Powers of attorney terminate upon the maker's death.

It is very common for spouses to name each other as their agent in a power of attorney. As soon as you've decided to divorce, you should take stock of your documents and decide whether you still want your spouse to be the person to make medical and financial decisions for you. If you don't, then you must execute new documents designating someone else to take care of your needs should you become incapacitated.

Guardian designations are covered in "Surrogate Decision Making: When a Divorcing Spouse Needs Extra Help" in Chapter 3. A guardian designation states who you want to serve as your guardian in case of your incapacity. Again, if you don't want your spouse to be your caretaker in the event you become disabled, you must designate someone else.

Even if you're separated, as long as you're still married, your spouse might end up in a position to make these decisions unless you explicitly designate someone else.

Dealing With Your Estate Planning Before Your Divorce

You can see that it's enormously important for you to know what your estate planning situation is. Before you file for divorce, know where your estate planning documents are. Make a copy of them for your divorce attorney. And know who your beneficiaries are—in your will, trusts, insurance policies, retirement accounts, and pension plans.

If you don't have a will, the laws of intestacy take over the distribution of property when you die. This usually means that your spouse stands to receive one-third to one-half of your share of the marital estate, as well as possibly a share of your separate property, and will probably be first in line to manage your estate upon your death. The fact that you and your spouse are in the process of a divorce won't change these rules. If you're planning for divorce, it might be wise to make a will that reflects your current wishes, before you file papers.

During: Watchdogging the Status Quo

Filing for divorce does not automatically revoke your estate planning documents, but temporary restraining orders might limit your ability to make changes in some types of these documents. There also might be reasons for reaching agreements early on about these matters. Your role in the divorce will determine where you stand on this issue:

- You might be the one who wants to modify estate plans that were made in happier times. After all, your marriage is on the rocks, and perhaps you do not want your spouse to gain from your death, much less manage your estate if you die or if you are incapacitated. You want to be able to make changes.

- On the other hand, you might be the spouse who does not want to be left out in the cold should your soon-to-be-ex-spouse decide, perhaps in a moment of anger, to write you out of a will and change life insurance beneficiaries. You depend upon your spouse's income and expect that to continue after divorce. Besides, people can die during a divorce. You want all changes frozen until the divorce settlement is negotiated.

The question of whether you can make—or prevent—changes in spousal estate plans depends on the rules where you live.

Death While Divorce Is Pending

In most states, the death of a spouse during a divorce will stop the divorce in its tracks. If you and your spouse are in the process of a divorce and one of you dies, the other inherits just as if the divorce filing never happened (unless a will provides otherwise). This is why estate planning decisions made prior to a divorce need scrutiny as soon as you know that a divorce looms in your future. This is also why you need a will if you have not gotten around to writing one before now.

Prohibitions on Making Changes

Many divorce courts issue automatic restraining orders when a person files for divorce. You might see a provision that states: "You are prohibited from changing or altering beneficiary designations on life insurance or retirement benefits while this case is pending" or something even broader, prohibiting either spouse from acting upon any general or specific powers of attorney signed by the other spouse.

These orders are designed to maintain the status quo—in other words, to leave everything the same as it was before the divorce was filed, to protect both spouses' rights during the divorce.

If you want to make changes before the divorce is final, ask your attorney before you do anything, or you risk angering the judge and ending up in court for violating the orders. If you are using a collaborative process, carefully read the governing agreements that you signed. It's very likely you've agreed to status quo provisions. Even if it is not a court order, a collaborative law participation agreement is a binding contract and you don't want to violate it, even inadvertently. (See Chapter 4, "Your Divorce Options," for more about collaborative divorce.)

If you live in an area that doesn't have automatic restraining orders and you're worried that your spouse might make changes that will affect you, ask your attorney about getting a court order to keep your spouse from modifying these important documents. You and your spouse might have entered into contractual agreements in a prenuptial agreement or during the course of estate planning that might prohibit unilateral changes. Again, discuss this with your attorney.

The Role of Trusts in Divorce

Trusts pose some interesting challenges during divorce. Revocable trusts can be dissolved or modified in the course of a divorce. A trustee might even become a party to the divorce, if there's a dispute over characterization or division of property that has been transferred to a trust.

Trustees as Third Parties

A divorce court can bring a trust into a divorce suit by making the trustee a third party to the divorce. This could happen if a spouse creates a trust that includes marital property without the other spouse knowing or consenting. In that case, the validity of the trust might be in question and the trustee might be made a party to the divorce action.

A trustee might also become a third party to a divorce suit if the trustee fails to comply with trust terms or with state law regarding income distribution. Even when the property in the trust clearly started as one spouse's separate property, trust provisions might require income from the trust asset to be distributed to that spouse as a beneficiary. And state law might characterize such income as marital property, available to be divided in the divorce. If the trustee isn't distributing the accumulated income according to the terms of the trust, a judge might bring the trustee into the divorce as a third party and order the trustee to comply with the terms of the trust.

Third-Party Trusts

If either you or your spouse is the beneficiary of a trust created by another person (the third party), the existence of that trust could impact your divorce. Its very existence might be relevant to the division of the marital estate, and there could also be questions about characterization of income generated by the trust.

EXAMPLE: You know that you are the beneficiary of a trust created in your parent's will and that you will receive the trust assets in the future. Right now your parent is alive, so you have a mere expectancy that you'll receive the asset down the road. That expectancy is not part of the marital estate, but a judge could consider it when dividing the marital estate— especially if the trust will provide you substantial wealth after your divorce. As discussed in Chapter 5, "Marital Property: Steps to a Fair Division," your separate estate (including an expectancy) is one of those equitable factors a judge can weigh when dividing your marital estate.

Another issue about third-party trusts is the characterization of trust income. Let's assume that your spouse is currently receiving income produced by a trust created by a grandparent. Is this income your spouse's separate property or marital property to be divided in your divorce? The answer hinges on several variables: The law of your state, the terms of the trust, the intent of the grantor, and the extent of the trustee's discretion. Obviously, we can't address all of these questions here, so the takeaway for you should be that if you or your spouse is the beneficiary of a third-party trust, you'll need the help of an attorney to determine how the asset, income, or expectancy should be treated in your divorce.

Beneficiary Designations

A large part of your estate might be in nonprobate assets, such as life insurance, retirement accounts, and annuities. At some point in the past, you designated a beneficiary for each of these assets—the person who would receive the benefits or money if you die while you're still entitled to receive the funds. In most cases, your beneficiaries are your spouse or children. (If you don't know who your beneficiaries are, request a copy of the current beneficiary designation form for each account.)

Many retirement accounts, especially ERISA plans, require that if someone other than your spouse is the beneficiary, your spouse must sign a form indicating agreement with the beneficiary choice. For this reason, and also because of restraining orders that keep you from making changes on this type of asset, you can't just go in and change beneficiary designations. (See "Prohibitions on Making Changes," above.)

Beneficiary designations might become significant during the course of settlement negotiations. In some cases, they are used to secure alimony or property buyouts. In others, spouses agree to fund higher education for children and grandchildren through life insurance.

Don't lose sight of these assets just because they aren't available in the immediate present—they could be valuable.

After: Taking Care of Business

If you have not changed your estate planning documents during your divorce—or even if you did make an interim will—then you must create new documents immediately following entry of your final divorce judgment. It's true that many states have laws that automatically revoke bequests to a former spouse upon divorce, as well as laws that revoke your designation of your spouse as executor or trustee of your estate or trust. States also have laws that revoke beneficiary designations of a former spouse in wills, life insurance policies, and retirement plans. But you don't want to rely upon these laws, which could create confusion about which parts of your will are valid and which aren't. Instead, state your own wishes clearly by preparing an entirely revised estate plan for yourself in your new life. It's important that it be clear that your will was created after your divorce, when your legal marital status was single.

If your settlement includes your spouse's promise to redesignate you as a beneficiary of insurance or retirement plans after the divorce, be sure to include specific provisions in your divorce agreement, including all of the following terms:

- You have access to the insurance company or plan administrator to verify coverage and beneficiary designation.
- Every year, your spouse must provide you with proof of the correct designation.
- The divorce decree must specifically order your spouse to make the beneficiary redesignation by a specific date and provide you with proof of this redesignation.

Follow up to be sure your former spouse takes the required steps to ensure your beneficiary status.

There is nothing wrong with consulting an estate planning attorney before a divorce is final. You need time, as does the attorney helping you, to revisit your estate plan in light of the assets you're likely to receive in the divorce and to draft documents that address your new life circumstances. Leaving the courthouse after a divorce is granted and going directly to your attorney's office to execute your new will and other estate plan documents is perfectly fine and actually very smart.

After your divorce is concluded, you will likely have a sense of relief. The last thing you want to think about is dealing with another lawyer or additional paperwork. But think of your estate planning professional, whether it is your divorce attorney or a specialized estate planning attorney, as the one who is really going to wrap up your divorce. Make a commitment not to delay changing beneficiaries, financial account designations, wills, trusts, and powers of attorney. When it comes to creating a new plan, you are a step ahead, because the same financial information and records you have gathered in your divorce are useful to estate planning.

So, no excuses. Get this important task done and move on to Chapter 12, which addresses other details you should deal with once your divorce is completed.

CHAPTER

The End Game:
Finishing Up and Moving On

12

The last thing you'll deal with in your divorce is completing a marital settlement agreement, which becomes part of your divorce judgment. Once the court enters the judgment in the court records and you're finally divorced, you'll need to follow up on some details that will guarantee the smooth execution of the terms of the judgment. After that, then what? You are truly on your own, and you must continue the work you've already begun, of creating your new life. This chapter addresses all of these elements of your divorce and your postdivorce life.

The Marital Settlement Agreement

If your divorce case doesn't go to trial, as most don't, then one of the final tasks you'll deal with is working with your attorney to complete a written document that sets out the terms of your negotiated settlement with your spouse. This document is usually called a marital settlement agreement (MSA), and it covers all of the agreements you've made about support and the division of your marital estate. The MSA becomes part of your divorce judgment and, along with a QDRO (if you use one) is the governing document for any agreements you've made that will play out in the future, like payments to be made at retirement or when property is sold later. If problems or disagreements arise in the future, the MSA is the central document for enforcement—that's why it has so many details.

The MSA pulls all of the agreements that you've made through your mediation, collaborative process, or litigation into one document. In other words, whichever process you've used, you'll end up at the same place—with a written document that sets out everything you've agreed to.

If you mediated your divorce without using attorneys, this is the time to either consult an attorney to review the MSA that the mediator prepares for you, or to have an attorney prepare the agreement.

If you were in a collaborative or litigated process in which both spouses had attorneys, one of the attorneys will prepare a first draft of the MSA. The other attorney and each spouse will review the draft, and the drafting attorney will make the changes that everyone agrees on. You might end up back in negotiations over some small points that weren't clear to everyone, but, in general, the process of drafting, reviewing, and finalizing the MSA should go pretty smoothly. Give yourself plenty of time to read the MSA carefully. You might be eager to be finished, but try to focus your attention on making sure everything is as it should be.

If your case goes to trial, the judge's ruling will be reduced to a decree or an order and will decide the same issues found in an MSA, and you'll have the same opportunity to review the judge's order for accuracy and completeness before it is made final. Because settlement is so much more common than trial, this chapter addresses settlement agreements—but you should watch for the same issues if you're reviewing a judgment ordered by a judge after a full trial.

What's in an MSA?

Your marital settlement agreement should cover every point you and your spouse have agreed on during the divorce negotiations and should address how every piece of property you own is going to be divided or disposed of.

Marital residence. Your MSA should cover how you are going to deal with your family home—through a third-party sale, buyout, refinancing, or other arrangement. The document should be specific about the timing of payments and other details of the transactions you're planning.

If you're planning a future sale and your agreement contains details about things like a schedule for price reductions, remember to put these details in a separate document that's not filed in court records, and have your MSA refer to that other document. This side agreement should spell out who will have access to the residence and when; who is responsible for paying utilities and other maintenance services; who will pay the indebtedness on the property and whether that person will be reimbursed for any of these expenses at time of sale; who will be the listing agent; what happens if spouses disagree on an agent or sales price, including reductions in sales price, or other sales contract terms. If the parties disagree over these details (and others, such as repair budgets, which inspectors to use, and which parts of the closing costs will be negotiated), they can resolve them by having each spouse or their attorneys select a realtor who in turn selects a neutral realtor to decide the issues.

Personal property. The MSA should assign all personal property to one spouse or the other. Some of the property will be identified specifically (cars, bank accounts, and other valuable items); other things will be lumped together and you'll find that you're receiving "all the personal property currently in your possession." Be careful with catch-all clauses like that one, though. If you've agreed that your spouse will retrieve personal property that's still in your possession after the divorce, identify the items to be picked up, and nail down a date and time when that's going to happen.

Debts. Ideally, you will have already paid off all of your joint debts as part of a property buyout or other transaction during the divorce (see Chapter 8, "The Bad News: Debts and Taxes"). If you haven't, the MSA will assign them and should contain indemnity provisions and other terms (mentioned in Chapter 8's "Bankruptcy" section) that protects the nondebtor spouse if the spouse who takes on the debt fails to pay.

Property buyouts. If one spouse owes money to the other for a property buyout or to equalize the property division, the terms of the promissory note, payment schedule, and any other payment details should be in the MSA. (You should also have a separate promissory note, preferably secured by collateral, or a lien on the property.)

Alimony. The MSA must address the amount and duration of alimony, as well as any conditions required for modification or termination. It should also state how the alimony is going to be paid, what the consequences are for nonpayment, and whether there's security for the obligation.

Resolving disputes. Even if you think that your divorce settlement concludes any dealings you'll ever have with your spouse (which might be the case if the marriage was short and did not involve children), it's prudent to include a provision in the MSA that says how you'll resolve any disputes that do arise in the future—for example, by going back to mediation or to the same collaborative attorneys or by using an arbitrator.

Estate planning provisions. You and your spouse might have made agreements about your estate plans that require you to take steps after the divorce (for example, a spouse staying in the family home might agree to execute a will leaving the house to the other spouse in the event of the owner's death). If either spouse has promised to designate the other as a beneficiary after the divorce, spell out the promise in the MSA, and make sure it includes provisions allowing the beneficiary spouse to have access to records in order to verify that the designation is put in place and stays in place.

Health insurance. The MSA should address each spouse's future health insurance plans and obligations, especially if one spouse is going to elect COBRA coverage through the other spouse's employment.

Retirement benefits. Even if you are going to use a qualified domestic relations order (QDRO) to divide some of your retirement benefits, you should still address the issue in your MSA. In some cases, you'll need a QDRO for certain benefits, while others—like some 401(k) plans—can be divided through your MSA. If a QDRO is needed, though, make sure that the MSA addresses the issue of which spouse will prepare it and when. If you're the spouse who benefits from the QDRO, your best bet is to volunteer to take care of making sure the QDRO gets done now and done right, rather than leaving the task to your spouse, who might not have an interest in making sure it's completed. Ideally, the QDRO should be presented to the judge at the same time as the divorce decree.

Taxes. Although most transactions during divorce are tax neutral, depending on the date of your divorce and how you've been dealing with your finances, the MSA might provide these details: whether you're going to file jointly or separately for the tax year prior to your divorce, how you'll make that decision, who is eligible to claim specific deductions, how tax liabilities are to be allocated, and who will prepare your returns. If you expect a refund or loss carryforward, the MSA should include who receives it or how it's shared.

Boilerplate provisions. MSAs typically include numerous provisions that are the same for each MSA—things like a requirement that both spouses cooperate with signing any documents necessary to accomplish the provisions of the MSA, or a statement of which state's laws apply to the agreement, or an assurance that even if a judge finds that one paragraph of the agreement is invalid, others stay in effect. You'll know these when you see them in your draft, and you should be able to skim through most of them pretty quickly. One provision you'll always see is the statement that you are signing the agreement voluntarily and that you fully understand all of its terms—so take a moment to be sure that's true for you. If you do have any questions or concerns, raise them with your attorney before you sign the agreement. Once it's done, it's done.

Postdivorce Details

After your MSA is complete, the attorneys will submit all of the final paperwork to the court. You might have to appear in court for a final hearing at which the judge asks you questions about your settlement and judgment, or you might just wait to receive the phone call from your attorney or the notice in the mail telling you that your divorce is complete and you are legally single once again. This could be a bittersweet day, and you might want to prepare for it by planning some sort of ritual to acknowledge the change in your legal status—even something simple like taking a walk in your favorite place or meeting up with a good friend for dinner.

It might seem that having the judge's signature on your divorce paperwork completes your divorce. That's true enough as it relates to your legal status, but you must take care of some follow-up tasks to ensure your single future.

Get a certified copy of your divorce decree (order or judgment). A certified copy is one that the court clerk has stamped with a special statement saying that it's a true copy of the original judgment and MSA that are in the file. You'll be surprised how many times you will need a certified copy of the final judgment—to change retirement beneficiaries, obtain passports, and provide evidence of changes in property ownership.

Certified copies are available from the clerk at the courthouse where your divorce was finalized; if you had a hearing at which your divorce papers were signed, you could get certified copies that same day. If you received your final judgment in the mail, you might need to make a trip to the courthouse and ask for (and pay for) a certified copy. You could also order certified copies by mail or, in some places, from the court website.

If your divorce involves a QDRO, the attorney representing the alternate payee is responsible for sending a certified copy to the administrator of the retirement plan and for tracking its approval process.

Sign all property transfer documents. The settlement terms might require that you complete deeds, car title transfers, stock transfer documents, liens, notes, or security/collateral documents. For every piece of property assigned to you, be sure that you have a valid document of title, and be sure that transfers to your spouse have taken place as well, so that you're not considered responsible for property—or debts—that your spouse was supposed to take care of. Be sure to keep photocopies of documents that assign property or debts to your spouse.

Transfer IRA and other retirement account funds. The actual transfers of retirement funds from one spouse's account to the other's must occur after your divorce is final. Remember, if ownership of an IRA or a 401(k) changes, do a trustee-to-trustee transfer into a new account—don't distribute funds directly to the recipient unless that spouse is prepared to pay the taxes on that distribution.

Check utilities. Be sure utility deposits are properly assigned. Change the name on utility accounts—cable, satellite services, electricity, water, garbage, gas, telephone, Internet—so they are the same as the new owner's.

Change beneficiary designations. This includes your retirement plans as well as any insurance policies you own. Be absolutely sure to do this after the date your divorce becomes final.

Protect health insurance and meet COBRA deadlines. For COBRA coverage, stay on top of all notice deadlines. If you are changing insurance carriers, be sure you have no gap in coverage.

Check auto insurance. Be sure policies reflect the correct owner's name.

Complete change of address forms. If you're moving, change your address with the post office as well as all of your credit cards and other accounts. If you're staying in the family home and you haven't done so already, you might still want to do a change of address form to make it clear that your former spouse no longer lives in the house.

Deal with safe deposit boxes and distribute property. Close safe deposit boxes or change ownership so that only one spouse has access, and return contents that belong to the nonowner spouse.

Retain historical documents for assets you receive. Ownership documents should follow the assets. Whether it is an art authenticity provenance or remodeling receipts on the home you are keeping, get all the historical files and records pertinent to each asset you receive.

Create good record-keeping systems. Be sure you keep all the financial records you created or acquired during the divorce, along with all correspondence generated. You could put them in a box in the recesses of your garage, but keep them! You never know when you might need to refer to them, especially if enforcing the MSA becomes an issue in the future.

Moving On

The previous section covered the practical details of your postdivorce life—but of course, there's a whole separate aspect of it that's about your future as a single person and the choices you'll make in your new life. Chapter 13, "Survival Stories," consists of first-person accounts of the ways that some other late-life divorcees have experienced their divorces, their transitions, and their postdivorce lives. You might find that some of them resonate for you, or you might be having an entirely different experience. Either way, the bottom line is that your life is changing gears.

Taking Care of Yourself

My suggestion is that you take things slowly after your divorce. A late-life divorce is a big event, and you are likely still recovering from all of its challenges. Don't make hasty decisions about anything—where you'll live, what you'll do for work, or what uses you might have for your settlement money. Just sit on all of it for a while and let things percolate.

After all, you've been through a major life transition. Mental health professionals speak of divorce as an experience of loss that creates the same cycles of grief as do other losses. Many of my former clients continued counseling or joined a postdivorce recovery group to work through the emotional and social fallout from divorce. They've described their group experiences as a positive way to share the reentry into singlehood, rediscover strength and a sense of humor, support others, and be supported.

New Relationships

In my view, the advice to take it slow applies to new relationships as well. Some people cannot imagine dating or remarrying when they've just come out of a divorce, but others are ready and raring to go. I always advise my clients to wait a while after the divorce is final before jumping into a new commitment, and especially before jumping into remarriage.

But perhaps you've been waiting for what seems like—or what literally has been—years to wed your new partner, and you're ready to remarry right away. In that case, I'll encourage you to consider a prenuptial agreement.

A Word About Cohabitation

Cohabitation—which generally refers to romantic partners living together—is no longer an outlier. According to a Pew Research Center survey, the fastest growing demographic for couples opting to live together rather than marry are those over 50. Since 2007, the number of cohabiting adults aged 50+ grew by 75%, the majority of whom have been previously married. The scenarios for living and financial arrangements fall over a wide spectrum. While most cohabiting couples have talked about whether and how to share income and daily expenses, few have plans for care in case of serious illness or a financial catastrophe.

If this less formal relationship is in your partnering plans, consult with a family attorney. States have varying definitions for cohabitation, and their laws also vary in terms of potential legal consequences of cohabiting—from being a criminal offense or creating an unintended common-law marriage, to enforcing rights in the financial and estate planning portions of cohabitation agreements.

Remarriage and Prenuptial Agreements

A prenuptial agreement—also called a premarital or antenuptial agreement, or simply a prenup—is a contract that a couple makes before getting married. Its purpose is to structure the financial relationship between the soon-to-be spouses, both during the marriage and in the event they divorce in the future. A carefully crafted prenup could lead to a less expensive and less combative divorce if it does happen—and if you've just been through a contentious divorce, you could see the value of having such an agreement.

A premarital agreement could address a single issue or a multitude of them. It is up to the people involved to determine the degree of complexity. Even if a premarital agreement speaks only to one issue, both parties should understand how the treatment of that one issue interacts with the laws governing related, but unaddressed, issues. Some issues you might decide to address include how you'll deal with your property and income during marriage (as each person's separate property or marital property); how you'll share responsibility for household expenses; who has responsibility for premarital debts and for debts you incur during the marriage; whether a less-wealthy spouse should receive a lump sum payment at divorce, if it occurs; whether a wealthier spouse will agree to pay alimony and if so, the amount and duration; and whether the prenup expires after you've been married for a certain time. You can cover many more issues; this section is just intended to be your introduction to the concept of prenups. For more information, consult your attorney and take a look at *Prenuptial Agreements: How to Write a Fair & Lasting Contract*, by Attorney Katherine E. Stoner and Shae Irving (Nolo).

You don't want to see a proposed prenup for the first time on the church steps or in the hallway outside the office of the justice of the peace (in many states, such an agreement wouldn't be valid, anyway). Make time to discuss and negotiate from an unhurried, informed perspective, not at the last minute. This is a business transaction that requires forethought, independent legal advice for each party, and concentration on all of the what-ifs. The more closely the agreement reflects the interests of both parties, the more effectively it will operate to provide solid underpinnings to the marriage.

Why Consider a Prenup?

Many life experiences and concerns lead people to seriously consider a prenuptial agreement, especially later in life.

Fear and a desire not to repeat mistakes. If you have been divorced, you might want to avoid another unpleasant, unfair, and costly experience. Or, you might recognize clues that suggest the wisdom of having a prenup. For example, if your future spouse will bring debts into the marriage, you want to be sure you're not liable for those debts.

Providing for future generations. You want assurance that specific assets will end up in your children's or grandchildren's hands. It is not unusual for estate planning to occur when prenups are being drafted.

Independence and equality. People sign prenups to preserve independence within their marriage framework—what's mine is mine, and what's yours is yours. If both people are of similar backgrounds with comparable premarriage estates, they can make a clear distinction between what they bring into the marriage and what they want to build through joint efforts. Prenups can create clarity in how marriage partners share their support duties to each other. Perhaps you and your spouse-to-be agree to share expenses pro rata, based upon your respective incomes and resources, rather than equally, because that better suits your beliefs and balance sheets.

Laying bare hidden expectations. You want to move beyond pillow talk and be clear about how your financial relationship will be managed, by putting in writing your expectations of lifestyle, handling of obligations, accumulation of wealth, and plans to retire debt.

Security. With the odds so high that a marriage (especially a second or third marriage) will end in divorce, you're courting a degree of risk in walking down the aisle, especially later in life. A prenup could specify exactly which assets will be divided at divorce, and how much support will be paid by one spouse to the other. For a wealthier partner, a prenup provides the security of knowing exactly what property might be forfeited if a divorce happens. For the less-wealthy spouse, the prenup offers an assurance of receiving something if the marriage ends.

Encouragement from others. Friends or family members, especially those who have gone through divorce or death of a spouse, might strongly urge you to make a prenup.

"Crammed Down" versus Collaborative Prenuptial Agreements

For decades, prenups were viewed as documents drafted by one future spouse and handed to the other future spouse, who is told to sign or else. This approach is called a "crammed down" document. That way of doing things is changing.

Prenups are just as amenable to negotiation as any other contract. I have used the collaborative negotiation process successfully in negotiating prenups, and I encourage you to consider that avenue. In one case, after starting to negotiate the financial terms, the couple realized that they had very different views on living expenses and budgeting—something they had not realized about each other before. They paused the collaborative process while they went into joint counseling to try to reconcile their significant differences. Frankly, I wasn't sure they would return to the prenup discussion, much less marry. But they did, and both expressed their gratitude for that opportunity to work through what could have been issues that derailed their marriage.

You, Divorced

Through my decades practicing family law, I noticed that the person sitting across my desk at our last appointment looked very different from the person I first met: a calmer, more relaxed person, with a touch of fatigue, tempered by the hint of a smile. The change in demeanor was often remarkable.

RESOURCE

Recommended reading. Deidre Bair's book, *Calling It Quits: Late-Life Divorce and Starting Over,* is a collection of interviews about the late-life divorce phenomenon. Bair is a highly acclaimed author who experienced a divorce after 43 years of marriage, and she synthesizes a lot of material with astute observations.

Survival Stories

Y ou've worked your way through learning about the significant financial and legal issues of your divorce. But even though I am a lawyer and not a therapist, I am well acquainted with the reality that for most people, divorce is first and foremost an emotional experience. It is one of the most significant life changes a person can experience, and it can bring with it some valuable self-knowledge. Many of you reading this book are in the eye of the storm, wondering where you will land when things quiet down. This final chapter is intended to give you a glimpse into the lives of others who have been where you are, and a view of the possibilities awaiting you after your divorce.

The stories here are written by men and women who have experienced late-life divorces and lived to tell the tale—with humor, intelligence, common sense, and hard-earned wisdom. The contributors come from all over the country and from a range of economic circumstances. When asked to write about their late-life divorce experiences, they wrote from their hearts. Their stories may reveal some of the realities behind the questions "Why is this happening ... now?" and "What will happen to me?"

What's fascinating to me (and encouraging) is that, although these folks were not asked to write anything in particular and certainly weren't instructed that they should present a positive spin, over and over, their stories were upbeat, encouraging, and hopeful. This corresponds to my experience working with clients who find ways to survive, and thrive, after a late-life divorce.

Survival Stories

These are a few of the stories I received in response to my request that people write whatever they wanted to about their late-life divorce experiences, as if they were talking to a person facing the same prospect.

Becoming a Self-Governing Entity

My world is spinning completely and totally out of control. I have left my safe and secure position in the universe and am no longer orbiting

Planet Bill the way I have so steadfastly done for the past thirty years. I am, according to my family, friends, and even casual acquaintances, a woman dangerously out of control. "What is wrong with her? Is it menopause? Is she crazy? Bill is such a nice guy. She'll come around. Just wait and see," they say.

It is absolutely true, and I am loving every single minute of my out-of-control free fall. I feel like I am finally on a zip line experiencing life in the way I did so very long ago ... without a plan, by the seat of my pants, impetuously, impulsively, with a wide-open mind and no destination ... just a journey ... the journey, MY JOURNEY!

A Controlling Marriage

I married when I was 25 and my husband was 36. You may think that's not a big age difference, and it wasn't. Not at first. In fact, not for the first 25 years. But then it slowly and insidiously became a huge difference. He became old and I became ... well, me. It wasn't that the marriage was so bad, or that he battered me, either physically or emotionally. What he did do was CONTROL me. What I did was allow him to control me. I mirrored his likes and his dislikes. I shared his obsession for fitness, his love of sports, his food preferences, his time schedules, his politics, his prejudices. I made his life my life. I altered, changed, rerouted, redirected, shifted, rescheduled, and compromised. Compromise is probably too kind a word. I became the Stepford Wife of all Stepford Wives. He controlled me so secretively and silently that no one knew. No one noticed. Not even me. Even today he denies it. "Haven't I given you everything you ever wanted?" That oft-repeated statement, alone, was controlling.

From Dentist to Divorce

One day about a year ago, I came home from a dentist appointment and told my husband I needed two new crowns. He became angry and replied, "How can you do this to me right now?" I was stunned and looked at him for the longest time. "What?!" he yelled. I continued to look at him like I had never seen him before. It's not like I was out shopping for jewelry or a new poodle. There I stood, feeling guilty for having two bad teeth. That moment was a catalyst. It was the straw that broke the camel's back. I knew then that I didn't want to be married any longer.

During the month that followed, I became obsessed with the idea of divorce. I was angry all the time. The resentment and despair was a physical presence in our house. I was always sad. While I am sure my husband felt it, he chose to ignore it.

Getting out of a marriage is rough. The initial disclosure of your intentions to your spouse is like walking off the edge of a cliff. You have instantaneously lost all of the comforts and continuity in your life. For me, the legal and financial complications were secondary to the hurt and pain I was causing in that initial moment. The conversation went something like this.

"Don't you think we should talk about our marriage?" I asked.

"Yes. Maybe we should just get a divorce," he replied.

I knew this was a test, and he never in a million years expected me to say, "Yes, I think we should."

This, my friends, is the most difficult part of the process. Don't get me wrong. The days and weeks that follow will test your will. But once you verbalize your intentions, you can never go back to that same place you were yesterday or a few moments ago. Even if you decide to remain in your marriage, it will be irrevocably changed.

I know my husband loved me, but at the same time, I knew that I could never again love him in the way of happily married couples. I, of course, rationalized that this was for his benefit as well as mine. I genuinely hope that this will prove true one day. I am his biggest fan and will encourage him every step of the way. How odd this sounds, but really, what purpose does it serve to be angry and bitter? Negativity only prolongs the healing process. It will drag on and on.

Collateral Damage and Collateral Growth

There WILL be collateral damage. It just happens. Be prepared to lose some friends, and expect your spouse's family to be conflicted ... even after

30-plus years. Because my children are stepchildren, I feared that I would lose them as well as my beautiful grandchildren. I was reassured, and cried, when my stepson said, "You will always be Grandma. We love you."

I am also fortunate to have a core group of girlfriends. We've seen each other through death, divorce, addiction, and depression. The men have come and gone. These girls have been my constant. Use your friends. That is what they are there for. You've always been there for them, haven't you?

There are moments, hours, and sometimes days of pure terror. Can I do this? Can I handle this loss? Can I bear the possibility of a single life? What if I get lost? What if I can't program the smart TV? What if a pipe breaks? What if I lose my confidence? What if I get sick? They say that it takes a year for every four years of marriage to recover. I simply don't have time for that. I'm taking one step at a time, one day at a time, one crisis at a time. Dig deep to find whatever way works for you.

I was determined to remain friends with my ex-spouse, and in doing so I pretty much gave away the farm. This I do not recommend, unless you are financially secure and willing to walk away from your comfort zone. All of our property, with the exception of a few family heirlooms, was expendable to me. In fact, I wanted to redefine myself and in doing so I was willing to let go of things that I would've fought like a cat for a year ago. I think it is all a part of the cleansing process that continues today.

Retooling

I have taken on the daunting project of reeducating myself. I am back in school. My friends all find this amusing since I was a pretty lousy student 35 years ago. I am also working in the field of early childhood development, yet another source of amusement amongst my friends and family. I am so fortunate to have found something to channel my energy and passion.

Thirty years ago, I made a regrettable choice. Over the years, I shed a thousand little pieces of myself like a dog sheds its coat. What grew back was not me. It was a reflection of my husband. Now when I look in the mirror, I see myself—Grandma, teacher, friend.

I am so very fortunate. I made that leap of faith. They say that more regrets come from indecision than from bad decisions. Divorce was absolutely the right decision for me. No doubt. I admit that I have a long way to go before I feel totally comfortable in my own skin. There is uncertainty and fear, times when my self-esteem fails me, times when I am consumed with guilt. When this happens, I think about the woman I have become and return to living the life I want. I also think about these four lines written by Helen Keller:

> *The million little things that drop into your hands*
> *The small opportunities each day brings*
> *He leaves us free to use or abuse*
> *And goes unchanging along His silent way.*

Every day when I wake up, I ask myself, "Is this going to be a good day? Or is this going to be a bad day?" I DECIDE to be happy!

* * *

Collaborating While Dismantling

"Hey guy, good news! After almost 40 years of marriage, including a couple years of separation and a year of dickering with lawyers, Suzie and I were divorced last month."

My friend, Tom, was incredulous. "Divorced? Man, you're 65 years old! Isn't it a little late in life to be starting over?"

"Not really, considering Suzie and I did almost everything backwards. I got my adopted daughter the same year I got my AARP card, remember? Now I'm 65 years old with half a pension, an ex-wife, and a teenage daughter. Piece of cake!"

Well, almost.

After three years of marriage, Suzie and I started saying both of us were too stubborn to admit we couldn't make it work. It took us 35 more years to acknowledge the truth and decide to end the marriage.

The first postdivorce lesson I needed to learn was that the past cannot be changed. While the death of a relationship always involves grieving, it need not include resentment and bitterness about what can never be changed. More to the point, it offers an invaluable opportunity for increased self knowledge, maturity, and, dare I say it, better behavior in the future. I'm starting to get me some of that!

I'm not a Boomer. I'm a Pearl Harbor baby, born nine months and one week after the Japanese bombed Pearl Harbor. When I was a kid, people didn't get divorced. It took a while for me to understand that my sense of myself as damaged goods because I had been divorced—rejected as defective?—was a product of values from a time and society long gone. Most certainly not true about me!

Suzie and I divorced using the collaborative process, which probably saved our lives and our daughter's. We were so angry when we parted—or is it more accurate to say we were so hurt and miserable?—I think any suggestions from either of us would have been rejected out of hand by the other. Collaboration let us deal with the issues we had to deal with only when we were ready and able to deal with them.

Yes, it took longer and cost more than it might have had we not been so defensive. After a while, though, with a great collaborative team supporting us, we were able to get to a settlement acceptable to both of us. Anyone who has gone through the process will not be surprised to hear that Suzie and I are better friends now than when we lived together, and our daughter is thriving. It certainly is not all roses, but it is livable because we have no regrets and no resentments about how we went about dismantling something we had lived in for two thirds of our lives.

Though alcohol problems were not directly involved in our marriage, our counselor sent me to Al-Anon to do some twelve-step recovery work, which I continue and expect to continue for the rest of my life. I learned there that many things are not under my control. I learned that I could not expect to make our divorce turn out exactly like I wanted it to, and that I could not expect to make the process move along on a schedule to my personal liking. Without belaboring the point, I learned to simply go with the flow—participate in the process, be clear, but undemanding about my preferences and expectations, and have faith that the end point I could neither foresee nor control would turn out to be all right.

And it did.

* * *

Reconciliation

Involving our two children in our divorce was not something that I wanted to do or even planned. My husband pulled them in by telling them, before me, that he had filed. Neither I nor my two kids wanted our family to split. My kids and I tried to process things together.

Then the reality of another woman came true. The kids had questioned him on this, and he lied to them. But it wasn't just the lie; it was compounded by who the other woman was; she was working at our family company where our son was employed. After months went by, our son approached his dad and made the ultimatum—it was either him or her. Dad chose her over his son. After our son left the company, it was almost two years before he saw his father again. His parents were divorcing, and his father betrayed him, too. How much worse could it get?

The effects on my daughter weren't as dramatic because she wasn't involved with our company. She didn't feel the betrayal that our son did. But she was hurting. She had always been "Daddy's Little Girl," and he wasn't treating her in the same way. She could see that I was really struggling, so she made the move back home to be with me. At first, neither of us saw what she was doing, but she had become my second mother. I accepted it readily because I wasn't seeing anything clearly. Sleeping at night was impossible and was replaced by crying. My daughter overheard me one night, got in bed with me, held me, and cried with me. Soon, she, too, cut her dad out of her life because of an embarrassing scene he caused at her workplace.

The kids saw their mother falling apart and their dad driving around in a new red Porsche with the Other Woman. My, how our family picture had changed!!

Getting to the Other Side

I never thought in my entire life that I would be forced to hire a divorce attorney. I called a good friend who had recently divorced. This was my first step in going public. I wasn't about to look in the yellow pages for an attorney. After I retained my attorney, my husband tried to talk me out of hiring her; I stuck to my guns and felt some sense of empowerment. I learned quickly to hold on to those moments as a defense—yes, he could leave me, but he wasn't going to get the best of me.

I also went public to my family, friends, and tennis team. I wrote this email to my tennis team: "My husband left me, filed for divorce, and bought a new red Porsche. What do you think I should do?" The comments came back in a fury, and one friend in particular advised me to think of him as a tennis ball. "Hit him where it hurts," she said, "and I don't mean just the pocket book." I used this mental picture repeatedly during my tennis matches, and that also empowered me. My tennis stroke even improved!

I asked another good friend, who was also a psychologist, to recommend a counselor. In the early sessions the counselor helped me to understand my husband. Midlife crisis was the diagnosis and a protracted one at that. Even though the counselor told me that he was acting out his hurts and it wasn't about me, it was hard to grasp. After so many years of marriage, how could he do this to me? Why did it hurt so much? For me, my husband's midlife crisis was a selfish form of depression. It was all about him, and he couldn't see it or the consequences of his actions. For him, it was a new red Porsche, new apartment, women, and spending money. For the rest of us, it was agony and pain and coping with the changes in his behavior that he inflicted on all of us.

My husband was invited to attend a counseling session because I needed closure. My counselor wanted him to tell me good-bye, and I was to do the same. He got to go first. But he couldn't do it; he broke down and cried in my arms! But he also didn't want to commit to a year of working with the counselor saving our marriage. This exercise was empowering because I could see he did love me, but was definitely in a midlife crisis and pretty messed up!

We had been separated for over a year and still no divorce or reconciliation. There had been several attempts at reconciliation, but none worked. My husband was still spending money and running up credit cards. At this point, my attorney advised me to get an independent audit of the family company; we learned that the company wasn't in good financial shape. Even though I knew my husband still loved me and I still had feelings for him, I needed to protect my assets and get on with the divorce. No one could tell me how long this crisis would last.

Everyone advised me to get the divorce finalized, including the kids. Who knew when my husband would snap out of this and if there would be any assets left? So I went to my attorney for advice—mediation or collaborative law? I opted for mediation for two reasons: One was that I didn't feel I could trust my husband; and the other reason was that if things didn't work out in a collaborative process, I would have to find another attorney.

Forcing mediation was the impetus for me to take a good look at my life and start planning for it financially. During this time, my son was a great help to me. His finance education really paid off. He organized all the assets on a spreadsheet and helped me analyze our entire portfolio. We sat down together and did a monthly budget. Next, he helped me think through which assets to ask for and how to invest funds so that I could meet my monthly expenses.

We reached an agreement in mediation. I would have the house and other assets. So, I immediately started doing repairs and getting appraisals so I could list it for sale. Downsizing was the plan, and invest the difference. Essentially, we were done with the divorce. All we needed was for the attorneys to complete the asset transfer documents, then we would go before the judge. The date was set, but my husband let us know the day before that he wasn't going to show up, and we had to schedule a new date.

Somewhere during this last phase I started dating, but soon realized I was in over my head and was not ready. I decided that dating would just have to be on a friendship basis after that. The thought of kissing anyone else, let alone jumping into the sack, was revolting.

Reconciliation

Communication was rare between us during the last stages of the divorce process, and what communication we had with each other wasn't very good. To list the house for sale according to the settlement, I had to get my husband's signature. This started an email dialog between us. Yes, he would sign the listing papers, and he also wanted to know how I was doing. I told him I was dating. He replied that he needed to talk with me, and it had to be in person. After thinking on it for several days, I agreed.

The bottom line was that he was waking up and realizing that he had messed up big time. We went out to dinner and talked for hours, the way we used to communicate so many years before. He still loved me and wanted me back. And yes, he was very sorry and would do anything to stop this divorce. I agreed to think about it. After spending the weekend thinking, I came up with a list of things that he would have to agree to if this reconciliation were to happen:

- Fire the Other Woman, and cut off all communication with her.
- Start counseling.
- Have the chief financial person with our company issue me a report on the financial condition of the company and give me access to talk to the other executives at the company.
- Give me all of his IDs and passwords for email accounts, bank accounts, and credit cards.
- Give me copies of his monthly cellphone bills.
- Answer any questions regarding the Other Woman any time I wanted answers.

He agreed to all of my demands and the next day he fired the Other Woman!

Shortly after this new twist in the divorce, I called my attorney and she suggested several options. I chose the option to dismiss the divorce, and my husband agreed. It's been three years since we reconciled. This has been a long, arduous process on the road to trust and forgiveness. He has reconciled with our children, and we are now first-time grandparents to twins. We have spent countless hours talking about the painful things, such as his affair and the effects it had on all of us. When he woke up, the pain came crashing through, and he now has to live with it every day. His pain is more real now than mine is. I don't feel sorry for him though—I have just come to a better understanding of it all.

This summer we will be celebrating our 40th anniversary, and repeating our vows in front of our children and friends. Luckily, Karma, God, or maybe even our patient attorneys were part of the plan for two best friends finding their way back to each other and to love.

* * *

Ambivalence

We met two dozen years ago. I was 47, never married, childless. If I didn't marry her she'd find someone else, I thought. That was in a fit of temporary insanity that will have endless repercussions.

We agreed things would start better in our new life together if we quit drinking. That lasted about six months, during which we found a home, got jobs and a cat. We began the idyllic illusion of American matrimony. I worked a lot, loving my job. She transitioned from outside employment to manager of our domestic affairs. I worked more, barely noticing the resumption of her drinking. I started again too.

It gradually became obvious that alcohol was wrecking my life. In January 2010 I quit for good. Two weeks later a routine colonoscopy revealed she had Stage III squamous cell cancer. The treatment, particularly the chemo, messed her up bad.

Time in bed filled with fear, pain and way too much Internet began to erode her happiness with me and our life together. I worked more. I stayed clean; she drank more. Bad combo. The marital dysphoria grew to the inevitable and tragic climax.

The unravelling culminated at the end of September nearly three years ago. Court-mandated urine testing, counseling, and supervised probation commenced. She'd called the cops, hoping to scare me. I was sober and bleeding; she wasn't. All on me, except ... not this time.

Divorce

The divorce was handled better than I could have hoped. Assistance from the court and its facilitators was great. Helpful advice from friends, neighbors, and books made the process clear if not entirely simple. But I won't go through it again.

She continued living here, even after the divorce was final, packing and smoldering. A week before her sisters arrived to help her load the U-Haul and go, I moved into a tent by the river. I returned home when I was sure she was gone. The house was on my side of the ledger. I've smudged, chanted, prayed, and rearranged space ever since. The arrangement of furniture, eye-candy on the walls, food in the fridge: It's all my choice now. I can entertain whomever I wish at any time. No slamming of doors, stomping of feet, or loud swearing will be tolerated.

The texts, emails and phone messages began almost immediately after she left. She was sorry, wanted to come back, hated where she was. At first I waffled, sympathy and foolishness overriding reason; but I also laid down conditions.

As her pleas and contrition continued, my resistance grew. I had thoughts about selling the house and moving, getting a restraining order, and even resuming the whiskey habit I'd abandoned for nearly a dozen years—that's pretty much a daily thing. I stopped responding. Days, then weeks and finally months passed without attempts at reconnecting.

The Latest: Discussion with Self

Ten days ago she showed up sober and glowing. I was charmed, sympathetic, bushwhacked. And now, clearheaded and healthy, she's at least as irresistible as she was two dozen years ago. When she left yesterday we were starry-eyed and grateful for a second (or twenty-second) chance.

I still love her, but love's not enough. Pheromones, an aberrant amygdala, or temporary insanity? The cause is irrelevant. We agree, this house is too small for both of us. It's possible, likely even, that she's imagining moving back in anyway. Her gauzy vision of our rainbows-and-unicorns future must inevitably acknowledge the cold, hard truth of the situation. Her opinions are welcome until they become an angry tirade. We are not married now, so the laws are in my favor. She would dwell here again with my consent and permission, which could be withdrawn at any time for any reason.

If this list of rules and conditions seems unnecessarily harsh, she's free to live somewhere else. I won't ask her for rent while she's here; I will require her to adhere to standards of polite behavior. I would remind her that my 401(k) is essentially gone, hers is to spend as she deems appropriate. This is a sober, civilized home. It will remain so as long as I'm in it. Want to live here? Follow the rules and mind your manners. (Welcome home, Sweetie.)

Many situations require the restriction of an individual's treasured "freedom." You get a job, you do as the boss says or you're gone. When we thank our "essential-service workers" we are in part celebrating their willingness to subsume their individual whim for a greater purpose.

I reiterate: Love is not enough. It's all you need? It's the essence of life? Maybe. But I'm too old to let teenage fantasy and half-baked theory dominate what's left of my life.

We'll have this discussion before she moves in. I'll be annoyingly alert to the distant flutter of a crimson banner. Trust is crucial and— once reestablished under a mutual agreement—precariously fragile. Don't know what's to come; never did. Unbidden, undeserved blasts of pure-G grace might save some resurrected contentment for us. Or not.

Selfless versus Selfish

When I filed for divorce from my wife of 30 years, shortly before my 60th birthday, it was without a doubt the most selfish thing I had ever done. My action radically altered the trajectory of the lives of my then wife and our two adult children. In its wake were lost relationships, social status, and financial security. My selfishness hurt loved ones deeply and to this day, there are those who remain baffled by it. It also saved my life.

For decades I defined myself as the caretaker-provider. Always the selfless one, I wore the badge of taking care of everyone else with pride. That was my defense against the repressed feelings and emotions that were increasingly difficult to keep at bay.

Several years before I filed for divorce, our marriage counselor of eight years rather casually remarked that selfishness is a good thing. Without it, she said, as children we would not survive. As adults it provides physical health, occupational success, and protection from danger. I came to realize that, in fact, it is chronic selflessness that is potentially harmful. It erodes and can destroy the self.

During the run-up to my divorce I learned that for us to survive as healthy, whole human beings, we need to find, liberate, and celebrate our authentic selves. That is our truth, as in "seek the truth and the truth shall set you free," "if you love someone set them free," and "freedom's just another word for nothing left to lose."

What is paradoxical, is this: Selfishness is not easy. We are taught to repel and avoid it. As children, we are punished or shamed for being selfish. As adults, our social institutions, our churches, and our political leaders trumpet and glorify selflessness.

Well, I say be a radical, be selfish. Do this for yourself, not for your spouse, not for your children, not for anybody or anything, but for you. Give yourself permission to be yourself.

At our age, it is still early. There is plenty of time to celebrate yourself, to accept yourself with enthusiasm and experience pure joy. There is still time to embrace life with passion (with or without Viagra). There is still ample time to have meaningful relationships, even a joy-filled and loving marriage. But you can't do it selflessly; my advice is: Don't even try. Be completely, unabashedly, guiltlessly selfish.

Let ending a lifeless, and perhaps emotionally or physically abusive, marriage be the beautiful question about who you are, not the answer. Of course, there was no salvation in my divorce any more than was in my marriage. But in my divorce, there was deliverance.

* * *

The "A" Word

I met him in 1991 at a business conference. I had been divorced for over a year and my only child was a junior in high school. He was professional, attractive, funny. He was nine years older than me and very charming, with a wonderful Southern accent. He went to a prestigious college and had been a Marine. He had lots of friends and three sons in high school.

We lived four hours apart, and dated long distance for four years before we decided to get married. My company agreed to transfer me to his town if I took a demotion. I took the leap. We sold his house and bought a new one together. Three of our kids were in college, and just his youngest boy was at home. I was thrilled to have found him. The first couple of years were fine. We traveled, visited friends, and enjoyed having all our kids and their friends visit as often as possible.

Then he started to change. He was very forgetful. He would leave things in hotel rooms when he traveled for business, and his secretary had to call and arrange to get them for him. He left a brand-new camera I bought him in the airport. He left his glasses in the golf cart. He would leave the house for work and leave the front door standing open. I decided he was the absentminded professor type.

But his personality changed next. He became suspicious of everyone. People were trying to "cheat" us—our tax man, the plumber, our financial adviser. Then he turned on me. He was sure I was cheating and hiding things from him. We began to argue a lot, and he started hitting me.

I finally talked him into going to a geriatric specialist, who diagnosed Alzheimer's. My husband was told he should be very careful practicing his professional career because of malpractice. He was told that he should put his finances in order. It was estimated that from diagnosis to custodial care, we were looking at about eight years.

He was in total denial, as were his sons and his siblings. To make matters worse, my husband found a neurologist who told him he didn't have Alzheimer's, but had been experiencing a series of ministrokes. He hung on to this different diagnosis and stopped taking his Alzheimer's medication.

Things continued to worsen. He thought I was trying to take his money. We were working on putting together a will, and he didn't even want me to get half of the house. We fought a lot. After he hit me one time, I left and went to stay with my sister for a couple months. Every day he and I talked. We then decided I would return home. Two months later, on my birthday, he slapped me across my face. The next day, I found a lawyer.

The Divorce

We used the same divorce lawyer. I knew his boys would need all of his assets to take care of him in the future. I only wanted half of the house, and he finally agreed to this. When I moved out, he checked every box and followed me everywhere to see if I was taking anything of his.

I was fortunate that I had a sizeable 401(k) account for my future retirement. When I left my company after nineteen years, at his request, I took my pension and savings plan in a lump sum. I could not take my health insurance, but I was covered under his plan. When we divorced, I had to find an individual policy. It is extremely hard to find health insurance at 55. There are not only the health issues; but if you have ever had any kind of counseling, some insurance companies will deny you coverage.

Life After Divorce

My daughter now lived in the California Bay Area. I called my former company, and they allowed me to come back to work. So I moved west. After the divorce, my ex-husband visited me a lot. He was going downhill, but could still travel on his own and do things. We had fun in the Bay Area. We traveled to Vegas. But I always had to be in charge and make sure he was okay. He was still in denial.

He has now been in a nursing home for Alzheimer's patients for a year. I think of him every day and miss the wonderful man he was. I do have lots of guilt for leaving him and have gone through counseling for it. I get lonely and wish things could have been different. I stopped drinking because I found myself killing my feelings too many times.

My daughter and her husband and my two grandchildren live down the street from me, and they are a big part of my life. I have a great job and terrific income. This summer I took a cruise with seven other women and had a ball.

Life goes on.

* * *

Peace Through Long-Term Separation

Why did I make the decision not to file for divorce when I left my husband? Good question. And I am not sure I really know the answer. It took me at least 25 years to come to the decision to leave him, and at the time I left, I had no idea what he would do. Although he was never physically abusive to me, he had such a volatile temperament that I was never sure how he was going to react. My family and friends were concerned for my safety. He was very upset but did not become violent. At first, I was so relieved he wasn't screaming and yelling that I didn't want to do anything to cause him to react angrily.

Fifteen years earlier, I had filed for divorce. He talked me out of it —promising to quit drinking and to get counseling—so I didn't follow through with the divorce. His promises lasted only about six months. This time, I planned in advance without his knowledge. I left before he had an opportunity to change my mind. My counselor was very helpful in predicting his reactions and helping me deal with them.

I was 62 years old at the time I moved out of our home, which was within two years of being paid for. He continued to live there. I was the one to move because I had so many unhappy years there, and I knew it would be an awful hassle to get him out of the house. Eventually I asked him to pay me half of the home's appraised value. He agreed and did so over the next two years. After a year and a half, I bought a townhouse and settled into a good life.

I actually believe that the reason he didn't create a lot of flak over the finances was because I did not file for divorce but left our status as separated. In hindsight, I am convinced that I took the easy way out because I had lived in such an explosive situation for so long, with so much verbal abuse, that I did not want to get back into it. My new life seemed so calm, and I wanted it to remain that way.

His objective in staying separated instead of getting divorced? To win me back. My objective? To keep the peace. So I settled into a new kind of serenity. My life became one of spending time with friends and doing what I wanted to do, when I wanted to do it. My two children were happy that I had made the decision to leave. They had grown up in that turmoil and knew it well.

As time passed, it was as if we were divorced but still had an amicable relationship. Neither of us made our friends choose sides, and we both continued to participate in activities with our friends. I became comfortable with the status quo, and we each went on our separate ways.

Because I was still married, there was a sense of security in that I was not in the market for another man in my life. Actually, when I look back on the past years, I am convinced that this kept me from making mistakes that I would probably have regretted later.

My family background played a role in all of this. My mother knew how bad my life had been with an alcoholic, but she never wanted me to get a divorce. She always said that he would change when he got older. It didn't happen. Her influence also kept me in the situation. It was only after her death that I got the courage to leave.

I also had several years in Al-Anon and individual counseling. Both helped me find my inner strength to decide to leave. Some days I think that if I had it all to do over again, I would probably file for divorce after things cooled down. But sometimes we can't redo those kinds of decisions. We just do the best we can, trust ourselves, and trust a higher power when we go through something like this.

Although I've not filed for a divorce since moving out 15 years ago, I know that option is still open to me. I would never say "never." My life has been rich and full since I left my husband. My husband and I remain on good terms. He is now more involved with our two children than he ever was before we separated. We have mutual friends, and from time to time we attend events together, celebrating weddings, birthdays, etc. I remain very close to his family and he considers my family a part of his family. We have had disagreements over the past 15 years, but have resolved them over time.

Finally, I know for sure that I could never live with him again. I am at peace with the decision to leave him that I made 15 years ago. Whether I should have filed for divorce is still a question I may never fully know the answer to.

* * *

Flying Solo

My late-life marriage began when I married at age 52 and my ex-husband was 70. Our marriage was short and we divorced three years later. At age 59, I am reflecting upon those few years. I would say that our marriage was canceled due to lack of interest. In short, there was no "there" there.

Disaster from the Start

After marriage counseling, I realized that our marriage was a situation in which he was CEO (chief executive officer) and I was COO (chief operations officer). He married me so that he would have someone to maintain the house, make the plane reservations, and download electronic files he needed regarding his investments. Once I was installed in my new position, his life went on as before.

A Cooperative Divorce

Shortly before our marriage, I was asked to sign a prenuptial agreement and I refused. Our divorce was done cooperatively with our respective CPAs doing the negotiations. Because the vast majority of his wealth was acquired prior to marriage, there was minimal marital property to share. The negotiations were complete in about three months and I spoke with him once by telephone and have not spoken with him since.

Jump-Starting a Career

By the time I picked up my settlement check at his attorney's office, I was well underway in restarting my life. My challenge was coping with the anxiety of jump-starting my career at age 55 in a new town where I knew no one. I had moved across the country to a rural area to marry, and I decided to move to a city nearby and begin my life anew.

I had a professional license but I needed to get relicensed in my new state. One day while doing online course work to gather enough hours to activate my license, I looked out the window and saw a bird on the wooden railing and wrote this poem:

A Bird With One Leg
Out the window
On the wooden ledge
A bird with one leg
Standing,
Balanced in the wind
Feathers puffed out, alert
Then, suddenly, gracefully
Flying away.
And I, with only one heart beating now
Now that he's flown away
I must stand on two legs, alert,
Feeling the winds around me
Ready to fly.

While waiting for all the licensure documentation to be processed, I learned of a new training in a specialty area. I quickly registered for the course, and jumped in the big old truck, and drove 500 miles to take the important training that launched me on my new career path. Shortly, I received my new license in the mail, scheduled my move, and joined a divorce group in my new town. There I met a woman who was also in transition who offered to share her apartment with me while I got established. In a year's time, I lived in three different places until I finally found my own home. During all this time I made contacts, established my new business, and never looked back.

After the Divorce

My postdivorce lifestyle is full and I have made friends, joined groups, and gotten to know my new town. I often travel to visit old friends and do career-related travel to conferences. I live a more frugal lifestyle than I did while I was married, but still have fun and go out with friends. Although I weathered the storm and learned to fly again, I would say that I am not as optimistic as I once was. I know I can handle risk in the professional arena with positive results, but am not as eager to take on risk in the world of personal relationships. When my peers discuss retirement or minor money worries, I know that I will probably not ever be able to retire. I am lucky enough to enjoy my work immensely and to be in a profession in which aging is a positive, not a negative.

* * *

Learning to Skip Again

On our 28th wedding anniversary, his usual behavior was distant, aloof, morose. But his new behaviors, smugness and condescension concerned me. So I confronted him, and he gleefully replied, "I can't help it. I don't love you! I never have!" Thus began the most stressful event of my life.

We met when my husband was a medical student and I was an undergraduate. Following my graduation, we married. I supported us through the remainder of his medical school years. After his residency, our two daughters were born. He worked while I stayed home to care for the children, house, and family issues. When the girls were in high school, I attended graduate school, continued my family and household duties, and cared for an elderly parent.

I graduated, accepted a job, and was thrilled about contributing to the family financially. I was delighted to have found a vocation that provided me satisfaction, as our daughters progressed through college and into their own lives. This is the point when our late-life divorce occurred.

The Divorce

Despite our long-term, emotionally distant marriage, I did not foresee it ending in divorce. I didn't know where to begin after he uttered that he did not love me, never had. My appetite disappeared, and I rapidly lost 25% of my body weight. I knew this was about survival. Finally I started putting one foot in front of the other, trying to look out for my future.

While I scrambled to determine what to do, my husband cut off my access to our money. I had one credit card, and I was petrified to use it for fear it might be canceled. Then came the crowning blow—a phone call from my doctor. I had a sexually transmitted disease (STD), compliments of my husband and who knows. The next several months brought a series of constant battles in litigation and embarrassment, while my husband publicly displayed his mistress.

Life After Divorce

Professionally. Shortly before the conclusion of the divorce, I took the best job I could find. Even with a master's degree, my limited work experience limited my salary. I realized I had a choice. I could continue to exist on that low salary, deplete my savings, and ultimately become a financial burden to my daughters. Or, I could establish my own business, incorporating a lifetime of experience, education, and skills, and do something truly meaningful. I chose the latter. Lots of hard work and several years later, I have no regrets!

Personally. Six weeks after my husband left our home, as difficult as things were, I found myself skipping to the kitchen one morning. This was the moment when I first realized the impact of living so many years in an emotionally distant relationship. I've been on a personal growth journey ever since and enjoying every day of my life.

Lessons and Advice

Why now? My husband's midlife birthday was a time of extreme depression for him. He observed our daughters become young women, developing intellectually and enjoying youthful relationships. I think he longed for youth and romantic excitement. Since my own divorce, I have observed this phenomena many times. My husband was going to do what HE needed to do without any regard for me. Divorce and a new partner were his answers to his dilemma. While I spent time contemplating what I could, should, and would have done differently, I've since learned that my mental struggle was irrelevant.

Process. I truly believe that family relationships should be preserved if possible, especially where there are children; they will always be connected to their parents. The collaborative law model of divorce was not available in my part of the country, but I have since learned that it offers one of the best ways to resolve a divorce. If it is not available in your area, read about it and vow to adopt a mindset that will foster amicable future relationships.

Guidance. Guidance through this late-life divorce can come from many sources. A good attorney, for starters. But there were mental health and financial professionals who steered me, as well. As I watched my body become thinner and thinner and my obsession with the divorce overpower me, I knew I needed help. Through counseling, I faced my situation and identified ways to avoid repeating the same mistakes in the future.

While my own background was in the financial field, I knew I was too stressed to think clearly. Outside opinions and guidance of financial advisers were invaluable to me in budgeting, asset division, retirement, and separate property issues. Every case is different; but if you become educated and informed, it will prepare you to negotiate an equitable settlement.

Dating. I promised myself that I would not date for a full year following separation. My idea was not to depend on one man and repeat the same behavior. My theory was a good one. Since most dating adults are on their best behavior, the positive attention can be mistaken for deeper feelings and lead to a premature commitment. There is really no need to hurry.

In the meantime, I still find myself skipping into my kitchen with a grin.

* * *

From Denial, Through Despair, to Love

Fifteen years ago, I was premenopausal, overweight, depressed, and mourning my mother's death. But let me tell you about the hard part. Because as painful and difficult as all this was, being newly divorced was a new low. I literally thought it might kill me. It was a wounding torment that threatened to engulf and destroy me, and I couldn't understand how it had happened. I knew it happened to other people, but I had done everything right, given it my all, yet here I was, facing the biggest challenge of my life.

Through determination and a spiritual perspective, I not only survived, but I thrived. I moved through the devastation of divorce to enjoy a fruitful, fulfilling life. Along the way there were many lessons: What doesn't kill you makes you stronger; your expectations and attitudes determine your life; you determine the depth of your own suffering; sometimes you have to learn the hard way.

At the time I saw none of this. Divorce is a type of death, and indeed it felt like one. It was the death of my marriage; my dreams; my trust. It was also the death of the self I knew. I had been a woman with a neatly planned life. I would put my stepchildren through school and take care of my husband into old age. I envisioned rolling him around in his wheelchair, the dutiful, good wife. Now I was to be a divorced woman, alone.

I felt devastated. The stress of my parents' divorce had killed my father and caused my mother to die a bitter woman. As she took her last breath, I held her hand and vowed that I would not die filled with bitterness and resentment as she did. Yet here I was, facing divorce and feeling angry, betrayed, and yes—bitter.

The Marriage

When we first married, I was delighted with my ready-made family. The youngest of his five children was 13, the oldest in college. After the divorce, I was abandoned by these—my—children. Another death.

I had taken on many responsibilities, financial duties, and most of all given them lots of love. I never begrudged financing their college and living expenses, and continued to do so postdivorce, not out of obligation but because I loved them. I knew they were not obliged to give back to me, but it still hurt when they didn't. Only one of the five children and I are close now. Divorce has far-reaching, unforeseen consequences and ripples.

There were many signs that things were falling apart, but I didn't want to see them. Denial still reigned. It's easy to ignore little things, but later I learned little things are not so little, but rather the tip of an enormous iceberg (and I was the Titanic). Then things changed.

He stopped laughing with me. He wrote big checks to himself for unexplained items. He met new friends at bars downtown. He wanted to go to church alone. As queen of denial, I kept thinking we could get back on course.

We planned a vacation. Whatever I wanted to do, he didn't. He sulked and nixed any suggestion I made. Finally, I lost it. I told him what a selfish, abusive, belligerent jerk he was. In a huff, he stormed off and sat in the airport the rest of the day. I enjoyed wienerschnitzel and a glass of local Riesling, relieved to have him gone. When we returned from Germany, he threw a few things in a suitcase and slammed the door on the way out.

How did it go so wrong? How did my ten-year marriage crumble so fast? When did our love end? Why did he leave? I tormented myself with these questions. By now, I felt no love for him, only remnants of duty. I began to suspect another woman. He would deny it and then turn my accusations back at me, saying that I was angry, upset, and crazy. The best defense is a good offense, right? I have now learned that when you are angry or emotionally distraught, trust those feelings! Don't doubt yourself, because they are telling you something.

After my mother died, I started to take practical steps. I consulted with my lawyer, who said we would file on our terms—not his. I had an ally. After we filed, she explained that the next step was the discovery process, as I still suspected that another woman was involved. She requested all his documents: phone, business and property records, bank and income statements, and more. She told me to comb through the records because I might find something that would shed light.

I didn't know what I was looking for, but I shuffled through the boxes anyway. Finally there it was: a phone number called at all times of day and night from the car phone. I called it and discovered it belonged to a woman who worked at our company, for my husband. Now I was obsessed with verifying my suspicions and knowing the truth. I rented a van with dark tinted windows, packed food, a camera, and blankets, and set out to be my own private detective. Stealthily, one Saturday at dusk, I drove to where I thought they were living. I turned the headlights off, settled down in the van and waited for a sign. Call me Ms. Columbo.

I didn't see anything all night, so in the morning I went to the church to see if he came out of the 11 a.m. service. There was our car in its usual parking place. Then he emerged with her. A warm feeling engulfed me. I finally knew the truth and it calmed me. At the same time, I felt slimed.

I should have seen it coming, but I was blind because I trusted him. All the signs were there—his distancing, lack of respect, separate activities, blaming, and no sex. Even the phone records had crossed my path. Because this was how my parents' marriage was for 40 years, the behavior actually seemed normal. I didn't understand what any of it really meant.

The Mediation Tree

My lawyer has a brand new Lexus, and my divorce paid for it. And I'm glad. She was not only my lawyer, but my friend. She explained the process and the rules of property division. She guided me when I was depressed, self-indulgent, and crazy. She proposed reasonable, rational solutions and alternatives, but at the time I was too angry to be reasonable or rational.

At the end of mediation, right before we agreed to the financial specifics, I stumbled out onto the back porch of the office and cried hysterically "Is this all there is to this marriage? Is it reduced to a fight over money?" My lawyer comforted me, and we went back inside and settled. I remember a large oak tree outside the mediator's building. Its strength inspired me. I took a photo of it and sat it on my night table so I could see it when feeling weak. In the following months, that was all the time.

Crawling My Way Out

I began to fall apart. It felt like I had descended into hell. I was falling, tumbling, whirling in a vortex I couldn't see, but only feel. I was in a constant state of confusion. I came upon a poem by a Persian woman who crawled down a shaft in the earth into hell. But then she slowly crawled back out. This inspired me, gave me hope. Maybe I could crawl back out of hell, to life, too.

So I attempted to do constructive things, like go to volunteer meetings. But on the way I would become overwhelmed, suddenly make a U-turn, and head right back to bed. I began to draw. First I drew myself as a reptile. Not human, but a basic, emotionless creature. Then, as time went on, as I began to slowly heal, I drew myself as a woman. I crawled a little further out of hell.

I began the process of forgiving him, as my own path to freedom. But it was really myself I needed to forgive, for taking part in his deception and for thinking he would be who I wanted him to be, who I thought *should* be, instead of seeing who he really was. As my mind cleared I began to piece together what had happened and accept it. I saw the end of the dark tunnel. I felt reborn.

I began a journey of introspection and returned to psychotherapy. I realized that I was always doing instead of enjoying. I couldn't work in this mental state anyway, so I decided to enjoy. I wrote down all the things I wanted to do, but hadn't had time to—yoga, religious learning, volunteer organizations, classic literature, dancing, and deep tissue massages. I practiced yoga, meditation, and chants. It brought me peace. I had left my married life dressed in a blue suit with matching pumps and had arrived here, divorced, in mismatched yoga clothes with a white-robed guru. I had crawled out of the tunnel. Like the woman in the poem, I was free.

So here is one gift hidden in the suffering of divorce: It led me to develop my unique spiritual path. I admire Buddhism, and meditation helped save my life; and I'm Presbyterian. I am so thankful I was raised with the concept of a higher power. But my path out of hell was not specifically religious. It was about love, values, and ethics.

Six Dates for the Fee

I was finally healed enough to consider a new relationship. An introvert, I wasn't going to a bar, especially in my fifties. None of my friends knew any single men to recommend. So I called a dating service. I felt like a teenager. It had been decades since I even thought of dating! I quizzed them: "What percentage of men are over 50? How many have college degrees?" Surprisingly, there were lots of them. The woman said I would get six dates for the fee.

The first date was so bad the service said it wouldn't count; the next two were nut cases. On my third date, I was late. I walked into the restaurant and there he was, waiting for me. A jolt went through my system. I was in love at first glance. We ate and talked and talked and laughed. We shared many values and interests. We had both experienced similar divorces, with spouses who walked away. He called me after a few days, and we went out again. I acted like a teenager with her first boyfriend. I spent my birthday weekend with my sisters in Santa Fe, and they laughed at my abnormal effervescence.

For two years, we were in the infatuation stage, but we had our issues. We dumped our pasts on each other, survived it, and grew out of it. It took three years to work through our baggage, but we made it. Now we've been together 12 years, married nine. We have each met our match. He tells me he loves me and shows it every day. And so, another gift hidden in the suffering: the wisdom that led me to go for what I wanted and deserved, to do what it took to get it, and to not settle for less.

So, divorce didn't kill me after all. Instead, I survived and thrived. The truth is, I wasn't slimed. My ex-husband's choices were his, and he's responsible for them, not me. The suffering, however, was my own doing. I did it to myself. But I'm no longer a victim, and I won't die bitter. On the contrary, I'm grateful I finally learned the lessons I needed to have a blissful life. Now I thank God I was divorced. If I had gotten what I wished for at the time—to remain married—I would be miserable now. Interesting how life works.

* * *

Your Survival Story

You've made it this far—now it's time for you to write your own survival story. Your late-life divorce was an ending, and it's also a beginning. My best to you on your journey.

Janice Green

Inventory of Assets and Liabilities

Instructions

Look for the assets listed in each category, and gather the requested information for each asset you have.

Even if you do not know or have access to detailed information, identify those assets and liabilities that you know about or that you think might exist. Keep a running list of information that you need to obtain from your spouse or your financial institutions.

REAL PROPERTY (including time-shares and other vacation property)

Address or street location _____

County and state _____

Legal description (or location of legal description, such as on property deed) _____

_____

Current fair market value (and date of valuation) _____

Name of mortgage company and account number _____

_____

Current balance due on mortgage _____

Other liens against property _____

Net equity in property _____

MISCELLANEOUS REAL PROPERTY INTERESTS (cemetery plots; minerals separate from land, as in oil/gas leases and royalty interests, and working interests)

Name of interest/lease/working interest/well _____

_____

Nature of interest _____

_____

County and state of location _____

Legal description _____

_____

Name of operator/producer/lessee _____

_____

Total annual income for last 12 months _____

Current value (date) _____

ACCOUNTS IN FINANCIAL INSTITUTIONS (savings, checking, cash, deposited funds with third parties, and certificates of deposit; do not include brokerage or retirement accounts)

Name and location of financial institution _____

_____

Account name _____

Account number _____

Names on withdrawal or signatory cards, including payable-on-death payees _____

_____

Type of account _____

Current account balance (date) _____

Terms (such as CD term or other restrictions) _____

_____

BROKERAGE ACCOUNTS (nonretirement, mutual funds, stocks, ETFs, bitcoin and other cryptocurrency, and bonds)

Name and address of financial institution _____

Account name _____

Account number (including subaccounts) _____

Names on withdrawal or signatory cards, including payable-on-death payees _____

_____

Type of account and subaccounts _____

_____

Tax basis (cost and date acquired) for each security _____

_____

Margin loan balance (date) _____

Value of interest in each account and sub-account (date) _____

_____

STOCKS, BONDS, ETFs, AND OTHER SECURITIES (not held in retirement accounts or brokerage accounts)

Name of security _____

Number of shares _____

Type of security (bonds, common stock, or preferred stock) _____

_____

Certificate numbers _____

Held by _____

Exchange where traded _____

Pledged as collateral? _____

Tax basis (cost and date acquired) _____

Current market value (date) _____

STOCK OPTIONS (vested, nonvested, exercisable, not exercisable, and with or without transfer restrictions)

Name of company issuing option _____

Date of option grant _____

Vesting schedule _____

Number of options for each grant _____

Are options exercisable? _____

Current stock price (date) _____

Strike/exercise price _____

Purchase price for option grant contract _____

Current market value (date) _____

BONUSES

Name of company _____

Date bonus expected to be paid _____

Type of bonus (individual or company performance based) and how measured _____

_____

Time period covered by bonus _____

Anticipated amount of bonus _____

RETIREMENT BENEFITS (Defined Contribution Plans: 401(k), 403(b))

Name of plan _____

Name and address of plan administrator _____

_____

Name of employer _____

Name of employee _____

Start date of credited service _____

Account name and number _____

_____

Account balance on date of marriage _____

Payee of survivor benefits, if any _____

Beneficiary designation _____

_____

Current account balance (date) _____

Current balance of any loan against the plan _____

RETIREMENT BENEFITS—Defined Benefit Plan (annuity payments per formula)

Name of plan _____

Name and address of plan administrator _____

Name of employer _____

Name of employee _____

Start date of credited service _____

Payee of survivor benefits _____

_____

Beneficiary designation _____

Benefits description _____

_____

_____

RETIREMENT BENEFITS—IRA (SEP)

Name of financial institution _____

Account name and number _____

Payee of survivor benefits _____

Beneficiary designation _____

Balance on date of marriage _____

Current account balance (date) _____

Are some or all funds not yet taxed? _____

RETIREMENT BENEFITS—Nonqualified Plan (Non-ERISA)

Name of financial institution _____

Account name and number _____

Account balance on date of marriage _____

Payee of survivor benefits _____

Designated beneficiary _____

Current balance (date) _____

RETIREMENT BENEFITS—Government Benefits (civil service, railroad, state, teacher, or local)

Name of plan _____

Account name and number _____

Plan or account administrator _____

Account balance as of date of marriage _____

Payee of survivor benefits _____

Designated beneficiary _____

Account balance (date) _____

If annuity, describe benefits _____

RETIREMENT BENEFITS—Military Benefits

Branch of service _____

Name of service member _____

Rank and pay grade of service member _____

Start date of credited service _____

Status (active/reserve/retired) of service member _____

Payee of survivor benefits _____

Description of benefits _____

_____

Monthly benefit payable _____

OTHER DEFERRED COMPENSATION BENEFITS (other forms of compensation, disability benefits, and workers' compensation)

Employee _____

Description of assets _____

Current value/balance (date) _____

CLOSELY HELD BUSINESS INTERESTS (partnerships, limited liability partnerships and companies, joint ventures, corporations, professional practices, and other business entities not publicly traded)

Name of business _____

Address _____

Employer tax ID number _____

Type of business organization _____

Percentage of ownership (or number of shares) _____

HEALTH SAVINGS ACCOUNTS, FLEXIBLE SAVINGS ACCOUNTS
(types of medical savings accounts)

Name of institution holding account _____

Name and number of account _____

Name and account number of high-deductible health insurance plan _____

Current balance (date) _____

LIFE INSURANCE (private and employment-based term, whole/universal, etc.)

Name of insurance company _____

Policy number _____

Name of insured _____

Name of owner _____

Type of insurance _____

Date of issue _____

Face amount _____

Cash surrender value on date of marriage _____

Current cash surrender value (date) _____

Beneficiary designation _____

Balance of loan secured by the policy _____

Amount of premiums _____

ANNUITIES

Name of company _____

Policy number _____

Name of annuitant _____

Name of owner _____

Type of annuity _____

Date of issue _____

Face amount _____

Beneficiary designation _____

Value on date of marriage _____

Current value (date) _____

Balance of loan against policy _____

Amount of premiums _____

MOTOR VEHICLES, BOATS, CYCLES, AND AIRPLANES (mobile homes, trailers, and recreational vehicles)

Year _____

Make _____

Model _____

Name on certificate of title _____

Who has primary possession of vehicle? _____

Vehicle identification number _____

Creditor, if loan secured by vehicle _____

Fair market value _____

Balance on loan (date) _____

Net value _____

RECEIVABLES—MONEY OWED TO ONE OR BOTH SPOUSES
(tax refunds and nonbusiness, personal loans made to others)

Name of debtor _____

Address of debtor _____

Debtor's relationship to you _____

Is debt reduced to writing? _____

Does debt have collateral? (If so, describe.)_____

_____

Current balance owed on loan (date) _____

HOUSEHOLD FURNITURE, FIXTURES, AND FURNISHINGS

In your possession (Describe and value each item)_____

_____

_____

_____

In your spouse's possession (Describe and value each item)_____

_____

_____

_____

ANTIQUES, ARTWORK, AND COLLECTIONS (coin and stamp collections, artwork, rugs, and so on)

In your possession (Describe and value each item)_____

_____

_____

_____

In your spouse's possession (Describe and value each item)_____

_____

_____

_____

COMPUTERS, ELECTRONICS, AND ENTERTAINMENT EQUIPMENT

In your possession (Describe and value each item)_____

_____

_____

_____

In your spouse's possession (Describe and value each item)_____

_____

_____

_____

SPORTING GOODS, ATHLETIC GEAR, AND FIREARMS

In your possession (Describe and value each item)_____

_____

_____

_____

In your spouse's possession (Describe and value each item)_____

_____

_____

_____

JEWELRY, FURS, AND OTHER PERSONAL ITEMS OF VALUE

In your possession (Describe and value each item)_____

_____

_____

_____

In your spouse's possession (Describe and value each item)_____

_____

_____

_____

LIVESTOCK AND PETS

In your possession (Describe and value each item) _____

_____

_____

_____

In your spouse's possession (Describe and value each item) _____

_____

_____

_____

FREQUENT FLYER AND TRAVEL AWARD ACCOUNTS

Name of airline _____

Name(s) on account _____

Account name and number _____

Current number of miles/awards _____

Current value (date) _____

SAFE DEPOSIT BOXES

Name of financial institution or depository _____

Address of financial institution _____

Box number _____

Names of persons with access and/or keys _____

Items in safe deposit box _____

STORAGE FACILITIES

Name of storage facility _____

Address of facility _____

Number of unit _____

Lease terms _____

Names of persons with access and/or keys _____

Items in storage unit _____

INTELLECTUAL PROPERTY

Type of property (copyright, patent, or trademark) _____

Describe property _____

Current value (date) _____

Potential future value (describe) _____

MISCELLANEOUS PROPERTY (tools, leases, crops, farm equipment, lawn equipment, construction equipment, tax overpayments, loss-carryforward deductions, season tickets and seat options, lottery tickets/winnings, and anything not listed elsewhere in this inventory)

In your possession _____

Description and value _____

In your spouse's possession _____

Description and value _____

CONTINGENT ASSETS (lawsuits by either party against a third party)

Nature of claim _____

Amount of claim _____

Parties involved _____

FEDERAL, STATE, AND LOCAL TAX LIABILITY

Amount owed in previous tax year _____

Amount owed in current tax year _____

CREDIT CARDS AND CHARGE ACCOUNTS (For each credit/charge account, furnish the following information)

Name of creditor ⎯⎯⎯⎯⎯⎯⎯⎯⎯⎯⎯⎯⎯⎯⎯⎯⎯⎯⎯⎯⎯

Account number ⎯⎯⎯⎯⎯⎯⎯⎯⎯⎯⎯⎯⎯⎯⎯⎯⎯⎯⎯⎯

Name(s) on account ⎯⎯⎯⎯⎯⎯⎯⎯⎯⎯⎯⎯⎯⎯⎯⎯⎯⎯

Current balance ⎯⎯⎯⎯⎯⎯⎯⎯⎯⎯⎯⎯⎯⎯⎯⎯⎯⎯⎯⎯⎯

Balance on date of separation ⎯⎯⎯⎯⎯⎯⎯⎯⎯⎯⎯⎯⎯⎯

ATTORNEYS' FEES

Incurred by you ⎯⎯⎯⎯⎯⎯⎯⎯⎯⎯⎯⎯⎯⎯⎯⎯⎯⎯⎯⎯⎯

Owed to ⎯⎯⎯⎯⎯⎯⎯⎯⎯⎯⎯⎯⎯⎯⎯⎯⎯⎯⎯⎯⎯⎯⎯⎯⎯

Incurred by your spouse ⎯⎯⎯⎯⎯⎯⎯⎯⎯⎯⎯⎯⎯⎯⎯⎯

Owed to ⎯⎯⎯⎯⎯⎯⎯⎯⎯⎯⎯⎯⎯⎯⎯⎯⎯⎯⎯⎯⎯⎯⎯⎯

OTHER PROFESSIONAL FEES

Incurred by you ⎯⎯⎯⎯⎯⎯⎯⎯⎯⎯⎯⎯⎯⎯⎯⎯⎯⎯⎯⎯⎯

Owed to ⎯⎯⎯⎯⎯⎯⎯⎯⎯⎯⎯⎯⎯⎯⎯⎯⎯⎯⎯⎯⎯⎯⎯⎯

Incurred by your spouse ⎯⎯⎯⎯⎯⎯⎯⎯⎯⎯⎯⎯⎯⎯⎯⎯

Owed to ⎯⎯⎯⎯⎯⎯⎯⎯⎯⎯⎯⎯⎯⎯⎯⎯⎯⎯⎯⎯⎯⎯⎯⎯

OTHER LIABILITIES NOT LISTED IN INVENTORY

Name of creditor ⎯⎯⎯⎯⎯⎯⎯⎯⎯⎯⎯⎯⎯⎯⎯⎯⎯⎯⎯⎯

Nature of debt ⎯⎯⎯⎯⎯⎯⎯⎯⎯⎯⎯⎯⎯⎯⎯⎯⎯⎯⎯⎯⎯

Account number ⎯⎯⎯⎯⎯⎯⎯⎯⎯⎯⎯⎯⎯⎯⎯⎯⎯⎯⎯⎯

Person incurring liability ⎯⎯⎯⎯⎯⎯⎯⎯⎯⎯⎯⎯⎯⎯⎯⎯

Is loan in writing? ⎯⎯⎯⎯⎯⎯⎯⎯⎯⎯⎯⎯⎯⎯⎯⎯⎯⎯⎯

Current balance (date) ⎯⎯⎯⎯⎯⎯⎯⎯⎯⎯⎯⎯⎯⎯⎯⎯⎯

CONTINGENT LIABILITIES (lawsuits pending against either spouse; guaranty signed by either spouse)

Name of creditor _____

Name of person primarily liable for debt _____

Nature of contingency _____

Amount of contingent liability _____

ASSETS CLAIMED AS SEPARATE/SOLE PROPERTY

List specific information about each asset (or liability) that you consider to be your or your spouse's separate estate (gift, inheritance, or owned or owed prior to marriage).

_____

_____

_____

_____

_____

_____

_____

_____

ASSETS HELD BY OTHERS

List information about each asset that a third party is holding for you or your spouse. For example, an asset is property that has been placed in a trust to which you or your spouse is a named beneficiary; or property that you or your spouse have inherited but which has not yet been distributed by the administrator of the deceased's estate. Besides a description of the asset, include the name and contact information of the person who is holding or managing the asset.

_____

_____

_____

_____

_____

_____

_____

Assessing Your Living Expenses

Reminder: This is a tool to jog your memory, but you must create your own notebook to list the expenses listed here. Use a page or more per category so you have room to make notes and run calculations. Give yourself plenty of time.

1. **Your residence.** Include rent, mortgage, homeowners' and neighborhood association dues, fees, and special assessments. If your monthly mortgage payment includes taxes and insurance, break out your annual property taxes and homeowners' insurance payments into a separate category. If your mortgage company allows, you may want to consider paying those expenses directly rather than escrowing them. Then include these same expenses for other real estate you own, as well as other property expenses listed below.

2. **Property insurance.** Not just homeowners' policies (if they're broken out from your mortgage), but also umbrella policies and special insurance endorsements you may have for contents, jewelry, and artwork.

3. **Property taxes.** If you pay property taxes separately from your monthly mortgage payment, find out whether you can make quarterly or semiannual payments. You may decide later to avoid annual hits of big bills and spread payments over time. Some taxing authorities do not charge interest on quarterly or semiannual payments.

4. **Utilities.** Gas, electricity, water, garbage disposal, and recycling charges.

5. **Household maintenance, repair, and services.** Swimming pool chemicals and maintenance; lawn care, landscaping, tree trimming,

gardening, and window washing; sprinkler systems; chimney sweep; vent cleaning; window cleaning; extermination. Include household help, and don't forget taxes owed for household staff. List security systems, including periodic fees and maintenance, carpet cleaning, seasonal checks on air-conditioning and heating units, air duct cleaning, and plumber and electrician visits.

6. **Communications (telephone and computer services).** Local charges; long distance services; land lines, cellphones, and Internet and Wi-Fi servers.

7. **Insurance.** Medical, dental, auto (and other motor vehicles), life, and disability. Include even if they are payroll deductions. Don't forget Medicare premiums, Medigap insurance, and prescription drug plans.

8. **Health care.** Regular annual check-ups with doctors, including internist, dermatologist, cardiologist, gynecologist, and so on. Prescription and nonprescription medication. Vitamins and supplements. Physical therapy, acupuncture, chiropractor, and therapeutic massage. Therapeutic equipment and aids. Medical laboratory expenses. Hospitalization. Dentist, periodontist, oral surgeon, dental cleaning, and orthodontist. Annualize health insurance deductible and copay amounts that you must cover. Mental health counseling. Live-in and part-time care and assistance.

9. **Groceries.** Food, water, and special dietary needs. Convenience store purchases and delivery services. Household items, including cleaning supplies. Wine, beer, and liquor. Catering. Cigarettes.

10. **Eating out.** Restaurants, fast food, take-out, and special event food (holidays and other celebrations); sporting event concession stands.

11. **Transportation.** Car payments; gas and maintenance; extended warranties; detailing; parking, tolls, and fines; license and registration; public transportation; taxi, limo, Uber, etc.

12. **Grooming.** Haircuts, perms, and coloring; pedicures and manicures; cosmetics and skin treatments; facials, botox, dermabrasion, laser, and waxing.

13. **Clothing.** Accessories, shoes, jewelry, and uniforms. Athletic clothing. Daily wear. Formal attire (including rental charges). Alterations and tailoring.

14. **Entertainment.** Cable/satellite services. Movie channel fees. Netflix and other movie rental and streaming charges and monthly membership fees. Cultural events. Season tickets. Sporting events. Podcast and other app entertainment subscriptions. Equipment purchases: TV; DVD; radio; sound and recording; stereo; camera, film, and development of film or digital printing. Sports equipment. Personal trainer. Books, music, and DVDs. Bookstore discount membership fees. Dues and fees for team memberships. Entry fees for competitions.

15. **Electronic devices.** Annual purchases for computers, notebooks, iPhones, iPads, software, downloads, games, apps, repairs, antivirus programs, utility programs, printers (and paper supply), scanners, and other hardware.

16. **Vacation and travel.** Family vacations, retreats, hunting and fishing excursions, spa weekends, educational and volunteer travel; include lodging, transportation, car rentals, meals, tips, and fees for sightseeing.

17. **Credit cards, charge accounts, and debt maintenance.** Fees, interest, and finance charges. While you are at it, make a list of credit card limits.

18. **Club memberships.** Dues, fees, and expenses for athletic, social, and country clubs, as well as dinner clubs, book clubs, and hobby clubs or groups.

19. **Religious affiliation.** Tithing, pledging, and special contributions; events and fees. Reading materials.

20. **Hobbies.** Lessons, instructions, instruments, equipment, and supplies.

21. **Finances.** Accountants; tax return preparers; software; asset management fees; bank charges; check printing; ATM fees, online banking fees, and overdraft protection.

22. **Subscriptions.** Newspapers; magazines; and online.

23. **Gifts.** Birthdays; anniversaries; religious holidays; rites of passage (bar and bat mitzvah); flowers for births, deaths, special occasions; and gift and note cards.

24. **Laundry and dry cleaning.** Regular and seasonal clothing. Special projects such as drapery, rug, upholstery, and bedspread cleaning.

25. **Charitable contributions.** Church, civic, and political.

26. **Furnishings.** Furniture and furnishings purchases, repair, and maintenance, picture framing, and upholstery and slipcovers.

27. **Income taxes.** Amounts withheld from pay; estimated tax payments; and federal and state income taxes.

28. **Savings.** Contributions to retirement accounts (IRAs, 401(k) plans, and deferred compensation). Earmarked savings and contributions to "rainy day funds."

29. **Emergencies.** The unexpected car repair, dental procedure, or need to contribute to a family member's financial misfortune.

30. **Pets.** Food, vet, supplies, training, grooming, and boarding.

31. **Personal fitness.** Trainers, club memberships, classes, clothing, and equipment.

32. **Miscellaneous.** Anything not included in another category; think about things like postage, loans to others, art and other collectibles, storage costs, and the piano tuner.

Index

breakdown of process results in new attorneys for litigation, 110, 111, 114–115, 116

bullying by spouse as potential downside to, 115

civil relationship with ex-spouse preserved in, 114

communications assistance by mental health professional, 112

cost of, 111, 114

equitable factors as consideration in, 138

facts revealed can be used as trial evidence if necessary, 116

four-way meetings (joint sessions), 111

generating options and reaching agreement, 113

inappropriate situations for use of, 115

information sharing, agreement for, 110, 111, 113

interest-based negotiations used in, 103–104, 111, 113

interests, identification of, 112

limits on what judges can do vs. creative solutions available through, 104, 113

minutes of meetings, 111

privacy and, 114

resource for, 116

state laws on, 108

status quo provisions, 306

team approach with specialists, 112, 113

time required for, 114

Collectibles and collections, 124, 214–216, 363

College savings account (Section 529) for spouse, 274

Commingled assets and tracing of, 132–133

Communications (telephone and computer services), as living expense, 370

Community property states

debts incurred as both spouse's responsibility, 221

and equal vs. equitable division of marital property, 137

married couples who work in their business qualifying as sole proprietors, 177

tax liability required on half of combined income, 231

Compensation

above market rate, and business interest valuation, 181

bonuses, 208, 357

deferred, 206, 360, 372

Competency issues. See Incapacity

Complaint. See Initial pleading

Computer Fraud and Abuse Act, 39

Computer privacy and security. See Electronic surveillance

Computers and related equipment, 124, 363

Confidentiality

friends and family are not bound by, 68

of mediation, 107

therapists as bound by, 68

See also Attorney–client privilege

Conflicts of interest. See Attorneys' conflicts of interest

Conservators. See Guardianships

Construction equipment, 365

Contested divorce

appraisals for business value in, 183

appraisals for home value in, 154

depositions as likely in, 97

 **NOLO**   *More from Nolo*

Nolo.com offers a large library of legal solutions and forms, created by Nolo's in-house legal editors. These reliable documents can be prepared in minutes.

Create a Document Online

Incorporation. Incorporate your business in any state.

LLC Formation. Gain asset protection and pass-through tax status in any state.

Will. Nolo has helped people make over 2 million wills. Is it time to make or revise yours?

Living Trust (avoid probate). Plan now to save your family the cost, delays, and hassle of probate.

Provisional Patent. Preserve your right to obtain a patent by claiming "patent pending" status.

Download Useful Legal Forms

Nolo.com has hundreds of top quality legal forms available for download:

- bill of sale
- promissory note
- nondisclosure agreement
- LLC operating agreement
- corporate minutes
- commercial lease and sublease
- motor vehicle bill of sale
- consignment agreement
- and many more.

More Bestselling Books

Divorce Without Court
A Guide to Mediation and Collaborative Divorce

Divorce & Money
How to Make the Best Financial Decisions During Divorce

Nolo's Essential Guide to Divorce

IRAs, 401(k)s & Other Retirement Plans
Taking Your Money Out

Prenuptial Agreements
How to Write a Fair & Lasting Contract

Every Nolo title is available in print and for download at Nolo.com.

www.nolo.com